Urban Migrants And Poverty Reduction in China

Chief Editors: Huang Ping & Genevieve Domenach-Chich
Proofreader: Michael Drake

Paths International Ltd

社会科学文献出版社
SOCIAL SCIENCES ACADEMIC PRESS (CHINA)

CONTENTS

1

Background

Zhan Shaohua

Since Reform and Opening up[1], China has witnessed an increasingly large scale of rural labor population mobility between town and country. This migrant crowd is due to the rural households, specifically referring to the "rural peasant worker" in the city who is engaged in non-agricultural economic activity. According to statistics from the agricultural department and labor and social security department[2], in 2004 the number of rural peasant workers reached about 120 million. Since the beginning of the 1990s, research circles have devoted much attention to this sociological group, Much of this research stresses the disadvantageous position of the migrant workers compared to the urban residents (*Hukou*).[3] Very few of the articles point out that poverty exists among the peasant workers, and very few researchers regard this poverty as a specialized topic that deserves serious investigation, analysis and theorizing. Moreover, the Chinese government in its helping of the poor and policy development, lacks expression concerning the problem of the impoverished peasant worker. This article, through the angle of poverty analysis, attempts to deal with China's problem of large-scale population mobility and its creation of an impoverished peasant worker population.

1.1 Poverty issues in China

After the commencement of Reform and Opening up in China in the late 1970s, the government began to use the word "poverty", referring to people who live in rural areas with an annual income less than the official poverty line (which fluctuates according to the price index). For instance, the line was set at 678 RMB (about 85 USD) per capita per year in 2004; about 26 million rural residents fell below this line, representing approximately 3.3

---

1 The Reform and Opening-up (*Gaige Kaifang*) is an umbrella term covering a whole range of policy areas to re-orient China from a planned economy to a market economy.

2 Quoted from a research report of the Ministry of Labor and Social Security in 2005; see also http://www.cass.net.cn

3 The *Hukou* system is a social control/administration system set up on the basis of households, whose members, either in rural or urban areas, must register at the local public security office as a legal resident. After registration, the households are issued a *Hukou* certificate, where all members of the household are listed in detail, allowing the local street office in urban, village or rural areas to closely control households.

percent of the total rural population. In addition to the establishment of the poverty line, the government used the "impoverished province" and "impoverished village" to come to define poverty. In 1994, 592 counties out of 3000 counties were labeled as poor; and after 2000, 148 thousands villages were officially labeled as "poor."

Rural poverty reduction became a main component of governmental policy after the middle of the 1980s. As a result of this policy, as well as economic development, the incidence of poverty dropped from 250 million in 1978 to 30 million in 2000, according to a governmental report.[4]

In contrast with rural poverty, urban poverty in China is called "new poverty" and did not attract public concern until the middle of the 1990s (Solinger, D, 2000). Part of the cause for this was related to the fact that in the middle of the 1980s and before urban reform, and even to the point of 1994 and the basic establishment of the socialist market economy and before the reform of State-Owned Enterprises (SOE), urban residents in general enjoyed higher income and better welfare than their rural counterparts and so they were basically not impoverished. However, since the middle to late 1990s, on the one hand due to SOE reform a large quantity of public workers were laid-off, and on the other hand the marketization strategy of "Making some people rich first" also contributed to the emergence of poverty in cities. This urban poverty caused policy-makers to follow this development very closely. In 1998, and in order to alleviate the "new poverty", the central government established the Ministry of Labor and Social Security to take responsibility for the employment and livelihoods of the unemployed population. Many cities established the laid-off employment service centers, where laid-off workers are provided basic living expenses according to monthly allotments, and which also helps them seek out new work. Another kind of measure to reduce the urban "new poverty" was to establish an official line that located the lowest level of social security. This began an urban experiment; in 1999 the State Council changed it into a nationwide policy, and the Ministry of Civil Affairs was responsible for implementing this policy. By the end of 2004, the number of people that were relying on social security had reached up to 22 million in urban China.

1.2 The Problems with Defining Poverty

On the surface, the governmental anti-poverty policy covers the rural and urban areas,

---

4 The Chinese government released a white paper on *The Development-oriented Poverty Reduction Program for Rural China* in 2001. See the English website: http://www.china.org.cn/e-white/index.htm

even to the point of possessing rural or urban residence and registration. But scholars point out that these policies neglect the great quantity of migrant workers that have emerged since reform and opening up. Although they live and work inside cities, they still only possess rural registration status, and they are not capable of receiving benefits from the rural anti-poverty policies and they are also not covered by the urban anti-poverty policy. Therefore, there exists a clear policy gap in the governmental anti-poverty policy (Huang Ping, 2004).

Furthermore, the governmental policies define poverty only in terms of economic or income dimensions. However, more and more researchers argue that poverty should not be defined and understood from a single dimension, but that we should go further, as some researchers argue, and understand poverty in terms of capability (education and health) (Sen, A., 1999; Zhang Xiaojun, et al, 2005) as well as social exclusion (Levitas, R., 1998). If so, the purposes of poverty reduction should also include strengthening capability and promoting social inclusion.

These discussions infuse the author with the idea to explore migrant workers' poverty in China from a new perspective. Moreover, the existing research has built a strong foundation for the study of migrant workers' poverty in this paper. For example, much of the research has discussed and studied migrant workers' disadvantages, social network (social capital), employment difficulties, rights protection, etc. (Tan Shen, 2003). Therefore, it is important to study the issue of migrant workers from the perspective of poverty analysis because it would provide a strong analytical and theoretical framework on the issue of migrant workers in China. However, two important questions should be raised to verify the following analysis.

First, what distinguishes migrant workers' poverty from rural and urban poverty in China in terms of causes and definition? Second, can poverty analysis provide a better analytical framework and posit policy implications regarding the issues of migrant workers?

These two questions lead to the assumption in this paper.

1.3 Assumption

On the basis of the existing research as well as the authors research, this paper presents the following (mobility-poverty) assumption[5]:

5 The relationship between "migration and poverty" is attracting more and more research concerns. A large amount of research emphasizes that poverty leads to migration, and that in the meantime migration can reduce poverty by pursuing a better life or by remitting money back home. But if they do not focus on involuntary migration, few studies realize that migration can contribute to poverty formation.

The remarkable migrant workers' mobility[6] is a main cause for their impoverished status. Moreover, external factors such as governmental policies and the labor market may influence the "mobility-poverty" relationship.

This paper will analyze and test this assumption with the collected (mainly qualitative) data.

1.4 Data Sources

The data used in this paper are derived from two sources: one is existing research results and statistics, and the other is from the author's fieldwork research on migrant workers in Inner Mongolia, Beijing, and Yunnan from 2003 to 2005:

1. From 2003 to 2005, the author continuously collected data on female migrant workers in Beijing that migrated from Chifeng Municipality in Inner Mongolia by adopting the methodologies of observation, in-depth interviews and questionnaires. More than 30 thousands migrant workers are included in this research.

2. In October 2003 and November 2004, the author went to Yunnan province in southwestern China and conducted one month of fieldwork on local labor migration and development. A designed questionnaire was constructed and about 20 thousand migrant workers were interviewed.

3. In December 2004, the author conducted research in the urban area of Chifeng, interviewing and investigating about 200 migrant workers. In September 2005, a home village of migrant workers was structurally studied to understand their families and communities.

1.5 Building up an Analytical Framework

1.5.1 Migrant workers' mobility

In contrast to the settled population, the migrant workers in China have a distinguishing feature: mobility in general, and employment mobility and spatial mobility in particular.

Employment mobility refers to migrant workers who have transferred from agriculture to non-agricultural sectors, but who still have the right to keep their farmland according to the governmental policy. Therefore, employment mobility can be seasonal/non-seasonal

6 In this paper "mobility" is used as an analytical concept referring to the changing process in people's position or status

and short/long-term; migrant workers could theoretically return to their farmland and agriculture as a safety net if they were to fail in the urban labor market.

Spatial mobility can be further categorized into two types: geographical mobility and social space mobility. The former refers to migrant workers that oscillate between rural area (villages) and urban area (cities). The latter indicates migrant workers who are disengaged, often in part, from family members and social networks in rural society, and who enter a new urban social space where there is no existing social network for them.

1.5.2 Migrant workers' poverty

The mobility feature makes it difficult to use current policies or poverty definitions to measure or analyze migrant workers' poverty.

On the one hand, the poverty line used to measure rural poverty cannot be applied to migrant workers, since migrant workers earn their income in the form of monthly/yearly salaries in the labor market. But the poverty line defines income mainly based on agricultural production, in which rural products can be sold for cash income as well as consumed by the households. In other words, their income is not very close to the market (labor or commodity market). As a matter of fact, almost all migrant workers' income largely exceeds the rural poverty line.

On the other hand, the standard of urban poverty is not applicable to migrant workers, since, migrant workers do not belong to the laid-off workers or the *Dibao* group who on the one hand possess urban Hukou, and on the other hand have their families in local cities (The Dibao policy only measures family/household income as a unit). However, migrant workers do not have urban *Hukou* or all of their family members in cities.

Therefore, it is necessary to define and understand the concept of migrant workers' poverty beyond the existing policy framework.

1.5.3 Defining migrant workers' policy

It is difficult to define migrant workers' poverty in terms of economic or income poverty. One reason is that there are two standards of income poverty in China[7], and neither of them is designed to measure migrant workers' poverty. Another reason is that migrant workers' poverty of income dimension is a relative one: their income is higher than rural residents, but lower than urban residents. Moreover, another important reason

7 The standards of income poverty vary not only between governmental policies, but also amongst academic discussion, especially those studies of development (Webster, A., 1984).

why this paper does not discuss migrant workers' income poverty is the fact there are a large number of rural people in China whose income is much less than migrant workers' income, even though some research has found that some migrant workers' income is lower than the standards associated with urban and rural poverty (Wang Fengyu and Li Lulu, 2001).

Therefore, this paper emphasizes that migrant workers' poverty should be understood more in terms of human capital and social integration than in economic terms. Thus, analyzing migrant mobility provides significant insight and understanding into the migrant workers' "poverty" in terms of these two factors.

First, mobility, specifically employment mobility and geographical mobility, creates migrant poverty in terms of demonstrated skill sets. Migrant workers intentionally leave their employment in agriculture and attempt to find jobs in non-agricultural sectors instead. This mobility makes it necessary for them to learn non-agricultural skills, however, only a small number of migrant workers demonstrate this ability or have access to this type of skilled training. In 2001, Governmental statistics revealed that only 18.6 percent of new rural migrants received sufficient training before transferring from agriculture to non-agricultural sectors[8]. Furthermore, the author's survey, implemented in Beijing in 2003, also revealed that 76.5 percent out of the 338 respondents expressed a strong need for training. In addition, geographical mobility forces the migrant workers to adapt to the specifics of urban society, meaning, they must understand the urban environment in terms of law, health, job seeking skills, city life, etc.

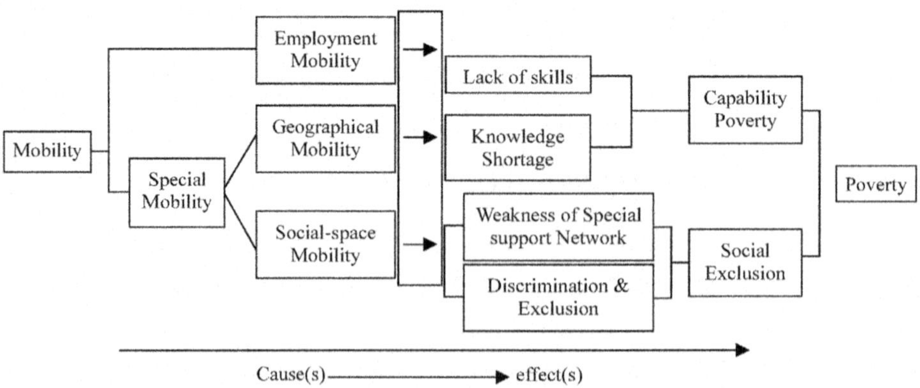

Figure 1.1 Migrant Workers' Mobility and Poverty

8 Please see: *The National Plan of Training Rural Migrants in 2003-2010*, issued by the State Council in September 2003.

Second, social-space mobility causes migrant workers to encounter social exclusion, which is divided into two parts in this paper: one is the weakness of a social support network; and the other is their discrimination and exclusion from urban society. The weakness of the social support network can be understood from the fact that migrant workers are disengaged from their original social network due to their mobility, but where they have difficulties in constructing and finding a new effective social support network in urban areas. Discrimination and exclusion indicates that the entry of migrant workers into cities causes tensions between the migrant inductees and the urban society.

Therefore, mobility in general can produce four types of migrant workers' poverty: lack of skills, shortage in knowledge, weakness in a social support network, and discrimination and exclusion. The "mobility poverty" relationship and corresponding types of poverty consist of the analytical framework in this paper (see Figure 1-1). However, it must be pointed out that, concerning the context in China, this paper uses the concepts of skill sets and social exclusion in different senses. To some degree, it compares China to that of Sen's analysis and of policies preventing social exclusion in some European countries. In this paper, migrant workers' skill set poverty cannot be separated from their quality of mobility. Although migrant workers are usually those more educated and skillful rural laborers, they still suffer from skill set poverty because their employment and geographical mobility leads to insufficiencies (non-agricultural skills and knowledge) relative to urban society. Also, migrant workers' social exclusion is derived from their social-space mobility, not from the exclusion of labor markets, which is heavily emphasized in some European countries, especially England [Berghman, G, 1995; Rodgers G, et al. (eds.), 1995]. But migrant workers in China can find jobs in urban labor markets, or else return to rural areas where they have a piece of farmland (even if very small) to rely on.

1.6 Four Types of Poverty

In this part, four types of migrant workers' poverty will be analyzed and discussed based on collected data.

1.6.1 Lack of Skills

Migrant workers' lack of skills is an elusive concept because anyone, even an advanced computer engineer, may insufficiently meet a certain expectation. Thus migrant workers' lack of skills could not be correctly understood if one adopted an individual perspective and not a social or group perspective.

As mentioned above, migrant workers' lack of skills mainly rises from their employment mobility from agriculture to non-agricultural sectors. The mobility is closely in line with socio-economic development in China: the large-scale rural-urban labor migration emerged in early 1990s, especially after Deng Xiaoping embarked on his southern tour and posited remarkable speeches. The event led to a significant increase in investment and produced a high demand for laborers. From 1992 to 1994, the number of migrant workers increased from less than 20 million to more than 60 million. Undoubtedly, most of the migrant workers had not participated in any training programs and therefore had to learn these skills through individual practice. In the middle of the 1990s, "Three Rural Problems"[9] became more and more serious and as a consequence a large number of rural laborers left their farmland from which they could make little profit, and joined the group of migrant workers. But in the process of this migration and transformation, many migrants experience a common problem: many migrant workers have not been trained before they enter cities simply because they are not able to afford training or do not know what skills should be learned.

As a result, the lack of skills in part shapes migrant workers' employment structure: much of the research and statistics show that migrant workers are often seeking jobs and are employed in the sectors which require low skill sets or even no skill sets at all. As a result, they work in sectors where they experience low wages, such as construction, domestic service, pipelining, etc. Table 1-1 shows that in comparison with the national scale, the western areas represent the highest concentration of migrant workers in these sectors.

Table 1-1 Migrant workers' employment structure in 2002

Regions	Cons	Industry	Restaurant & hotel	Commerce	Tran	Donestic service	Agri	Others
West	25.00%	22.00%	18.60%	6.70%	7.30%	1.60%	3.30%	15.00%
National	14.41%	37.22%	11.93%		5.86%	?	1.50%	29.08%

Source: MOA, 2003

Note: "Cons. " means construction and "Agri. " means agriculture; "Tran. " means transportation.

Although a lack of skills did not prevent rural laborers from migration, it did increase the degree of migrant workers' poverty. Therefore, the migrant workers developed a strong desire to improve their skills; however, if they are not able to satisfy this requirement to increase their skill level, then they are likely to continue in an impoverished state.

9 "Three Rural Problems" refers to the problems facing rural China, including problems of rural products, rural community and rural people, which became an umbrella word covering all challenges for rural development.

According to the author's research on Chifeng female migrant workers in Beijing in 2004, out of a survey of more than 300 people, more than 80 percent of those interviewed expressed strong demands for training while those under 30 years old reached over 90%. In another example in 2003, the government of Diqing Prefecture, Yunnan Province, started a training class with a capacity of 70 students, but the registered migrant workers exceeded 200 people. Moreover, almost all government operated training classes, which are free of some charges, faced similar situations: the supply greatly falls short of the demand. There are many reasons why the demand cannot be easily satisfied: an insufficient supply of training services from governments; migrant workers' affordability; low education; over-working of migrants, etc. For example, many migrant workers cannot participate in training programs simply because they must work more than 12 hours a day and are not free on weekends. Taking the domestic services sector in Beijing as an example, female migrant workers in this sector have to stay in their employer's houses all day long, and only have two days free a month. It indicates that many migrant workers must not only pay for their training, but also are required to give up their current jobs if they decide to attend a training course. Thus training becomes impossible for many migrant workers since they earn a relatively low income in cities and at the same time carry the responsibility to remit money back home. However, despite these difficulties, some migrant workers still make efforts to participate in training programs in order to acquire a better career (Box 1).

Box 1A: A Story of Training

ZYQ and CZH are two female migrant workers, who came from the same township in Chifeng Municipality in 2002, and who work in the domestic service sector. Employment in domestic service can earn some good money but "you cannot make it a career because you cannot do it all your life", CZH said. Both of them are eager to find an opportunity to develop important skills.

After 3 years of employment in cities, their willingness became so strong that they decided to give up their current jobs and register for a training course. One of ZYQ's aunts opened a hairdressing business in a county of Chifeng and ran it very well, thus, she suggested that they attend a course on hairdressing and other related skills. They in fact agreed with ZYQ's aunt. In May 2005, ZYQ participated in a course on beauty culture and CZH joined a hairdresser training program. After two months, they graduated and started to seek new jobs. With her sister's support, ZYQ found a job in a company related to beauty culture Although it asked for 2 months

It is It is

probation without any payment, starting from September, she has earned a higher salary (more than 1000 RMB a month), which is much higher than before (500 RMB per month). Unfortunately, CZH cannot find a suitable job and had to return to the domestic service sector.

The cost of training is very high. ZYQ paid about 1500 RMB and CZH paid 4000 yRMB for their training. Furthermore, they must pay for their daily expenditure and housing during the training. Since CZH did not find a good job, she now owes about 2000 RMB to her friends.

It is

It is necessary to point out that the lack of skills also has impacts on labor markets. For instance, migrant workers' shortage in southern China in 2004 can be seen in part as a result from migrant workers' lack of skills. On the one hand, due to the migrant worker's low level of skills, it is difficult for the department to employ migrants at relatively high wages; thus, under the circumstances of agricultural production and the improving of village employment forms, some migrant workers would rather return to farmland or rural areas. On the other hand, there are vacant positions in the labor market, but problems have surfaced in the fact that applicants have received insufficient training and do not conform to the requirements of skilled workers for the labor market.

1.6.2 Knowledge shortage

Geographical mobility causes the migrants to enter the cities from the villages. However, there are many differences between these two societies in terms of law, health, daily life, etc., and after they enter the cities this causes them to have no other choice but to undergo re-socialization. In this process, it is required that they obtain knowledge regarding the aspects of social life, such as necessary laws, health and everyday city life. Without this type of knowledge, the migrant continues in a state of impoverishment (Bai Nansheng, 2003).

One type of knowledge shortage lies in the difference between the laws of rural and urban societies. In this paper law is defined in a broad sense and includes the formal and informal norms of social life. For example, in China, a village is an "intimate" society in general where people put a high degree of trust in each other and usually do not need a written contract when they reach an agreement, which is actually seen as a sign of "distrust". However, the urban society is considered a "stranger" society and the trust between people is to a large extent guaranteed by the issued laws and paper contracts. But many migrant workers who enter the cities fail to embody an awareness of these differences, and therefore, they are unable to adapt to the city's social life. Particularly, when they encounter urgent circumstances, they are not able to use legal means and knowledge to protect their interests. Most of them are not accustomed to signing a contract for their employment and are reluctant to posit a request for a wage increase when it is suitable and necessary. According to the author's interviews of female migrants in Beijing, most of them do not know how to take advantage of their rights because they fail to separate out the relationships in the internal space of employment and the external space outside of employment (such as seemingly friendship, kinship-like intimacy, etc.).

Another type of shortage is that migrant workers do not have enough knowledge in terms of health to protect themselves from diseases in cities. It is obvious that an urban society is more populous than most rural communities, and as a result that people in urban areas are more vulnerable to some diseases, such as hepatitis, diarrhea, skin diseases, etc. There are no statistics concerning the incidence of diseases among the migrant workers, but according to the author's small-scale interviews, migrant workers easily acquire diseases such as diarrhea and skin infections. Another supporting example is that many migrant workers know little knowledge of self-protection: they do not know that tap water is undrinkable in cities; and they don't know how to protect their faces and hands in winter, or how to keep themselves from harmful insects in the summer, and so forth. Furthermore, most of the migrant workers live in basements and crowded shelters that also correspond to a very dirty environment – and this makes them more vulnerable to diseases. Moreover, they are not likely to see a doctor or purchase medicine because their income level is not sufficient enough to cover the high-cost of medical care.

It is also necessary to point out that migrant workers to some degree lack the knowledge of urban life, including the knowledge of traffic rules, how to seek help, how to recognize false advertising, and so forth. For example, some migrant workers even do not know that they should dial 110 (police) and 120 (medical emergency) when it is necessary. According to several interviews conducted by the author, in the spring of 2005, several migrant workers were swindled out of a large amount of money due to their credulity in believing the a false job advertisement. It is surprising in that some of them have worked and lived in cities for years but still lack the knowledge to distinguish between "good" and "bad" information.

1.6.3 Weakness of the social support network

From the perspective of spatial mobility, migrant workers experience geographical mobility as well as social space mobility. This social-space mobility leads to the weakening of the original social support network based upon the rural community, and subsequently, the gradual change of its functions.

Three functions, if not more, of migrant workers' social network are changed due to the social space mobility. First, the rural family no longer provides protection for the family members working outside as migrant workers. When the author implemented research in a village of Chifeng Municipality, many families expressed strong concerns over fellow family members who had migrated, while at the same time stating: "It is useless to worry, and we cannot do anything helpful for them other than asking them to come back." Second, the network does not provide migrant workers with a sense of security and identity-as it did in their rural home environment. There is no denying that migrant workers recognize this (see Box 2); but these can only be obtained via the original network. Third, migrant workers can move to cities without losing part of the original social support network, i. e, they migrate together with their families, relatives, friends and neighbors. However, the remaining part of network will have some new functions according to migrant workers' new needs. For instance, migrant workers usually seek support from the part of the network related to temporary accommodation, job information, and the like.

Box 2: The Story of Diary Writing

Most migrant workers have a junior middle school (9 years) education, while a small minority is equipped with an educational level higher than junior middle school. After they leave their families and social networks in rural communities, it is difficult for them to find the opportunities for good communication, especially heart-to-heart communication. This is often the case for migrant workers employed in domestic services, who must stay in the employer's houses for a long time, and where almost all the people around them can be seen as the their "employers" to some extent.

As a result, they have few opportunities to say what they want and what they are willing to say. Instead, some migrant workers divert this communication into diaries everyday and express their fear, pain, happiness, sadness, etc. I was allowed to read hundreds of migrant workers' diaries and found that the topics of these writings are often related to their families and hometowns, which are described as beautiful pictures with love, safety, warmth, harmony, etc.

The other supporting evidence of a weak social support network is the fact that the network can no longer satisfy migrant workers' needs once migrated to urban areas.

According to a questionnaire survey among Chifeng migrant workers in 2004, more than 70 percent of migrant workers usually feel "helpless" as they work and live in cities. The result indicates that the network cannot provide enough support for migrant workers. Migrant workers usually make efforts to re-construct their social support network by building up or renewing social relationships among them, especially among those coming from the same rural areas, however, on the one hand, they are not all successful in re-constructing their social network, and on the other hand, if successful, they could not get effective assistance from the "new" network since it is mainly constructed among migrant workers who share the same advantages as well as disadvantages.

1.6.4 Discrimination and exclusion

The analysis of discrimination and exclusion against migrant workers is easily confused with that of class, for the reason that migrant workers possess two identities: the migrant group and low paid working class. Some of the discrimination and exclusion that they experience resonates from migrant workers actually rise from their position of low paid working class. In this sense, migrant workers are similar to urban laborers, especially those in low paid positions. For one, migrant workers share similarities with low paid urban laborers in terms of residence, housing, occupation, and life style. Moreover, according to some research, migrant workers are located in the same position of the social classification structure (Lu Xueyi, 2002).

However, migrant workers, as new inductees into cities, encounter specific discrimination and exclusion from mainstream urban societies, which can be observed in two ways: One is that migrant workers in general have less interaction and communication with urban societies. A survey carried out in Beijing, Shanghai, Guangzhou and Wuhan in 1997, showed that 18 percent of rural migrants felt strong discrimination from urban residents; 45 percent felt some discrimination from urban residents; and 66 percent of respondents expressed they did not dare to, and would rather not, make friends with local urban residents (Ling Yue, 1997). According to the author's research very, few migrant workers have developed a good relationship with local residents.

The other observation is that most of the migrant workers do not share the identities of the cities where they are working and living. According to the author's research in Inner Mongolia, Beijing and Yunnan Province, almost all migrant workers would rather see themselves as "outsiders" than local urban residents, which is very surprising. Some research labels migrant workers as "people of margin" in urban societies (Liu Kaiming, 2003), which indicates that they are excluded from urban society. However, it would be cursory to make the conclusion that migrant workers can keep their rural identities. I found that many migrant workers, especially the younger generation, do not regard themselves as "villagers" or "rural people." In this sense, they also belong to the "people of margin" in rural societies.

1.7 External Factors

Above all, the framework for this paper consists of a discussion and analysis regarding the "mobility poverty" relationship, however, it is important to be aware that factors beyond this framework may influence this relationship-specifically in a way that strengthens or weakens the analysis. These factors are called "external factors." Based on the existing research (Huang Ping, et al., 1997; Huang Ping & Zhan Shaohua, 2005), this paper will discuss two external factors: governmental policies and labor markets (see Figure 1-2).

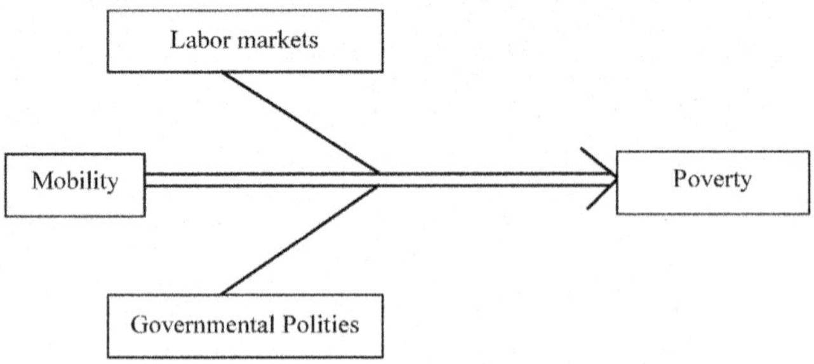

Figure 1-2 External Factors and the "Mobility Poverty" Relationship

1.7.1 Governmental policies

Governmental policies can be divided into those policies issued by the central government and those by the local governments. Prior to 2000, the central government issued many policies designed to control and regulate rural-urban labor migration (though the migration was not prohibited) because the government believed migration related to social disorder, which would endanger social stability and the normal urban life. However, after 2000, the government started to emphasize the positive effects of labor migration on rural development. Thus, rural laborers were not only encouraged to move to cities as migrant workers, but furthermore, government policy, provided more rights-protection and public services for migrant workers. The positive policies towards migrant workers can be generalized as follows:

(1) Strengthen migrant workers' rights to live and work in cities so that local governments (especially those receiving cities) cannot expel migrant workers (2003).

(2) Require the employers to pay migrant workers on time (2003).

(3) Provide programs for training and understanding urban social life, especially for migrant workers from poor areas in central and western China (2004).

(4) Provide more employment services for migrant workers (2005).

Although these policies should be further studied and assessed to find out whether or not, or to what degree, they can effectively support migrant workers, it is apparent that they will have some impact on migrant workers' poverty, especially their poverty related to a lack of skill and training.

Box 3: Migrant Workers' Home

In 2001, the CWF established an office called the Migrant Workers' Home (MWH) and hired a full-time and experienced staff to provide rights-protection and social services for Chifeng female migrants in Beijing, along with the financial support of some international NGOs and the Chifeng Municipal Government. The MWH is responsible for the following:

- Providing provisional accommodation for Chifeng female migrant workers who work in Beijing; and helping migrant workers find employment
- Holding discussions, lectures and other public activities once a week, and helping migrant workers strengthen their social support network
- Building a hotline to provide consulting services in terms of knowledge, law, health, job search, etc.
- Publishing and distributing monthly newsletters to highlight the issue of migrant workers' protection and to share experiences

1.7.2 The Labor market

In China, the environment and circumstances of the labor markets are closely related to governmental policies. Many local governments, especially the sending localities in western China, stressed the policy of rural labor migration in the middle of the 1990s as a main policy designed to reduce poverty and promote local development. Some local governments of sending places even issued these policies to protect and provide services for their migrant laborers. On the one hand, the "push" policy increased the degree of migrant workers' poverty because it turned more rural laborers into migrant workers; on the other hand, some good policy measures led to the use of peasants and therefore the reduction of migrant poverty. The establishment of the "Migrant Workers' Home" by Chifeng Women's Federation (CWF) can be seen as a good example in this regard (Box 3).

After Reform and Opening-up began in the late 1970s, the central government adopted the market economy and broke down the system of full employment (the so-called Iron Rice Bowl) in cities. As a consequence, the phenomenon of unemployment started to emerge in middle 1980s (Tang Jun, et al., 2003). Especially after 1990, on one hand the largely developed coastal areas of the Southeast needed a large quantity of laborers, and on the other hand, the deepening transformation of cities and SOE reform produced a large quantity of laid-off workers. Under this background, more and more migrant workers left their farmland for urban labor markets to seek job opportunities, and as a result competition emerged in urban labor markets between migrant workers and local laborers. Some city localities in the 1990s, in order to protect the local labor force and provide preferential treatment, drafted policies prohibiting non-natives from employment in certain professions. This labor market competition and unfair employment policies intensified migrant workers' poverty: they not only excluded migrant workers from some areas of urban labor markets, but also stigmatized them as "trouble-makers", and as a result aggravated the migrant worker's situation of discrimination and exclusion from urban societies.

It is necessary to note that China is facing significant employment pressure, based on the fact that there has been a rising employment population (see Figure 1-3). In particular, China is facing an increase of more than 12 to 13 million new laborers each year in the coming decade (Huang Ping & Zhan Shaohua, 2005). Therefore, on the one hand, a lack of job opportunities in rural labor markets contributed to the large-scale rural-urban labor migration, and on the other hand, severe competition in urban labor markets led to migrant workers' poverty in terms of discrimination and exclusion.

Another example of the influence of labor markets on "mobility-poverty" can be demonstrated in the phenomenon of "peasant shortage" in the beginning of 2004. The shortage could be derived in part from improvement in agricultural policy, which increased farmers' income and job opportunities in rural areas, and therefore provided the rural laborers with the possibility not working outside as migrant workers. In September 2005, I discovered that many rural laborers would rather work on farmland and seek jobs in townships and counties nearby where they find job opportunities and earn a basic livelihood. In other words, the increase of job opportunities in rural labor markets causes migrant workers to choose to stay with their families and seek jobs nearby in order to reduce their poverty.

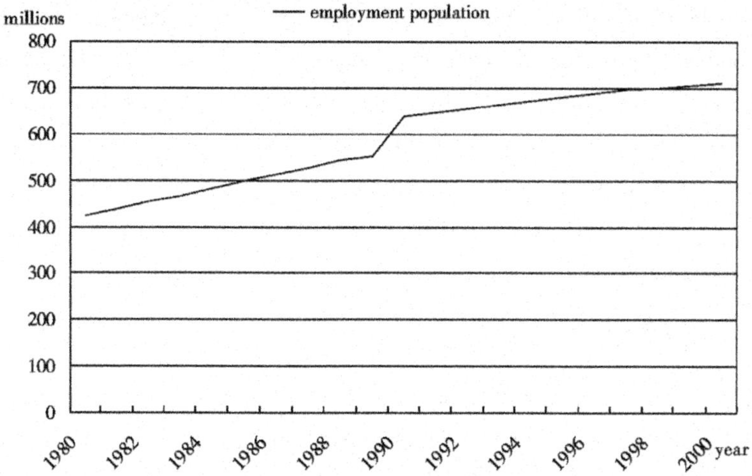

Figure 1-3 Employment Population in China: 1980~2000.

Source: NBS & MOLSS, 2001: p 8.

1.8 Anti-poverty Practice and Policy Implications

1.8.1 Summary of the poverty analysis among migrant workers

On the basis of the analytical framework and discussions above, this paper concludes the following:

(1) Migrant workers' poverty should be distinguished from rural poverty and urban poverty in China. Their poverty mainly includes capability or competence poverty, which consists of a lack of skills and a shortage of knowledge shortage of the urban social life; and social exclusion, which exists in the weakness of their social support network and their discrimination and exclusion from urban society.

(2) Migrant workers' poverty is caused by their mobility and the "mobility-poverty" relationship can be influenced by external factors such as governmental policies and labor markets.

However, it is important to understand the policy implications behind the analytical framework on poverty among migrant workers. This author will attempt to analyze research initiated by UNESCO and CASS in order to explore what can be learned from the above framework in issuing effective policies in China.

1.8.2 Strategies of poverty reduction

As emphasized above, poverty among migrants doesn't emerge as a single economic phenomenon, but instead as a multi-dimensional one and includes poverty in terms of capability and social exclusion. Therefore, as far as poverty reduction for migrants is concerned, the object should not only focus on increasing rural migrants' income, but more importantly on improving their capabilities and promoting social inclusion between migrants and urban societies as well as among different groups of rural migrants. Three strategies of poverty reduction should be developed in order to target the four types of poverty among migrants:

1) Capacity Building

Capacity building can at least reduce two types of poverty among migrants shortage of non agricultural skills and lack of knowledge of law, health awareness, urban life, etc.. It is known as an effective way to provide migrants with training in order to improve their shortage of non agricultural skills; and it is necessary for rural migrants to have access to knowledge in terms of law, health awareness, urban life, etc..

2) Network Building

It is evident that a social support network can help to reduce poverty. In order to strengthen migrants' social support network, a policy or project can promote social or institutional network building between "sending and receiving areas" on the one hand, and can promote network building among pro-migrant organizations (or potential ones), such as governmental agencies, private sectors, NGOs/NPOs, researchers, social actors, etc., on the other.

3) Social Inclusion

Social inclusion for migrants in this paper refers to migrants' inclusion into urban society that includes not only social inclusion between migrants and urban residents but also among different migrant groups. It is evident that social inclusion can help to improve the difficulties related to social communication.

1.8.3 Practices of poverty reduction

With the understanding that most of migrants are living in poverty, UNESCO initiated a project to reduce this kind of poverty in 2002, in cooperation with CASS. The overall project selected 8 pilot sites across the country, including metropolitan areas (Beijing and Shanghai), large-size cities (Dalian in Liaoning Province, Chengdu in Sichuan Province and Kunming in Yunnan Province) and sending areas (Chifeng Prefecture in Inner

Mongolia, Diqing Prefecture in Yunnan Province, Zhuolu County in Hebei Province). The project intended to last 4 years from 2002 to 2005, and tried to explore innovative ways and examples to reduce the four types of poverty mentioned above.

In the CASS-UNESCO project, different pilot sites were selected to observe and cope with various situations for migrants in different cities. Among the pilot sites were those located in western and eastern China, as well as some specific "sending and receiving areas." Moreover, some areas were ethnic regions, while others were of non-ethnic (with Han background) characteristics.

Also, different organizations were selected as local partners in pilot sites: three were governmental agencies (Dalian Bureau of Public Security; Diqing Bureau of Agriculture and Livestocks; and Zhuolu County Government); three were academic institutions (Yunnan Academy of Social Sciences in Kunming; Sichuan Academy of Social Sciences in Chengdu; East Normal University in Shanghai); and two were NGO/NPO (Female Migrants' Home in Beijing and Chifeng Women's Federation).

1.9 Two Key Features of Poverty Reduction Related to the Project

One key feature is that the project is not merely aiming at increasing migrants' income, but even more so, that it is improving migrants' capabilities and promoting their social inclusion in urban society. The second key feature is that it advocates alternative and innovative strategies and measures among governmental entities and various agencies at all levels.

1.9.1 Innovative methods and examples

1) Skill Training

Diqing pilot site, located in southwestern China and with a majority of Tibetans or those with other ethnic backgrounds, is facing challenges related to a lack of local training. Specifically, local rural laborers find it difficult to locate non-agricultural jobs in local labor markets where many job vacancies have been occupied by migrant laborers from outside areas. To help local rural laborers benefit from local developments, the project in Diqing provides training courses for Diqing rural migrants in order to help them find non-agricultural jobs in the local labor market. In the meantime, the project helps them in job search consultation and micro-enterprise activities. Amongst around 500 trainees from 2002~2004, more than 95 percent have found non-agricultural jobs and have run small enterprises locally.

2) Programs for Migrant Knowledge Acquisition

To increase migrants' knowledge of law, health awareness, urban life, etc., in each pilot site, the project has held training programs in order to educate the migrants. These programs have been carried out in different ways: training classes, participation discussions, brochures, exhibitions, consultation hotlines, self-improvement, network building among migrants, etc. Most of the trainees in different pilot sites expressed that they had benefited from these programs, according to for instance, the reports of Chifeng and Diqing.

3) Network Building

Network building has been encouraged and implemented in some pilot sites. For example, the Chifeng Women's Federation has established a Chifeng Migrant's Home in Beijing and a Female Migrant's Center in Chifeng prefectural city. As a result that a network has been built up between rural areas of Chifeng, Chifeng city and Beijing, where a large number of Chifeng migrants are working and living. The CASS team, which is responsible for monitoring the project work in each pilot site, has released that the network has effectively linked Chifeng migrants with their original social support network, and built up a network between governmental agencies, NGOs, volunteers, and other actors. Moreover, the Chifeng Prefecture Government has realized the importance of network building for migrants and therefore has provided the political and financial support needed for this network building since 2004. Besides network building between "sending and receiving places", some pilot sites have made efforts to establish social support networks for migrants in cities. Taking Chengdu as an example, the pilot site has successfully established a social support network for migrants and their children. Many actors, including enterprises, postgraduate students, research institutions, governmental agencies, and migrants' children schools, were incorporated into the network in 2004. There is no doubt that it would not be successful in poverty reduction among such a huge number of rural migrants if all pro-migrant actors were not integrated and had not worked together in such a way.

4) Social Inclusion

Some pilot sites have been trying to promote social inclusion in different ways. In the Kunming pilot site, for instance, Yunnan Academy of Social Sciences has in cooperation with local authorities attempted to get rural migrants in Jinniu Neighborhood socially included into the urban society. Jinniu Neighborhood of Panlong District is one of the areas where ethnic people live, and most of its residents are of Hui background. In 2004, the project established an organization called the Committee of Ethnicity Friendship in the neighborhood, which is joined by 27 work units (Danwei) in the neighborhood. The ethnic migrants can express their voices and suggestions through this Committee. Moreover, the project provides public services for the migrants, such as legal aid, access to kindergarten, training classes to educate the migrants on law, health awareness, urban life, etc., and activities of social communications between the migrants and neighborhood residents. Kunming is a city where a number of ethnicities work and reside; thus, the project design has focused, to some degree, on how to promote social inclusion between migrants and local urban residents from an ethnic perspective, which means not only considering the factor of ethnicity but also utilizing cultural and customary advantages among the ethnicity groups in the project's implementation.

Beijing is another example of promoting social inclusion among different migrant groups. The local counterpart, Female Migrant Home, with support of the project, has been holding regular activities among female migrants in Beijing, such as group discussions; self-organized improvement activities; lectures on law, health awareness, urban life, etc.; field visiting activities, and so on. The female migrants who have participated in these activities come from different provinces, such as Gansu, Inner Mongolia, Henan, Anhui, and so on. In fact, Female Migrant Home has created a sort of public space for rural migrants that helps promote social inclusion among them.

1.10 Policy Implications

China has experienced rapid urbanization and at the same time the government has emphasized a more balanced, comprehensive, and sustainable development plan since 2003, which is described as a new paradigm for development (Xinde Fazhan Guan), covering all dimensions in social, economic, cultural, political and environmental domains. Nonetheless, there are many challenges, problems and risks. For example, the gap, between rural and urban, eastern and western, rich and poor, can pose a serious threat to the future of development; and the gap between migrants and urban residents, and social exclusion of rural migrants are exactly part of the threat. Therefore, it is important to reduce poverty among migrants. Fortunately, the Chinese government has realized the implications of this problem, and in September of 2003, the State Council issued The National Plan of Training Rural Migrants (2003~2010). Six ministries provided for hundreds of millions of migrants through training programs on non-agricultural skills and knowledge of law, health awareness, urban life, etc.. The Sunshine Project (Yangguang Gongcheng), which was initiated by MOA in 2004, is part of this Plan. On the basis of above analyses and project practices, some policy implications can be realized:

First, the government will demonstrated its ability to generate poverty reduction policy more inclusively so that it covers rural migrants in urban areas. On the one hand, the governmental experiences of poverty reduction in past decades can to some degree be helpful to future policies in reducing poverty among rural migrants, and on the other hand, future policies can be further improved from the existing ones: in addition to the training programs, policies can be drafted with the intent of promoting social inclusion. For instance, on the basis of the practice of the CASS-UNESCO project, the policies can be made to emphasize and strengthen capacity building, network building, social inclusion within urban neighborhood communities, establishment of public space, etc..

Second, the government will set out more practical macro policies related to the process of urbanization in order to ensure that cities will not absorb an unhealthy level of rural migrants, i.e, the residents in cities, regardless of their urban or migrant resident status, should have adequate employment opportunities, social support systems, and public services so that they will not fall into poverty. On the other side of the coin, most of the migrants should keep their arable land before they become permanent urban residents, so as to prevent falling into poverty and in order to help them strengthen their social support network in "sending and receiving areas."

Third, the government will encourage a more realistic strategy of urbanization where on the one hand, the rural laborers can seek non-agricultural jobs in urban areas and become urban residents, and on the other hand, they can also be socially included into local societies wherever they live. One of the strategies is to balance rural-urban balanced development (*Chengxiang Yitihua*), which means that the urban development will not be at the expense of rural decline. There are at least two preconditions which should be met for this strategy: one is to promote local development to help people find employment opportunities in nearby townships or cities; and the other is to improve the rural laborer's non-agricultural skills so that they are capable of receiving employment. The development of the Diqing pilot site, supported by the project, is a typical example.

References

[1] Bai Nansheng, "Interviews on Issues of Migrant workers.." *Dushu*, 2003, 12 (9).

[2] Berghman, G. "Social Exclusion in Europe: Policy Context and Analytical Framewor." In *Beyond*

the Threshold, ed. G. Roots, 10-28. Bristol: Policy Press, 1995.

[3] Huang Ping, et al. *Xunqiu Shengcun* [Seeking Survival]. Kunming: Yunnan Renmin Chubanshe, 1997.

[4] Huang Ping. "When Young Farmers Leave the Farm: What Will Happen to Rural Development in China When Rural-Urban Migration Takes Place at a High Pace under Impacts of Globalization?" In *Globalization and Its Impact*, ed. Cecilia Lindqvist, 56-67. FRN, Stockholm, 2000.

[5] Huang Ping, 2004. "Strategic Thinking." In *Together with Migrants*. Beijing: UNESCO Beijing Office, 2004.

[6] Huang Ping and Zhan Shaohua. "Internal Migration in China: Linking it to Development." In *Migration, Development and Poverty Reduction in Asia*. Geneva: International Organization for Migration, 2005.

[7] Levitas, R. *The Inclusive Society? Social Exclusion and New Labour*. London: Macmillan Press Ltd, 1998.

[8] Ling Yue, 1997. "Chongtu Yu Kuanrong" [Conflict and Endurance]. Zhongguo Qingnian. January 18.

[9] Liu Kaiming. *Bianyuan Ren* [People of Margin]. Beijing: Xinhua Chubanshe, 2003.

[10] Lu Xueyi. *Dangdai Zhongguo Shehui Jieceng Yanjiu Baogao.* [A Research Report on Social Classes in Contemporary China]. Beijing: Social Sciences Academic Press (China), 2002.

[11] MOA. "Migration Trend of Western China," *Jingji Cankao Bao* [Economic Reference Daily], June 4, 2003, http: //www.cass.net.cn/webnew/file/200306126929.html.

[12] NBS and MOLSS. China Labor Statistical Yearbook 2001. Beijing: China Statistics Press, 2001.

[13] Rodgers, G. *Social Exclusion: Rhetoric, Reality and Responses*. Geneva: ILO Office, 1995.

[14] Sen, A. *Development as Freedom*. Oxford University Press, 1999.

[15] Skeldon, R. "Migration and Poverty." *Asia Pacific Population Journal*, December, 2002.

[16] Solinger, D. "The Potential for Urban Unrest." In Is Unstable?, ed., David Shambaugh. NY: ME Sharpe.

[17] Tan Shen. "Nongmin Gong Yanjiu Zoushu" [A synthesis of Studies of Rural Migrant Workers]. *Sociological Research* 6, no. 2 (2003).

[18] Tang Jun, et al. *Zhongguo Chengshi Pinkun Yu Fanpinkun Baogao.*[A Report of Urban Poverty and Anti poverty in China]. Beijing: Huaxia Chubanshe, 2003.

[19] Wang Fenyu and Li Lulu. *Zongguo Chengshi Laodongli Liudong: Congye Moshi, Zhiye Shengya, Xinyimin.* [Labor Migration in Urban China: Employment, Career, New Migrants]. Beijing: Beijing Press, 2001.

[20] Webster, A. *Introduction to the Sociology of Development*. NJ: Macmillan, 1984.

[21] Zhang Xiaojun, et al. *Capabilities and Poverty*. Beijing: Social Sciences Academic Press (China), 2005.

2

Rebuilding Rural Migrants' Communities*

Zhan Shaohua

The issue of rural labor migrants (*Nongmin Gong*) has become one of most significant public and policy concerns in China in recent years. Since 2000, the state has adjusted its policy from passively controlling and regulating rural migrants to actively protecting and helping them in cities (Bai Nanshen, et al., 2002; Huang Ping &. Frank Pieke, 2003). In 2002, the central government in an official document promulgated a "16 word" principle as a general policy guide on rural migrants: "Fair Treatment, Reasonable Consultation and Suggestion, Comprehensive Management, and Better Service" (Gongping Duidai, Heli Yindao, Wanshan Guanli, Gaohao Fuwu). However, under this general principle, there have been many different opinions on how to protect and help rural migrants in practice, who are regarded as a disadvantageous group in comparison with urban laborers. Still, the central government and many local governments are waiting for practical policy proposals. This paper will critically review the existing policies and on going discussions in this respect, and propose rebuilding rural migrants' communities as a new strategy to deal with the problems relating to rural-urban migration in China.

2.1 Policy Framework and on-going Arguments

2.1.1 The *Hukou* system

The Household Registration System (*Hukou* System) was established in 1958 and became a strict system preventing rural-urban labor migration before 1984. After 1984, the *Hukou* system has become more and more flexible and has become gradually divorced from other institutional arrangements, such as the food supply, education, employment, health care, social security, etc.. In 1997, the Ministry of Public Security announced that rural people could apply for their urban *Hukou* in townships and small and medium-sized

---

* This paper is drafted by Mr. Zhan Shaohua and with the help of Professor Huang Ping, Dr. Chen Xin and Ms. Pan Jie of the CASS team.

cities if they have been working and living there for more than a year. Since June 2003, a new policy for wandering homeless people and beggars has acted to prevent local urban authorities from sending migrants back home. In last two years, many provinces (such as Chongqing, Zhejiang and Hebei) have abandoned the separation of urban *Hukou*.

However, most rural migrant laborers in cities still have rural *Hukou* and that is why they are called "*Nongmin Gong*" in Chinese. Indeed their *Hukou* distinguishes them from urban residents and to some degree excludes them from urban social policies, such as social insurance, public relief, education.

However, the *Hukou* system has still been a main target of critics. The most radical opinion attributes all migrants' miseries to the *Hukou* system, and argues that only by abandoning it completely could rural residents, migrants and urban residents be treated equally. However, the opposite argue that the *Hukou* system has been modified greatly since 1984 when an official document was issued to allow farmers to seek jobs and run businesses in cities; thus, it is not a main barrier against migration and social equality any more. Moreover, the *Hukou* system has some positive effects in protecting the disadvantaged groups, such as farmers and migrants. For example, it provides the farmers and migrants with a piece of farmland, which is a source of their livelihood and can reduce their risks in the urban labor market. Ultimately, authorities express that the *Hukou* system should be further modified but not abandoned completely, according to the announcement of the Ministry of Public Security in 2002 (Please see: http: //www.china.org. cn/chinese/2002/Feb/111419.htm).

2.2 The Labor Market

With the withering away of policies excluding rural migrants from some sectors, adopted in some large cities in the late 1990s such as Shanghai, Beijing, Shenzhen, etc., rural migrants can in principle be employed in any sector in the labor market. However, a large proportion of rural migrants still find their jobs in the so-called "3D" (dangerous, dirty and difficult) or informal sectors with a low salary, partly due to their shortage of human capital. For instance, some research shows that almost 90 percent of workers in the construction industry are migrant laborers, 80 percent in the mining industry, and 50 percent in the service sectors (The People's Daily, 2003). Thus, the issue of protecting the migrant laborers has become much more important and has attracted the public and governments' concerns. In September of 2003, the Ministry of Labor and Social Security (MOLSS) and the Ministry of Construction (MOC) jointly issued another "Notice on

Resolving the Problem of Delayed Wages of Migrant Laborers in Construction", and in September 2004, the two central agencies issued another document attempting to institutionalize wage payment among migrant workers in construction and to ensure that their wages would not be delayed. Moreover, the MOLSS demanded in June 2004 that the employers must purchase work injury insurance for migrant workers, especially in the dangerous and risky industries such as construction, mining, etc..

However, even though the government has set out positive policies, many researchers have expressed their doubts over whether the policies could be implemented effectively partly because of governmental administrative constraints. For instance, labor inspection is one of the important measures ensuring that the employer obey the laws and regulations, but it is quite difficult to inspect and stop a wide range of unlawful behavior even though labor inspectorate has been established at all levels and consists of 43000 officials across the country. Here the key problem is that migrant laborers (to some degree all laborers) are quite powerless in comparison with the employers, and thus it is important that they are empowered to a certain degree.

2.3 Social Security

Except for work injury insurance, thus far the central government hasn't formulated any policy that incorporates migrant laborers into the existing urban social security system. Nonetheless, some local governments began measures to do exactly this, such as in Shanghai, Beijing, Shenzhen, etc.. But it has only covered a very small part of migrant laborers (less than 5 percent) and its effectiveness and feasibility have been widely doubted[10]. Actually, some research has insisted that farmers and migrant's farmland should not be privatized because it can serve as a kind of social security for them, instead of pushing them all into the official social security system, especially given that the government has not enough capacity to provide social security for all (Wen Tiejun, 2000a; Li Changping, 2003).

2.4 Pro-Migrant Policies

As a result of strong political will, governments at both central and local levels have

10 The doubt is substantiated by the fact that a large number of urban laborers have not been covered by the social security system. By the end of 2004, about 122.4 million urban laborers paid for their pension insurance, 93.3 million for medical insurance and 105.8 for unemployment insurance. Please see the official website: http://www.1m.gov.cn/gb/news/2005-02/02/content_61863.htm.

implemented pro-migrant policies to help migrants. In January 2003, the State Council issued a document titled "Notice on Management and Services for Rural Migrant Workers", which established some general principles of pro-migrant policies on skill training, education for their children, work injury insurance, housing, health care, transportation, etc. In September 2003, the State Council promulgated The National Plan of Training Rural Migrants, 2003~2010, to provide hundreds of millions of migrants with training programs on non-agricultural skills and knowledge and skills for urban life. The Sunshine Project (Yangguang Gongcheng) initiated by the Ministry of Agriculture (MOA) in March 2004 is part of this plan. Also in September 2003, the State Council issued another document on education for migrants' children, in which the urban education system is responsible for migrants' children. With the implementation of these policies at the central level, most of the local governments similarly followed suit and have begun to implement policy at the local level. Although the public and researchers speak highly of these positive policy changes, it is also widely believed that this process would be time consuming and require more efforts and innovative measures.

2.5 Remaining Challenges

Despite positive policies and on-going arguments, three challenges still need serious attention:

One-effectiveness: many people worry about whether or to what degree migrant workers can benefit from the positive policies mentioned above. Even though the Chinese government has a comprehensive and relatively efficient administrative system, which reaches the township/street level and even has a strong influence at village/neighborhood level, migrants are outside of this system in the sense that they move out of the rural area while failing to become integrated into the urban administrative system. Apparently it is too risky and unrealistic for the government to expect that the employers or the labor market would settle all migrants' problems, especially after the reform and, to a strict extent, the breakdown of Work Unit (*Danwei*) System in cities in the early 1990s. The precarious status of migrants in employment and settlement makes it more difficult to cover migrants within the urban administrative system which is mainly based upon the residents' location. Therefore, the key point here is that a system or measure should be developed to integrate the migrants into the administrative system if these positive policies are to be fully implemented and effective.

Two-social exclusion: although much of the research has paid attention to the exclusion of rural migrants from existing social or public policies, research and policy has seldom touched upon social exclusion between migrants and urban society. The problem has become very serious with the wide-range social discrimination and high ratio of migrants' criminal behavior. What social policy should be implemented in order to promote social inclusion of migrants in urban society?

Three-limitation of resources: another important question is whether or not the government has enough resources (such as financial support) for migrants seeing that as of 2004 the population of migrants has reached more than 110 million. However this might be less significant if we remember what was accomplished during/under the planned system before 1978 when the country had much less resources: industrialization, the wide coverage of basic education and medical care, the comprehensive irrigation system, etc.. Therefore, the key point in this respect is how to develop an effective and innovative institutional arrangement for the socialist market economy.

In attempting to approach the challenges above, community rebuilding is recommended as one of the strategies in this paper.

2.6 Community Rebuilding for Migrants

In this paper, community is regarded as a collective and/or network of ordinary people, who therefore share, to a great extent, identity, security and solidarity. Community will thus work, among other things, as a network and safety net for individuals (or families), linking them with outside forces, such as political agencies, market forces, etc.

2.6.1 Rural community

Before rural laborers become migrants, they live in rural areas consisting of about 680 thousands villages across the country. After the establishment of the People's Republic of China in 1949, the political and administrative forces permeated the village level in rural areas, but official institutions, such as the People's Commune (*Renmin Gongshe*), the Production Group (*Shengchan Dui*) before 1978, and village committees after 1978, were basically established on the basis of rural communities/original natural villages (*Ziran Cun*). Most of them were untouched and therefore to a certain extent autonomous before the era of "modernization" started in 1840 and had strong social support effects (Wang Xiaoyi, 2000; Wen Tiejun, 2000b). Many rural communities were built up based on the kinship system. Even after the reform and opening-up, rural communities have still played an active role with social functions such as supporting the disadvantaged and the elderly. However, after the farmers leave rural areas and become migrants, they face the problem of insufficient social support in comparison to the rural communities.

2.6.2 Urban community

Before urban reform was initiated in the middle of 1980s, most urban residents had been basically organized on the basis of their work units (*Danwei*). Their work unit not only provided them with jobs but also social welfare, including retirement pension, medical care, housing, amusements, etc.. Thus, urban communities emerged on the basis of this work unit system where employees not only worked together but also lived together. However, after the reform or, to a strict extent, the breakdown of work unit system in the early 1990s, especially after the reform of the State-owned Enterprises (SOEs) in the middle of 1990s, many workers were laid off from the SOEs, and the urban communities, which were mainly based on the work unit system, have been declining. At the same time, the urban governments have introduced new policies that act to build up a so-called "urban community" based on the neighborhood. But there are many doubts as to whether or not this type of administrative "urban community" can be regarded as the community since in such administrative communities many residents don't even have social communication and public activities, and as a result don't share a common identity. It is especially true when people move to newly built apartment complexes. Research has demonstrated that most urban residents seek social support from their social network (the network mainly consisting kinship or work relationship) instead of from this kind of community (Zhan Shaohua, 2003).

2.6.3 Rural migrants' community

Some of the migrants' communities did begin to emerge after a large number of migrants had arrived in cities in the 1990s. Most of these communities were identified with the name of the sending areas, such as Zhejiang Village, Henan Village, and Xinjiang Village in Beijing, because they were built up by the migrants themselves from Zhejiang Province, Henan Province, etc.. Moreover, the research has demonstrated that in the same community migrants' employment statuses were quite identical. For instance, most migrants in so-called Henan Village were rubbish pickers (Tang Can & Liu Xiaoshuang, 2000). These communities mostly located in the suburbs and seemed to possess geographical boundaries, but the studies revealed that these communities existed and functioned beyond these boundaries and in fact exhibited a strong social network with both sending and receiving areas. That is why some scholars called them "trans-boundary communities" (Xiang Biao, 2000).

However, most urban governments have regarded the emergence of migrants' communities as an abnormal phenomenon, and have made efforts to uproot them (though mostly unsuccessful), for the reason that they had been found with problems of insecurity, disorder, lack of harmony, uncleanliness, and so on, according to the standards of urban administrative communities introduced above. Nevertheless, the studies have demonstrated that the migrants' communities have played positive roles in protecting and helping migrants (Xiang Biao, 2000; Tang Can & Liu Xiaoshuang, 2000).

2.6.4 Community rebuilding for migrants

Migrant community rebuilding is an important objective within China's urban environment. On the one hand, migrants have left their original rural communities; and on the other hand, most of them have not built up their own communities in urban areas except for a limited number of rural migrants' communities. Thus, it is necessary to rebuild communities for migrants not only because it can provide social support systems for migrants but also it will meet the above three challenges:

First, community rebuilding for migrants can subsequently provide a platform for policy implementation. In this way, the positive policies mentioned above can reach and benefit migrants through the migrants' communities. Moreover, the community can also become the action platform of NGOs and other actors, which are willing to work with migrants. Obviously, this rebuilt community is different from those communities such as Zhejiang Village in Beijing, since it will be accepted by and actively interact with the local governments, NGOs, and other type of actors.

Second, community rebuilding can promote social inclusion for migrants in urban society. On the one hand, individual migrants can obtain social support and participate in social life in their community in order to reduce the ratio of migrants' crimes[11], and on the other hand, the communities can interact with urban society and take positive actions to reduce social discrimination from urban residents.

Third, community rebuilding can mobilize social resources among migrants and promote identity, security and solidarity. Thus the governments' resources, such as favorable polices and financial support, can be leveraged by the established communities to

11 Community building/rebuilding has been regarded as a useful mechanism in reducing criminal behavior, or what European scholars term the so-called "third way" (See Giddens, Anthony, 1998, *The Third Way: A Renewal of Social Democracy*. Cambridge: Polity Press.

support the migrants, and thus ensure that policies are more equal and effective.

Of course, in the realities of the operations of community rebuilding there exist some problems and challenges for the migrants. For example, the migrants' employment and residence is unstable, and the problems of mobile identities, social exclusion, and the migrants' disadvantageous position all hinder community rebuilding. Therefore, the migrants' community rebuilding needs to in practice carry out things slowly and experimentally. The following text will use an example of a project, summarizing and carding over this project in a three year period in terms of the practice and exploration of community rebuilding, and using this as the foundation to put forth an interest in the problem of migrant community rebuilding as well as attempting to understand a way to deal with these problems.

2.7 The Work of Community Rebuilding from 2002~2004

In 2002, the UNESCO and Chinese Academy of Social Sciences (CASS) initiated an action research project to reduce poverty among migrants in China. The project selected 8 pilot sites to explore and understand the problem of migrant poverty in different environments. In the passing of three years time, the project in practice explored or discovered three ways of community rebuilding.

2.7.1 Community rebuilding based on locality

In 2002, the Chifeng Women's Federation, the local partner of the Chifeng pilot site in Inner Mongolia, established an organization called the "Chifeng Migrant's Home" (CMH) in Beijing, one of the places where a large number of Chifeng migrants are living and working. CMH provides provisional accommodation for female migrants (most of them work as domestic servants), coordinates with the migrants and the employers (including the domestic service companies and households, for which the migrants are working), holds weekly activities on training or communication among migrants, protects migrants' legal rights and interests, helps with legal issues, health awareness, urban life, etc., and prints brochures for migrants. In fact, around 40 thousands female migrants are directly involved in the activities of CMH.

Researchers discovered that a community has been built up among the female migrants through CMH, even though they cannot communicate frequently with each other because due to their extensive household commitments all day long. Nonetheless, CMH has established (direct or indirect) social networks among them. More importantly, it is easier for the female migrants to acquire the same identity because all of them are from the same sending area-Chifeng.

Furthermore, CMH and the community gained the approval of local urban government to hold activities. It has also become a platform for the governments or other types of actors, such as CASS and UNESCO, to implement policies or hold training activities. For instance, the training programs are more easily and effectively carried out through CMH and the community, according to the project reports. Moreover, the community has empowered the female migrants and promoted identity, security and solidarity among them. Mutual assistance, happiness, risk-bearing, etc., have been experienced throughout the community.

In short, this is a realistic and feasible way to rebuild community for migrants as it helps them to easily obtain their common identities. The migrants' communities, such as Zhejiang Village, are obviously built up according to migrants' original localities. However, the CMH community, similar to Zhejiang Village, demonstrates its weakness in the fact that it struggles to promote social communication between migrants and urban residents. More than 80 percent of members in the community have not made friends with local urban residents. Thus, mechanisms should be developed to promote positive interaction between the community and local urban society.

2.7.2 Community rebuilding based on cultural resources

Since 2003, project researchers discovered another type of community rebuilding in the Kunming pilot site. The local partner, Yunnan Academy of Social Sciences has, in cooperation with local authorities, tried to integrate rural migrants into the urban community. It is not easy in most urban areas because social exclusion widely exists between rural migrants and urban residents. However, the urban community, officially called the "Jinniu Neighborhood of Panlong District", is one of the areas where the ethnic people live, and where most of the residents have ethnic backgrounds. Therefore, the migrants who share similar ethnic backgrounds can be relatively easily integrated into the existing urban community on the basis of their ethnicity. In 2004, this project promoted the establishment of the "Ethnic Minority Friendship Ties Committee" inside the community. Through this committee, the migrants and the urban residents were able to increase their interactions, participate together in the work of community policy, and ultimately, migrants successfully merged into the urban community.

The example of the Kunming pilot site has illustrated that cultural resources can play a positive role in community rebuilding. Agencies or organizations in other areas of western China, where a large number of people with ethnic background dwell and reside, can learn its lessons and experiences. However, this way of community rebuilding cannot be adopted if common/similar cultural identities fail to exist among migrants and urban residents. Of course, deserving attention is, in addition to the ethnic minorities interrelated cultural identification, they also have other many cultural resources that they use, such as language, religion, customs, etc.

2.7.3 Community rebuilding based on governmental policies

In the Dalian pilot site, from 2001 on the Dalian Bureau of Public Security advocated apartment building for migrants with the primary purpose of reducing the migrants' crimes. Compared with the migrants' scattered residence circumstances, the training activity and the dissemination and carrying out of policy are more effectively implemented inside migrant apartment complexes. In 2003 and 2004, the Dalian Government attached great importance to the issue of apartment building for migrants as well as to the CASS-UNESCO project. In order to encourage private investment in migrants' apartment construction, the Dalian city government issued many advantageous policies, such as tax exemption and reduced prices on electricity and water. As a result, the influx in apartment construction (52 apartments in 2004) has greatly reduced the migrants' crime rates in the city.

Some migrants' communities were rebuilt based on these policies. A noticeable example is the community which emerged with the Sihai Migrants' Apartment, which is located in the Ganzijing District and originally established in 2002. With support of local authorities, the community organized frequent public activities for migrants, and more importantly, a public fund was established (used as legal aid for those in lawsuits) and every member in the community contributed to it. Apparently, the fund was established according to the identity and solidarity within the community, and in turn, it can promote identity, security and solidarity among migrants. Unfortunately the apartment building was demolished in 2003 due to urban expansion.

However, to some extent, local counterparts in the Dalian pilot site have yet to realize the importance of community rebuilding. Therefore, as far as policy is concerned, they still are without the encouragement and support of rebuilding migrant communities.

2.8 Suggestions for the Project

Despite the achievements on community rebuilding for migrants, the CASS-UNESCO project should go further and take community rebuilding as one of its most important strategies. On the basis of the above introduction and analyses, five suggestions are presented for the future work and action of the project in terms of community rebuilding:

First, under the general principle of poverty reduction and action research, the new strategy of community rebuilding can be used as another important measure to reduce poverty among migrants. A more detailed schema should be designed in the future in terms of a new strategy, including its principles, methodologies, indicators, etc.

Second, the project should give priority to the 8 pilot sites to practice the new strategy, especially those that have already made progress in the way of community rebuilding for migrants, such as the pilot sites of Chifeng, Dalian and Kunming that were mentioned above.

hird, the project should learn from the various projects on rural or urban community building/rebuilding, which are hosted by either governmental agencies or NGOs/NPOs, and should try to hold joint actions with them, if at all possible.

Fourth, migrant community rebuilding is an advantageous strategy for realizing the fusing between migrants and urban residents, and thereby, reducing migrants' social exclusion. Migrant community rebuilding is also advantageous to overcoming the scattered condition of migrants' employment and residence. It increases the capacities of migrants in their urban life and environment, and it hastens the birth of a social network between migrants. Thus, the migrant group is able to achieve a certain level of empowerment. Active community building is unlikely to cause migrants' communities to become an enclave within the urban community, or a slum. Conversely, this kind of community building can lead to reduced migrants' crime rates (using the Dalian project as an example), and in turn reducing antagonisms between the urban residents and the migrants. Therefore, through this community platform, and even further through measures such as policy formulation or project policy strategies, mutual communication and assistance can be effectively formed between these groups. So here it is suggested that in future policy formulation and project strategizing, these measures need to use various kinds of advantageous conditions to strengthen mutual activity and help between the migrants' community and the urban residents, such as, the Kunming project which used ethnic minorities cultural understanding as the foundation for carrying out community rebuilding and merging the migrants into the urban community.

Finally, migrants' community rebuilding needs support from specialized governmental departments that organize measures and carry out management. From this train of thought we can discover that the various governments can select a path that is currently different than urban community building. On the one hand, in the local conditions they can combine together the migrants' community rebuilding and the urban community building; on the other hand, through subsidizing or helping establish grass-roots or non-governmental organizations, they can encourage the goal of community rebuilding. In wishing to carry out the work of this project, they need to have specialized government departments that organize these measures and provide responsible management. But at present, they still do not have specialized governmental departments that carry out management and service with regard to migrants, and therefore, these conditions need to undergo changes.

References

[1] Bai Nanshen. *Huixiang, Haishi Jincheng? Zhongguo Nongcun Waichu Laodongli Huiliu Yanjiu* [Return or Go to Cities? A Study of Rural Migrant Labor Returning to Rural Areas]. Beijing: Chinese Financial Press, 2002.

[2] Giddens, A. *The Third Way-A Renewal of Social Democracy*. Cambridge: Polity Press, 1998.

[3] Huang Ping and Frank N. Pieke. *China Migration Country Report*. Beijing: DFID Research Report, 2003.

[4] Li Changping. "Shenyan Tudi Siyou Hua" [Careful to say Privatization of Arable Land]. *Dushu* 12, no. 6 (2003).

[5] Tang Can and Liu Xiaoshuang. "Henancun Liudong Nongmin De Fenhua" [Stratification of Migrants of He Nan Village]. Journal of Sociology 6, no. 4 (2000).

[6] The People's Daily, "Pingdeng Duidai, Wanshan Zhengce" [Fair Treatment, Better Policies], September 27, 2003. Also please see:http://www.people.com.cn/GB/paper464/10284/939913.html.

[7] Wen Tiejun. "Sannong Wenti de Shiji Fans" [Reflections at the Turn of the 20th Century on the Three Rural Problems]. Dushu 12, no. 1 (2000a).

[8] Wen Tiejun. *Zhongguo Nongcun Jiben Jingji Zhidu Yanjiu* [A Study of Rural Basic Economic Institution]. Beijing: Zhongguo Jingji Chubanshe, 2000b.

[9] Xiang Biao. *Kua Bianjie de Shequ* [Community Across Boundaries]. Beijing: Sanlian Shudian, 2000.

[10] Wang Xiaoyi, 2000. "Tradition and Transition: The Chinese Village since Rural Reform." In *Globalization and Its Impact*, ed. Cecilia Lindqvist, pp 44-55. FRN: Stockholm.

[11] Zhan Shaohua. "Dishouru Dongqi Jumin De Xingwei Xuanze Jiqi Bianyuanhua Hougu" [Behavior Choice and its Effect of Marginalization of Low-income Resettled Urban Residents]. *Social Policy Review*, 4, no. 4 (2003).

3

Poverty Issues of Migrant Laborers Under Market Conditions

Chen Xin

3.1 Introduction

One of the main purposes of the CASS-UNESCO project in the eight different locations is to experiment with strategies intended to reduce poverty and protect social/legal interests of migrant laborers, and in the end, influence the process of policy making at the different levels of government. However, in order to achieve this goal, the project's design and related activities attempt to understand the migrant workers' situation in depth in the market of urban economics, which is believed to play an increasingly crucial role in preventing improvement in the situation of migrant workers in urban areas of China. Since there is much debate on what the actual causes are for the present unsatisfactory situation of the migrant workers in urban areas, different ideas, suggestions, and policy orientations have been put forward in trying to deal with this matter. Therefore, this paper attempts to present a point of view related to the experiences and research derived from the CASS-UNESCO project and some data from wider recourses as well. First, the general background of China's migrant workers will be discussed in response to the ongoing argument, specifically referencing the findings of the CASS-UNESCO project following three years of experiences and observations. Second, a discussion will combine data from the CASS-UNESCO project in recent years. Third, the following section will discuss the issues and problems encountered in the project. Fourth, the following section will discuss suggestions for policy development and the future design of the project.

3.1.1 Insights on the Issue of China's Urban Migrant Laborer

China's urban poverty is mainly related to the living conditions of migrant laborers. Furthermore, in the long run, if this situation is not alleviated, an increasing number of urban laborers will join the ranks of poverty, creating new and serious levels of urban poverty. Of the more than 300 millions surplus rural laborers in China, about 100 million belong to the floating population travelling between urban and rural areas to work or do business, and over 100 million rural laborers are engaged in non-agricultural activities at home. It is predicated that in the next 20 to 30 years, there will be 200 to 300 million rural laborers entering the urban areas and that they will constitute the main problem in China's urban poverty struggle. Below, this paper first discusses some different views on the understanding of "migrant labors" and before exploring relevant policy suggestions.

The reality of "migrant laborers" tells us that the issue of "migrant laborers" belongs to the question of "rural laborers, agriculture and rural development" and also to the question of industrialization and urbanization. According to the mainstream view at home, the fundamental answer to the question of "rural laborers, agriculture and rural development" lies in cities instead of in the countryside, i.e., it lies in industrialization and urbanization. The background of this view is still related to the experience of western industrialized countries. The agricultural output value makes up less than 14 percent of China's GDP, and it is believed that at present China's urban population should not merely reach around 40 percent of the total population, but that it should mainly correspond to the proportion of the second and third industries' GDP; and that according to international experience, it should reach a level of 70-80 percent or higher. But because the question of "rural laborers, agriculture and rural development" in China is not identical with the experience of industrialized countries, the mainstream view more often attributes this problem to the domestic economic and social policies of the Chinese government. According to this view, social and economic policies have resulted in the characterization of "serious lagging behind" in terms of China's urbanization, and the concrete reasons are that the Chinese government has not loosened its domicile system control and that the government has not promoted active flow of rural population into urban areas. This paper does not intend to negate that the Chinese government still has positive initiatives in response to the question of "rural laborers, agriculture and rural development", and that both in the past and at present, there are still some major policy defects. However, the most widely held view is that the government has neglected a more essential problem behind the domestic policies of "rural laborers, agriculture and rural development", i. e. international factors related to home economic and social policies that have led to predicaments of the question of "rural labors, agriculture and rural development" on one hand, and the domestic labor market factor on the other hand. Fundamentally speaking, the issues of migrant laborers that relate to the question of "rural laborers, agriculture and rural development" are a reflection of the international economic and political pattern in China's domestic development. This does not mean domestic policies are exempt from their contributions to the problems (such as their failure to invest main rural development resources in the rural education, public health, rural community building and other social development fields), but rather that modernization, industrialization, and marketization is blindly promoted and practiced in the vast rural area. Under the impact of the globalization of the world economy and the subsequent domestic policy domination by the trend of marketization, surplus supply of rural migrant laborers has been directly contending with market forces.

In the past, criticisms at home often talked about governmental urbanization policies, stressing stagnation of urbanization development, focusing on domicile control policies and system hindrances that restricted flow of laborers and expecting that the problems would be resolved if 200 to 300 million rural labors entered cities. In the meantime, this view paid less attention to the discussion of market factors exerting a more and more unfavorable influence on the ever increasing surplus supply of rural laborers in urban areas, and it failed to mention much in the way of promoting education of the rural population, training for rural laborers, medical care and community building as necessary strategies for areas alleviating these problems. According to main lines of development of globalization, the question of China's urbanization is directly related with rural problems, but according to this logic, urbanization is further related to industrialization. Therefore, we must analyze China's rural problems including migrant labor issues by proceeding from the question of industrialization.

Generally speaking, China's manufacturing industry is at the middle and lower end of the international industrial chain. On the world scale, industries at this position are surplus in capacity, and in the past 20 years and for some time longer, China's industrial expansion will be situated at this position. China's industrial expansion in the past 20 years was not brought about by the fact that the international market had the room to accommodate China's huge production capacity, but by the fact that China made use of the comparative advantages of this position to make industrialized countries shift, actively or passively, traditional industries and labor intensive industries to China, and at the same time it was a result of the fact that China seized the shares of other developing countries. China's industrialization is in fact absorbing the existing production capacity of the international manufacturing industry and the key to the expansion of China's industrialization is to absorb international production capacity via the low cost of her labor force. Therefore in the international economic pattern, it is not so much the successful expansion of China's industrialization as it is the successful shift of traditional industries from developed countries and regions to China in relation to China's superiority of labor force price and production capacity. In the past 20 years, what has truly brought about new industrial expansion internationally is the so-called high and new technological industries, i. e. the "new economy." Only this new type of industrialization expansion represented by high and new technology can create new and increased open space in the international market. China's industrial development in the past 20 years was almost insignificant in this aspect. In 1995, high-tech industries accounted for 13.05 percent of the total industrial output value of the country; and occupied a total of 8.4 percent of the total workforce. A large share of them did not control core technology but only produced auxiliary equipment or did assembling or processing. Internationally speaking, this share of market production was about USD 3000 billion in 1996, accounting for 30 percent of the world market of products and services, whereas China only represented a share of USD 3 billion, which was negligible (See Table 3-1).[12]

Table 3-1 Distribution of Shares of the "New" Global Economic Market in 1996

Country/Region	Market Share (USD 100 Million)	Percentage
China	30	0.1
Japan	4000	13.33
Germany	5000	16.67
USA	7000	23.33
Other countries and regions	13700	43.33
Total	30000	100

China will still not be capable of such "new economy" expansion for quite a long time. Even if such capability exists, the expansion of the "new economy" represented by high and new technological industries excludes, rather than absorbs, nonprofessional or unskilled laborers. International figures have demonstrated that expansion of industry with high densities of technique and capital does not positively link to the employment of traditional economy and sociology. By 2030, China's population will gradually reach about 1.6 billion. Even if urbanization rates reach 50 percent as optimistically predicted, there will be 200 to 300 million rural laborers that will likely shift to urban areas and will cause serious pressure on urban employment. On the other hand, there still be about 300 million surplus laborers in the countryside and unemployment and land resources in the rural areas

12 *Knowledge Economy Countermeasures-Operation and Security*, Wong Yong (eds.), p. 468, 482. Beijing: China Cities Publishing House, 1998.

will continue to be a problem. Therefore, surplus labor supply will significantly constrain China's social/economic development as well as government policy in solving the problems of migrant labor.

Even if urbanization reaches 50 percent, what will be the basis for industrial expansion and employment increases? Obviously, in the future 20 years, the way out for China's realization of industrial "expansion", increase of employment and implementation of urbanization strategies is still to encourage industrialized countries to "move" traditional industries to China. Apart from other economic or political factors that have a bearing on this process, there is a key factor, i. e., China must continue to maintain its superiority in the price of its labor force. If hopes are placed on the expansion of traditional industries for the resolution of employing the future prediction of over 900 million workers, the present unfavorable position for the majority of migrant labor in the market will not be improved soon and space for government interventions would also not be very wide. With China's large working population and relatively low stage of economic development, unified labor market characteristics of a unified social security system in China still remain a a distant phenomenon. To be realistic, China's future social security system should just provide the minimum level guarantee, whereas stress should be put on social relief to migrant laborers rather than on an overall social insurance project dominated by the government in urban areas. In this way, the market-oriented economy in China could continuously absorb its increasing labor supply and therefore China's economic development could benefit the majority of its population.

On the other hand, China's lack of attention to the international economic system greatly restricted China's process of urbanization. If we want to compare with the progress of the developed nations whether or not China's urban population scale displays the problem of lagging behind in urban development, then it seems that when viewing the absolute and relative quantity of China's urban economy that shoulders the urban population, China's urbanization level is not insufficient but rather in excess. The per capita output of urban economic activities (the second and third industries) of major developed countries is 10 to 13 times more than that of China; and that of middle-income countries is 2 to 5 times more than China. That is to say that the per capita output of urban economic activities is much more efficient in the developed countries than in that of China. China's urban population is significantly greater than that of Britain or France, has over 70 millions more people than the total population of the whole EU, over 200 million more people than the total population of Japan, and over 100 million more than the total population of the United States, but the urban economic output volume is only on par with that of Italy. The relative magnitude of output of China's second and third industries accounts for 86% of the GDP, but the per capita GDP is only USD 3700 of the working population in terms of the second and third industries, and with the total magnitude of value standing at USD 1200 billion. According to the production efficiency of developed or middle-income countries, the nearly 400 million laborers (including 95 million migrant laborers and some laborers engaged in non-agricultural industries in the countryside) represent a superfluous amount. In comparison to the productivity levels of the US, Japan and Germany, the present urban economic output in China should require no more than 20 to 30 million laborers, and a maximum of over 200 millions laborers if calculated at the average productivity of some middle-income countries in Latin America and the Caribbean regions (See Table 3-2).[13]

We can see from Table 3-2 that the relations among the urban economic output, the corresponding working population and the per capita GDP of the labor force of major developed countries take the shape of a "U"; that of the Latin American and the Caribbean regions takes the shape of a flat "n"; and that of China represents an even more obvious "n" shape. This also reveals that China's urban-based employment and urbanization capacity have reached the level of saturation and over-saturation, and compared with international urban economic efficiency, China continues in the state of excessive urbanization. China's urban economy has not expelled the 100 to 200 million "surplus laborers" from the urban economy because of the low price of the labor force and the labor-intensive industries' absorption of great quantities of laborers. The rural land policies and domicile management policies that China has been practicing for a long time have prevented the appearance of large-scale urban slums that can be found in Bombay and some cities in Latin America.

Table 3-2 An Estimate of Urban Economic Output and Input in Different Countries and Regions

Country and Region	GDP ($1 Trillion)	Corresponding Labor Force (100 Million)	Per Capita GDP of the Working Population ($10,000)
USA	10.35	1.6	6.47
EU	7.54	1.68	4.49
Japan	4.09	0.69	5.93
Laing America and the Caribbean Region	1.53	3.20	0.48
China	1.2	3.7	0.32

13 Though figures in Table 3-2 are roughly calculated on the basis of GDP data of various countries in the world in 2003, they still reflect the basic situation.

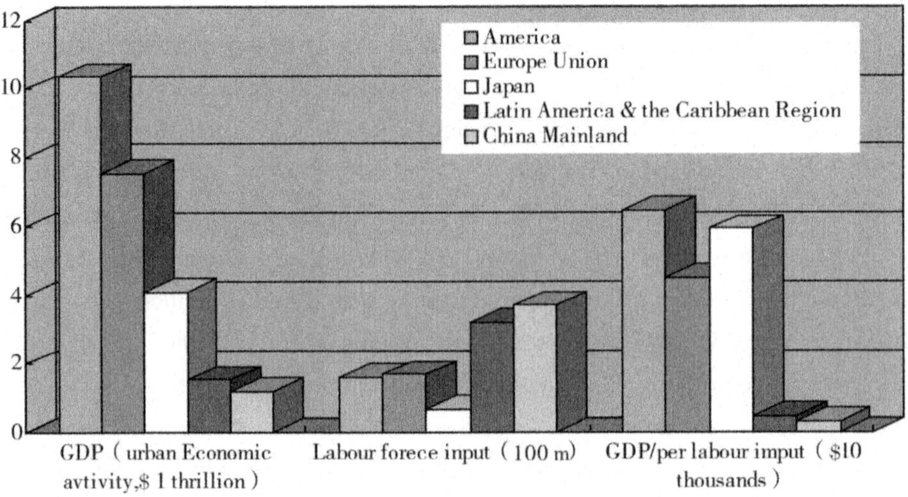

Figure 3-1 Urban Economic Output and Labor Force Input

It is not practical to solve the problem of "rural laborers, agriculture and rural development" and further to solve the problem of China's economic and social development through the quick transfer of rural laborers to the urban areas, unless a closed-door economic system is implemented. In other words, the assumption of realizing a unified labor market with a unified social security guarantee for the future 900 million laborers through the promotion of a so-called "free" transfer of large numbers of rural laborers to cities will lead to serious destruction of the existing "safety net" of the rural population, and to the complete collapse of the whole social "security network" and the existing social security mechanism in China.

The current and future danger of China's urban poverty is excessive urbanization in the above sense. The strategy to reduce this crisis is to promote the steady development of labor-intensive industries and at the same time to ensure in economic and social policies the role of the social "safety net" characterized by more employment, low salary and the most necessary level of security. The advantage of the low price of labor force should be used to promote the expansion of the second and third industries in the labor-intensive manner so as to expand the domestic as well as the international markets. In the meantime, blind and disorderly flow and transfer of rural population into cities should be restricted; and as a compensation for the gaps between urban and rural areas, redistribution of national income and other means of payment transfers, and the superiority of administration of the Chinese government, should be brought into play in order to strategically emphasize the support and promotion of agriculture, rural community building and rural social development programs in terms of education, health and sanitation, environments, etc..

Apart from the restricting factors of international trade and division of labor with regard to China's urbanization and industrialization, the quality of the domestic labor force is another restricting factor. The main contradictions in the field of employment in China are the contradictions between demand for employment and oversupply of laborers and their low qualities. Contradictions in total labor force supply and demand and structural contradictions in employment exist at the same time. Relevant statistics illustrate that out of the present working population, those with an education level below junior high school make up 79% of the population, and reaching as high as 91% in the countryside. From 1990-to 1999, the labor force increase to 189 million, and among this figure, only 3.5% represented college graduates and technical personnel, and only 14.5% represented senior high school or vocational school graduates. Moreover, 82% accounted for those with junior high school education or those whose education level could not meet the requirements of primary technology (see Table 3-3).[14]

From this we can see that the main task of human right promotion for China's labor in general, and for rural labor in particular, is to adopt various basic efficient measures to promote employment. In recent years in China, the supply of a low quality labor force is greater than the demand, and high-quality laborers are in short supply. Improving the quality of the labor force has become a necessary condition for the provision of economic and social development security for the urban and rural working population, particularly the rural working population. The primary work of human right promotion for the majority of Chinese working population is therefore to ensure that the present and future working population can receive better, cheaper and more convenient basic education and vocational and technical training opportunities, and in turn, greatly increase both the employment opportunity and the position of laborers in the market.

Table 3-3 Distribution of Work skills of the 189 million Laborers During the 1990s

Technical Skills of the Labor Force	Proportion (%)
Junior College or Higher	3.5
Technical Secondary School	14.5
Junior Technical School	46
Primary Technical ability or lower	36
Total	14.5

14 "On the Problems of Vocational Training and Ways for Improvement" (Zhang Lingxia and Ming Pu)

The significance of mandating education and training as the primary objective for the promotion of China's working population (with most of them representing rural laborers including existing migrant laborers) rests in the fact that the current price of China's development strategy to move centers of traditional industries of industrialized countries to China is costly: energy, raw materials and water resources are increasingly in short supply, and serious problems such as environmental issues and treatment of laborers are on the rise. Therefore, a strategic path for China is to greatly strengthen construction and development of its human capital in the labor force. Improvement in the quality of the labor force can act to achieve the dual development goal of promotion of employment-oriented economic growth and the upgrade of the industrial structure in order to pursue sustainable development.

3.2 Case Study of the Dalian Labor Market

In order to support the argument presented in this paper, a case study of the Dalian labor market will be used to illustrate the unfavorable position of migrant laborers in the urban labor market.

The "Dalian employment information and service center" provides employment information and service for the local labor demand and supply. The information from this agency reflects the overall employment situation and the structural relations between labor demands and supplies.

Box 1. Data from the 2004 Dalian Labor Market

Labor demands and supplies revealed that the labor supply was still in excess of the demands in the third quarter, in which the structural contradiction between the demand and the supply remained prominent. The supply was 99% higher than the market demand, decreasing by 1% percent from the last quarter and the same period the previous year. Under the impact of the structural contradiction of supply and demand, the employment center provided employment for 62,034 people, reaching only 39.14% of the labor supply, and representing a 7.05% percent decrease from the previous quarter. Laborers for technical work were also continuously in shortage. Computer programmers, solderers, sewers, lathemen, electricians, beauticians, and machine operators are listed in the top ten of those in the shortest supply. However, the top ten of those in highest supply are concentrated on non-technical type of work. Yet, the top ten professions where the demand was much less than the supply were the professions of accountant, secretary, cleaner, driver, clerk, cashier, gate-guard, and purchasers, representing a demand of less than 65% of the supply.

From the point of view of the supply and demand in the market, the supply of laborers with qualifications of education or vocational skills falls short of the demand, and the demand is virtually non-existent for those whose education falls below primary middle school. The demand for skilled labor of various levels contributed to 46.10% of the total labor demand in the market, with a concentration of those individuals representing middle or high levels of required skill. Undergraduate students, graduate students, and technicians easily found positions in the market, since the demand was around 11 times the level of supply. Laborers with middle or higher skill levels were in serious shortage and the demand of highly skilled labor reached 33.76 times that of the supply. In the third quarter, 98,000 labors applied for jobs, of which 56,000 persons had no skilled qualifications, contributing to 57% of the total.

Although the quality of laborers as a whole is much better in term of the level of education and skill set, both enterprises and laborers in Dalian confronted the same contradiction. Firstly, the information revealed that the total labor supply exceeded the total demand in the market on the whole, and secondly, that the structural contradiction in the labor demand and supply still caused many laborers to prove unsuccessful in finding jobs due to their lack of necessary education or skill level. It is generally understood that unless the participation of migrant laborers in urban labor markets can conciliate the above difficulties in the market, that migrant laborers will not be able to obtain better positions in urban areas.

Box 2 Data of Migrant Laborers in the Dalian Labor Market (The third quarter, 2004)

During the third quarter of 2004, Dalian witnessed for the first time market demands for migrant laborers that exceeded the supply. Enterprises invited 9,598 laborers' application for jobs of various kinds, and only 5338 laborers applied for jobs, representing a 5,694 decrease compared to the last quarter. This equated to a 25% increase compared to the previous quarter.. In addition to the shortage of vocational and skilled workers, laborers in primitive positions were also in short supply. The decrease in market labor supply (in Dalian) mainly stemmed from the following factors: rural policy improvement which directly lead to large numbers of migrants' decision to return to their rural hometown to work in local enterprises; in Dalian, the salary is not high for migrant laborers, with an average around 700 RMB per month; and poor working conditions as well as enterprise neglect of the migrants' rights and interests.

In the third quarter, a great deal demand of migrant laborers came from construction and restaurant industries, occupying about half of the total labor demand. Industries of manufacture, trade, transportation, and construction materials also required a large number of migrant laborers. The highest demand for migrant laborers occurred in the areas of restaurant service, domestic service, needlework, lathe man, welding, aquatic product's processing, public security, woodworker, loading and unloading, and machine operators; and private enterprises were in particular need of skilled workers. The salary and welfare provided by these enterprises were quite satisfactory, but under the impact of the overall short supply of migrant laborers in general and skilled workers in particular, the enterprises were unable to find enough laborers.

From information in recent years and from information in the third quarter of this year, the demand for housekeeping laborers has been on the rise. It is estimated that from now on a large number of domestic service laborers will be required in Dalian's the labor market. At the moment, there are only 151 registered domestic service laborers in the market and the gap between their supply and demand shows a supply that is deficient by at least 3000 workers.

Due to the 2004 introduction of migrants into the city, the so-called "worker shortage" phenomenon emerged, and many viewpoints believe that this was a crucial turning point in the improving of the migrants' unfavorable status. According to the CASS-UNESCO Dalian project and a number of other migrant projects, as well as exchanges with government departments, it is believed that this kind of optimism is premature. First, this articles main view is that the "worker shortage" is a two-fold and complex effect related to the government and market. It is possible to further support this article position to posit the reasonable retaining and energetic construction of a new type of "duality", that of a socioeconomic viewpoint. The new emergence of this "worker shortage" phenomenon in Dalian and other areas is facilitating an initial understand of its existence, as well as drawing greater attention to its development. This article attempts to summarize the following background elements:

(1) Although the total amount of migrant supply has provided for a continual increase, according to the expansion of manufacturing and processing industries in the coastal areas,

especially in the Yangtze River Delta's economic rise, the western areas large development and the start of vigorous planning measures in the northeast, the increased demand for migrants emerged nationwide. Therefore, the total increase of positions and migrant workers in the changing national regional distribution is one cause for the shortage of migrant workers in the coastal areas.

(2) The generation of rural laborers in the 50s and 60s has transformed into a new generation of migrant laborers in the 70s and 80s. The market is in the process of being faced with a generation that possesses different values, life-styles, and different income expectations.

(3) Government policy on rural areas has changed significantly, and therefore, many peasants continue in their agricultural industries and relinquish the idea of migrating to the cities for alternative work. This confirms an important point in this paper: an effective approach in improving the disadvantaged status of migrant laborers is to improve rural policy and strengthen rural construction.

(4) In recent years, the Yangtze River Delta has experienced higher rates of development than that of the Pearl River delta, and therefore, more migrant laborers transferred to the Yangtze River delta, which has caused a shortage of migrant laborers in the Pearl River Delta.

(5) A great deal of migrant laborers concentrate on the low-end of manufacturing, which provides little potential for salary increase.

There are 700 thousand migrants in Dalian and most of them work in positions with low salaries and poor working conditions. Through the CASS-UNESO project in Dalian, interviews with migrant laborers show that, on the one hand, a large number of non-skilled rural laborers still attempt to find such jobs, and, on the other hand, that they could no longer tolerate their working conditions. This was another part of the contradictory phenomena in Dalian's labor market. The shortage of supply of even non-skilled migrant labors in the market partly reflected this dilemma. It is also important to point out that the shortage of non-skilled migrant labor supply was also due to the improvement of the government's rural policies last year. This fact has supported one of the arguments in this paper that a proper policy on rural development could be another possible way to relax the problems associated with migrant laborers, which was not in agreement with the argument that the way out for rural development and for solving the issues of migrant laborers lies in the process of urbanization.

The perspective that the issues of migrant laborers in urban areas rests considerably in the restriction of the relationship between labor demand and supply attempts to point out that, under the market conditions, the government policy in various levels will inevitably meet its limitation if the residence registration system (*Hukou*) continues to be of first concern in solving the problem. However, while the majority of Chinese scholars still pay much attention to the *Hukou* system in considering the migrant labor issues, the government has stressed its new development strategy in terms of harmonious development between urban and rural areas, and between eastern and western regions (new development ideas) since 2003. This is a major breakthrough for the mainstream academic fields where the dominant opinion is try to make a copy of the paradigms on the basis of development experiences in western countries. The main differences concerning development between the government's new policies and the old mentality can be illustrated by following points.

1) Stress on empowering the human capital of rural laborers instead of blindly promoting urbanization while neglecting the absorbing capacity of the urban economy; 2) Stress on orderly transferring of rural laborers to the urban areas and refining the domicile (*Hukou*) management system rather than advocating a thorough abrogating of it to allow the free flow of 1300 million people in pursuit of economic efficiency and unrealistic "human rights"; 3) Stress on rural community rebuilding and social development in rural areas by assisting agriculture, education, health care and sanitation instead of stressing rural GDP increases in terms of rural industrialization, rural urbanization, and rural modernization, etc..

These initiatives are logical, since, after more than 20 years of unbalanced economic increases, it can be concluded that the paradigms of industrialization, urbanization, and modernization based on western experiences are not compatible with China and its huge population and limited resources. By promulgating the new development strategy, it is hopeful that China will pay more attention to pursuing human development by giving up the concept that the solution to the issues of abundant rural laborers rests in urban development in terms of industrialization and urbanization.

From 2003 on, a series of crucial documents have been promulgated by the central government of China to promote rural development and improve the conditions of migrant laborers in urban areas through comprehensive policy development. Some of the documents directly concern the provision of education and vocational training programs for rural laborers. These government documents include the following:

(1) In January 2003, the Notice on the Management of Services for Rural Migrant Workers, promulgated by the State Council, set up general pro-migrant policies related to skill training, education of children, work injury insurance, housing, medical health, transportation, etc..

(2) In September 2003, the State Council promulgated The National Plan of Training Rural Migrants from 2003~2010 to provide millions of migrants with training programs on non-agricultural skills and knowledge and skills for city life.

(3) The Sunshine Project (*Yangguang Gongcheng*) initiated by the Ministry of Agriculture (MOA) in March 2004 is a part of The National Plan of Training Rural Migrants from 2003~2010.

(4) In September 2003, the State Council issued another document on education for migrants' children, in which the urban education system is considered responsible for migrants' children. Under these policies of the central government, most of local governments have begun to mandate local policies that follow this trend.

Furthermore, findings from Dalian pilot site through investigation revealed some problems concerning training programs among the migrant laborers:

(1) The government dominates the training programs at different levels. Related government sectors tend to carry out the monitoring and organizing of the training programs, and therefore, it is difficult to guarantee both the quantities and qualities of the training programs.

(2) A large portion of migrant laborers are reluctant to participate in the training programs, partly because they already have jobs in Dalian, and partly because some of them have worked in Dalian for several years, and therefore, the training program is not a first priority.

(3) According to interviews with migrant laborers in Dalian, the best time to provide vocational training programs to rural laborers may be when they are still in their hometown or at the time of graduation from junior or high schools.

(4) The training programs would be welcomed if they were associated with job introductions. In other words, the training programs would be widely accepted if they were closely connected to employment.

(5) There is much space for utilizing social resources and professional organizations to conduct training programs. The vocational training must be developed into a professional sector and the government must pay greater attention to policy making and regulation building for supporting and supervising the training service activities organized by society.

The government's emphasis on human capital as a first priority in practicing poverty reduction among migrant laborers is after all representative of great progress in understanding the issues of rural laborers. Nevertheless, apart from education and vocational training, efforts at poverty reduction should include other domains, such as, orderly urbanization, labor market building and management, social security and safety net building, the rural land system, community building in both urban and rural areas, etc. The following part of this paper will express these concerns based on the experiences from the CASS-UNESCO project in China and other relevant research conducted by the team.

3.3 Policy Advice

3.3.1 Upgrading the rural labor quality

As a whole, the surplus of laborers, but especially the low quality of laborers, represent the real problem in China's urbanization. Another important factor is education, especially skill training. Thus, it is very important to reinforce education and skill training among the low quality labor force.

From the analysis above, we can see that the labor force price at home cannot be resolved solely by focusing on the domestic market. International competence and the developed countries are a big factor that influence our industrial development and the labor force price. Thus, if we simply cancel the *Hukou* system, it may yield very little positive results.

The government should improve the rural worker's human resources, lead the rural migrations flow in an orderly fashion, and help the rural migrants adapt to urban life. Above all, the government should invest more in rural education and train rural laborers, which is an urgent and effective strategy.

3.4 Rebuilding the Non-Market Rural Economy-Society

The dualistic relationship between rural and urban is a problem as well as an advantage.

The "dualistic" notion we use is different from the concept used in western scholarly circles. Lewis[15] pays more attention to the labor force supply under the free market conditions, but domestic criticism mainly focuses on the *Hukou* and its welfare. The research paper deems that the rural-urban divided resulted from special conditions in history: to resolve the food supplies and the funds of industrial development in the 1960s and in the 1970s. From this point of view, the rural-urban dualism of China was different from that of Lewis', and the difference was that the Chinese government planned the rural-urban dualism.

---

15 See A. Lewis, 1989, *Dualistic Economy,* Beijing: Beijing Institution of Economy Publishing House.

The rural-urban difference existed from ancient times in China, and not solely as a result of the planned economy. Today many countries are faced with similar problems, and some of them are even more serious than China.

In the past 10 years, China's *Hukou* system has had little restriction on the rural migration compared to that of the past, and the fact is that the income gap between rural and urban has increased to the extent that it is more extensive than that in the planned economy era. The reality is that there is much doubt over the market's impact on eliminating the gap between rural and urban areas.

Another related and broadly accepted point is to believe industrialization and urbanization

is capable of solving rural poverty. But the fact is that China has too large a population with limited space both for the development of industry and agriculture.

What China must employ is not one dimensional industrialization or merely provide compensation to the rural areas, but furthermore search for the coexistence of these two kinds of socioeconomic development. Above all, this paper believes that the market cannot solve the problems related to the rural-urban gap, but that only the government is capable of resolving this matter in China

3.4.1 The Rationality of "New Dualism"

In contemporary China, the mainstream opinion for addressing the problem of "rural labor, agriculture, and rural development" is to utilize the processes of industrialization, urbanization, and land privatization, and to build a unified social security system. This point of view seems attractive, but some basic realities must also be considered.

1) Under world market conditions, will the expansion of industrialization continue to lead to urbanization?

(1) Similar to the linkage between GDP and employment increase, the economic developmental trend of new technological concentration and knowledge concentration has weakened, and the linkage between industrialization and urbanization has also weakened. The root cause of this is the restricting mechanisms of market competition and international trade.

(2) China has a population of 1.3 billion people, and a population that is projected to reach 1.6 billion in the near future. This implies that 800 million to 1 billion laborers will enter the manufacturing or service industry. This is not only a problem for China, but at the same time it also is a global problem. Therefore, the government's abolishing of the *Hukou*

system, or implementation of comprehensive policy that frees the mobility of the population, cannot simply solve this problem.

Due to resource, technology, capital, market, and environment restrictions, industrialization space in reality is very limited. Moreover, the ability of the labor force to participate in the development of industrialization is also limited. The former inseparable relations of urbanization and industrialization relations, and moreover, industrialization's effect of ending the traditional significance of rural areas and peasantry, is precisely due to the breaking apart of China's industrialization and urbanization with the different experiences of former developed nations. Therefore, many people do not believe that the experiences of the small number of developed nations and the industrialization population of many developing nations lack universality. They should pay more attention the individual country's governmental policy, believing that it is mainly the government policy that leads to the lagging behind of urbanization and the migrant problem. Amidst this, the *Hukou* system, labor force mobility and migrant wages bear the brunt of the problems.

2) Is Urbanization Blameless?

Even if urbanization is not opposed, it is important to determine why urbanization is implemented and what type of urbanization should be implemented. If the connection of rural labors with their land and village is cut, their situation will worsen. As a result, there will be thousands of landless, homeless, and jobless migrants in urban areas.

3) Perfecting the urban-rural labor force migration flow model

Through field work in Dalian, this paper believes that over a long period of time China cannot solve the problem of "rural labor, agriculture, rural development" by employing the methods of developed countries, such as industrialization and urbanization. A more realistic method is:

(1) To reserve and respect the different life styles between rural and urban areas, and to stabilize the rural-urban migration model.

(2) Using rural communities and implementing a system of rural land ownership and employing methods (the need to further perfect, and not privatize the land), is in fact the foundation of the kind of mobility pattern. Land is the basic living guarantee for rural migration; and it uses the urban economic department to supply the rural labor force with non-agricultural employment, increased income and urbanization opportunities.

(3) To promote public goods in rural areas through the government's transfer payments.

Through this model's shifting of monetary payments and redistribution, it can provide social security for rural migration, and it is the reason why so many people have migrated to the cities in the past 20 years to work. It can also explain why the impact of the 1997 Asian Financial Crisis on China was less than that in other Asian countries: thousands of people returned to the land when they lost their jobs in the urban areas. After the crisis they returned to the cities for work, and part of their income strengthened and replenished the economy and society in rural areas. Thus, this kind of dualism economy not only enforced the flexibility of social security when facing the crisis, but it also reduced the urban government's risk.

On the other hand, because it supports the rural land and village, and because the Chinese labor force represents low costs and a superior advantage in the international market, eliminating the rural-urban dualism in the short term is unfavorable for the rural laborers and Chinese manufacturers.

3.4.2 Mixed Dualism Economy/Social Harmony Development

This article attempts to reach a conclusion regarding the concept of "dualism", namely, that a non-antagonistic nature of the economy-society development should become China's reply to international and domestic markets. Firstly, it is unrealistic to eliminate this kind of dualism in the short term; secondly, this dualism pattern has positive significance.

Build a new type of village is the key to the problem of "rural labor, agriculture, and rural development" and rural migration, which is different from that in other developing countries.

The core content of building the new village is developing the public goods in rural areas, including education, training, medical treatment, sanitation, environment and community rebuilding, instead of the village policy of industrialization. So the goal of the new village is to provide more countryside public goods and public service, and not to merely enhance income.

There are some realities that show the needs of the new dualism:

(1) There is no alternative to the current land system that is capable of supporting such a large rural population.

(2) The urban market's labor force under the context of the second and third industries, and under the conditions of long-term employment, are still not capable of accommodating a huge rural labor force and improving migrants' income.

(3) The structure of the rural labor force cannot change fundamentally in a short period of time, and it worsens with economic globalization.

(4) The validity of the modern social security system is doubtful when facing economic crisis.

(5) While the Chinese city's social security system is still in the process of construction, it cannot work efficiently considering the factors of economic crisis and rural migrations.

(6) There still exists the possibility of the national income redistribution, but the chief emphasis is on enforcing rural education and skill training.

(7) Past experiences have testified the validity to mechanisms such as the land security system, family safeguard function, inter-personal assistant system, community management, etc.. All these successful practices can be good complements to industrialization and urbanization.

(8) Finally, in the long term our nation still is likely to experience large numbers of the rural population that are unsuitable or incapable of entering the cities, and yet, in the wake of the continuing rise of the urban industrial economy, these conditions are not only not likely to be mitigated, but on the contrary, they are likely to become even heavier.

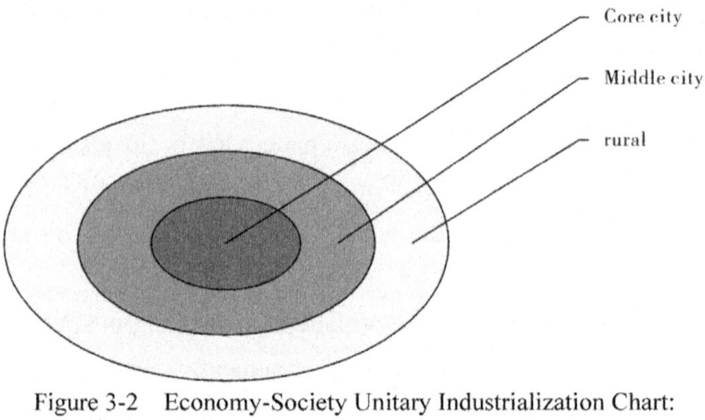

Figure 3-2 Economy-Society Unitary Industrialization Chart:

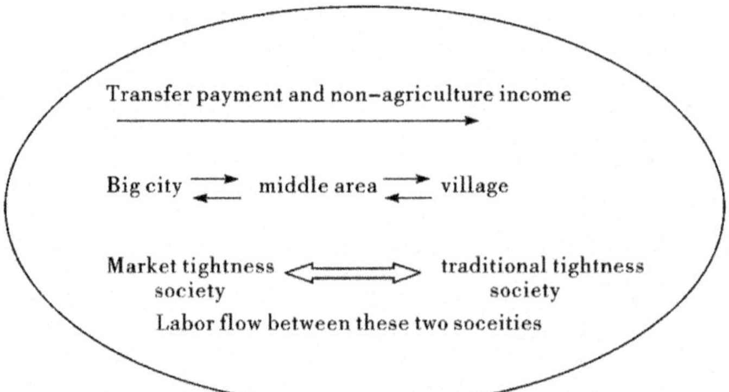

Figure 3-3 A Mixed Type of Economy-Society Chart:

3.5 Rural Labor and Flexible Urbanization

Flexible urbanization refers to maintaining the social-economical linkage between rural migrants and their hometown, which is another kind of pattern compared to mainstream models such as rigid urbanization. The flexible urbanization model can avoid urban poverty, which is an outcome of rigid urbanization.

China's goal in the coming 30 to 50 years is that the urbanization rate rises to 60%-70%, which means that nearly 1 billion people would live within the modern manufacturing and service industries, and would represent an urbanization scale double of that achieved in the west in the past 300 years. As discussed earlier, such a large population entering into the modern market system is not Chinese wishful thinking, and China has little advantage in the international political/economy field. Even if China could acquire the advantages experienced in the west, it could not traverse along the western route, which would bring a new round of global political/economy crisis. Thus, the dualistic situation between rural and urban in China must continue for some time, and the development policy of the Chinese government must strengthen its activity. The first step is to reduce the gap of public goods and services between rural and urban areas; it is the foundation for implementing the flexible urbanization model.

3.5.1 The content of flexible urbanization

- According to the limitations of social securities, implement a shift in the rural population to urban areas.
- According to the market needs, guide rural laborers to work in various branches of the urban economy.
- According to changing market conditions, improve the rural-urban mobility mechanism of the rural labor force and corresponding policy.
- According to the social needs, strengthen education levels and skill training in rural areas, and improve the labor force structure.
- Furnish relevant services and support systems for the rural migrations in urban areas.
- Promote village construction according to the needs of the rural population, accommodating the rural population that has not yet entered the urban branches of the economy.
- Stabilize and perfect the implementation of the rural land ownership system,

limiting the land going into the market.

- Ensure the rights and interests of land for the rural population.
- Establish consistent social security items for rural migrations.
- Improve the conditions of rural labor mobility securities in terms of employment, lifestyles and rights, stressing the strengthening of their employment and skill training.

3.5.2 The significance of flexible urbanization

- By giving the rural migrations equivalent treatment as city residents, the cities are able to attract capable rural inhabitants who have the ability to work in cities.
- Provides high quality rural labor force to cities, which is favorable to enhancing the ability of competition and promoting economic development.
- Avoid the rural migrations from entering blindly into urban areas.
- Enhance the consciousness and enthusiasm of the rural migrants in participating in the social security system.
- Promote the needs of special skills for the rural labor force, which can enhance productivity.
- Explore Chinese human resources further.
- Relieve the worries of rural migrations, and reduce their personal risks.

3.5.3 The promotion and management of rural labor flexible urbanization

1) Urbanization of Rural Laborers

Lewis' dualistic model represents the correlation of several sample theoretical variables. The "traditional department" and "modern department" overlooked some important background factors, such as policy, institution, culture and the international political economy, etc..

The urbanization of China's rural labor force must be carried out step by step and in a planned and controlled manner, so as to avoid serious urban poverty problems that have cropped up in some Latin American countries and India.

The issues related to migrant laborers concern the processes and results of urbanization. The healthy development of urbanization is a result of industrialization and the constant upgrade of the industrial structure. If the objective of urbanization is to achieve high levels of prosperity and low levels of poverty, then the key is not to deregulate domicile control, but instead to focus on the improvement of the quality of the labor force so that they can find jobs and produce in society. In light of the present quality structure of the rural labor force, it is impossible to fundamentally solve the problems of employment and the treatment of rural laborers under labor market conditions. Even mitigation of unemployment is out of the question. Under the conditions of serious imbalances between the structure of the labor force supply and that of the labor force demand, deregulation of domicile control will, without a doubt, cause the hidden unemployment of hundreds of thousands of scattered rural laborers to turn into an observable unemployment concentration in cities. What is most important to note is that if their existing relations with land and the traditional rural community are severed completely, the living conditions of most of them will further deteriorate and many of them will enter the ranks of the new city poor: landless, homeless, jobless, without any property, without a stable income, without social security, without a good education and without any community mutual support network.

Another possible way to improve the condition of the rural population and the migrant laborers is to find a way out in terms of non-agricultural economic fields. As for the problem of social security for the over 100 million migrant laborers, discussions must proceed from the situation of employment of the second and third industries, from the feasibility of the economic and social policies of national income distribution and from the actual economic situation of migrant laborers. The actual problems are as follows. In the first place, in such as short period of time it is impossible for the country's total economic volume, government revenue and existing infrastructure to provide migrant laborers' social security and welfare similar to that provided to urban residents, Of course, that does not mean that all the special treatment enjoyed by urban residents at present cannot accommodate migrant laborers. Some discriminative labor policies can and must be changed, but on the whole there are still many difficulties, and strenuous efforts are needed for the resolution of these difficulties. Second, there is spacious room for the adjustment of the re-distribution of national income and to set up and improve assistance mechanisms for migrant laborers. But the focus is not on the provision of so-called "equal rights" or national unified social security in the modern sense for rural laborers, but rather on input in education and training for professional skills as a feasible strategy. Third, the functions of the existing social security for migrant laborers under the actual economic conditions should be consolidated. The present rural land collective ownership as a fundamental security system for rural population as well as for migrant laborers, family security functions, personal mutual help and community building (including the previous rural communities and the living and working conditions of migrant laborers in cities) are practical means and potential resources that cannot be neglected. Below this paper posits some principled suggestions for the gradual integration of migrant laborers into urban areas and for the improvement of their economic and social rights and interests.

Improvement of the state of economic and social rights and interests of migrant laborers is now one of the most effective ways for poverty reduction among the rural population. There are currently more than 98 million rural laborers working outside their hometowns, and in a positive sense, many of them have been employed in cities for years and therefore have some working skills, stable incomes and a residence. Orderly integration of the rural population into cities should start from this group of people. This group may be assisted with integration into the cities through stages and batches, and in a planned and controlled way by establishing certain standards and procedures. For instance, temporary resident permits may be changed into long-term residence permits; and the focus of this policy should firstly be placed on those migrant laborers with some technical skills or a stable job, or with the ability to find a job in the urban economy. This must, however, be carried out side by side with a relatively complete urban social security system.

The above standards apply to big cities and megacities with a wider scope of employment, higher demands for working skills and higher living costs, whereas medium and small cities and towns can formulate relevant standards in light of different economic and social development levels and demands for a labor force. All these standards must correspond to working skills, income, and educational background, so as to prevent the emergence of a new and large group of poor people in cities mainly composed of rural laborers. These people are without a job, without working skills, without an education, without an income, without a residence, without land and with no social security of any form.

2) Guaranteeing the Economic, Social and Legal Rights and Interests of Migrant Workers

In the process of integrating a part of the rural population into cities, the majority of rural laborers cannot acquire an urban resident identity for quite a long period of time. However, migrant workers in some areas have outnumbered the working population of cities, which is also the case for some medium and small cities. In the next 10 years, the population of rural laborers as the main component will exceed the number of the local residents. From the concept of social security in the broad sense, great attention must be paid to the guarantee of the economic and social rights and interests of migrant workers who cannot obtain a city identity, and a system guarantee must be provided to some degree.

Practice shows that the guarantee of the economic, social and legal rights and interests of migrant laborers can remarkably improve their working and living conditions, thus laying an economic and social foundation for the social security systems that are being established, such as elderly support, medical care, unemployment, industrial injuries and minimum guarantee. Therefore, the design of the social security system for migrant workers should take into consideration both the guarantee of rights and interests as well as protection against future risks. The present focus is on the guarantee of rights and interests and this is another "safety-net" that will be provided in the future to a possible new group of poverty-stricken people in urban areas.

3) "Safety nets" in China's Rural Areas for the Flowing Rural Laborers

If the problems in the vast rural areas in China are not alleviated, deterioration of new urban poverty will not be prevented, since China's future urban poverty will be associated with the development of the poverty situation in the countryside. The view which emphasizes increased urbanization as the way to solve the question of "rural labor, agriculture and rural development" has for a long time neglected the strategic significance of rural reconstruction for providing practical and feasible "safety nets" for the great quantity of rural population and flowing rural laborers as well.

Due to economic gaps between urban and rural areas, more than 300 million rural people will flow into the cities in the future 30 years, and it is difficult for many of them to settle down in the urban areas in a short period of time. Even for those rural people that can work in cities for a considerably long period of time, one must also consider ways out and security means under circumstances such as banking crises. Given the great quantity of the surplus rural labor force, it is impossible for the formal social security system to provide reliable guarantees to such a large population. International experience shows that during economic crises, social security can also fall into crises and even into the predicament of actual collapse. Therefore, in order for the more than 300 million rural to urban floating population to retain a last line of defense, namely rural land and rural community, China's social "safety nets" must implement a system plan.

At present, rural communities, particularly village level communities, have witnessed a serious decline in China. Concrete manifestations include continuous decrease of agricultural efficiency, slow growth and even negative growth of income in rural areas, adverse development of the local economy of rural communities, underdevelopment of the rural cooperative economy, increasing fragility of mutual relations within the community, basic collapse of the systems of village level public management, public economy, public finance and public goods supply, and lagging behind in rural social development fields such as health care, assistance and ecological environment. These problems explain why the contemporary economic and social security for the rural population and the function of the "safety nets" are more fragile than in any period since 1949.

With regard to the question of social security and "safety nets" in the vast countryside and for the 900 million rural population, special attention should be paid to its stability and being further brought into play in the existing rural social security mechanism. Concretely speaking, the most important social security system in China is in fact the village collective ownership and community of rural land plus the land contract system with the family as the unit. The main social security and safety mechanism in China's rural areas in the future should be based on the present rural land system and rural household economy, paying special attention to the promotion of rural social development, and curbing the declining tendency that has emerged in the rural community in the past 10 years. In order to use the present farmer household economy as the base to stabilize the rural economy, the current rural land system must remain unchanged for a long period of time. Under this premise we will consider how to develop various kinds of cooperative economy in the rural areas and realize the gradual transfer of surplus rural laborers under new circumstances. Advocating privatization and marketization of rural laborers' village and community land will disintegrate fundamentally the farmer household economy, and thus disintegrating the basic social security system for the 900 million rural population.

The design of the social protection system for flowing rural labors must, therefore, also proceed from China's reality and from the rural land system that has sustained and will sustain the social security system for the huge rural population. It is impossible for China to establish a social security mechanism for the rural population within a short period of time that can replace the existing rural land system. First of all, renouncement of the registered residence management system cannot automatically bring about human urbanization and effectively improve the conditions for the majority of the rural population, and this has been proved by the grim reality of some developing countries. At least up until to now, the core of the question of "migrant laborers" is not the registered residence management system, which is a false problem. The crux of the question of "rural labor, agriculture and rural development" rests firstly in the inability of the urban economy to provide jobs needed for the nearly 300 million surplus rural laborers and therefore it is impossible to get rid of the dual economic pattern in the urban and rural areas in a short period of time. Second, the relations between the rural population and rural economic resources, particularly land resources, are serious distorted. The efficiency of the agricultural economy, on which the 900 million rural population depends, is so low that China's rural economy is not at all agriculture in the modern sense, but in fact a last guarantee for subsistence.

Furthermore, land, as the basic social security resources in the countryside, cannot be deployed on the market as a general economic element. Reflected in the low efficiency of the agricultural economy is the amount of governmental tax revenue, which accounts for only 4% of the total tax revenue, and which corresponds to nearly 70% of the population. This problem is especially serious in the central and western parts of China. It is impossible for the government to maintain its governance over the rural area and to provide rural areas with necessary public goods enjoyed by most urban residents with such a disproportionate tax revenue and this is indeed the core reason why the rural population cannot enjoy "national treatment." On the other hand, the government is duty-bound to improve the living conditions of the rural population and remedy the seriously unbalanced economic development levels between urban and rural areas through re-distribution and transferring payment.

The existing rural land system is, generally speaking, still able to provide basic subsistence guarantees for the majority of the rural population for some time and there are no other resources available for guaranteeing the basic subsistence of the 900 million population in spite of the low levels of guarantee. There is, therefore, only one way out and that is to ensure guarantee through development. This is to say that the government and the whole of society should provide more input into the economy in order to improve the quality of basic education in the rural areas, to organize job training for rural laborers, to transform the structure of supply and demand of the rural labor force, to cut off the annual supply of the more than 10 million low quality labor force that is unsuitable for future economic and social development, to improve the ability of rural laborers to adapt themselves to the requirements of the labor market and finally to change the imbalance of supply and demand of the labor market instigated by the present imbalanced structure of the labor force supply. This work will achieve immediate effects and meet the medium and long-term development strategy goals. This is the fundamental way out for the resolution of the future employment and social security in China and also a necessary condition for the healthy development of China's urbanization and for the resolution of the question of "rural labor, agriculture and rural development", which hinders the economic and social development of China.

If the rural laborer's employment ability cannot upgrade effectively, then there will be no substantial foundation for the building of a social security system in the rural areas.

Thus, the government should put emphasis on helping the rural community develop an educational foundation, strengthen the skills and training of the rural labor force, and establish a medical treatment system, but it should not attempt to establish any significant modern social security system.

Therefore, the government should take the following steps:

(1) Through various levels of government and social circles, eliminate charges related to the 9-year compulsory education, and therefore, prevent the loss of household income in rural areas. At the same time, enhance the income of village teachers, stabilize their ranks and attract superior teachers to engage in rural education.

(2) Reform the rural education situation. The aim of the rural education should be skill-related education.

(3) Confirm and improve the family planning mechanism.

(4) Continue to preserve the industrial-engaged farmer's grain field labor for a long period of time, enjoying the same rights as the local farmers, and allowing them to voluntarily arrange the use of the land, but without changing the functions of the land.

(5) Construct the middle vocational education system in rural and urban areas. Encourage the rural students to go into middle vocational education after their 9-year compulsory education.

(6) The government should immediately draft policy, increasing the educational funds to 4–5 percent of the GDP, and 70 percent of the increased portion should be disseminated at the county level and below.

(7) Continue the collection of agriculture tax. All tax income should be allocated to pay the rural cooperation medical treatment or other social security items covering the region.

(8) Build village sanitation. The investment should be given from all levels of government. The objective is that within two years every village administration that represents a village below the poverty level (an income of less than 50,000 RMB) will be assisted in constructing and improving village sanitation (with a minimum target of 200,000 villages).

(9) Other various agricultural development as well as the basic establishment of policy measures.

This paper believes that emphasis should be placed on building rural society, which is the key to the problem of "rural labor, agriculture, and rural development", and the rural migrations. Today, China has emphasized city growth and development; but the future should place greater emphasis on rural development. If the two poles (rural and urban) develop, the interspaces will also naturally develop, and therefore, there will be greater overall development. Thus, the problem is not the dualism itself, but rather the imbalance between the two poles.

3.6 Conclusion

On the basis of the experiences from the CASS-UNESO project and some related information from other places in China, the most significant obstacles in the way of improving the conditions of migrant laborers in urban areas have been shifting from traditional institutional domains to market domains. Migrant laborers' unfavorable position in the market will increasingly rely upon the assistance of government policy. The most meaningful aspect of the CASS-UNESCO project is its cooperation with governments at various levels in testing and suggesting methods for assisting the migrant laborers and attempting to develop these experiences into policy articulation and formulation.

3.7 Epilogue

Western modernization was successful in very few countries and it occurred over several hundred years. It is not suitable for China, with its large population, to carry out all-round urbanization. What China must do is explore new ways to create a harmonious society and a harmonious global interaction, which in the end would be a great contribution to the world.

It would be useless to solve the rural migration only within this issue. We should put the rural migration into the practice of building a harmonious society. A long-term strategy that constitutes a kind of "non-urbanization, non-industrialization" society in rural areas is necessary for development. That is to build a new type of rural-urban relationship that is harmonious and that can demonstrate a mutual symbiosis. The core objective is to solve the "two pole" (rural and big cities), to promote the "middle" (county, town), and consequently form a multi-development situation. In order to accomplish this, China must first give up the urbanization and industrialization exclusive method of development.

References

[1] Huang Ping and Cui Zhiyuan. *China and Globalization: The Washington Consensus, the Beijing Consensus, or What?* Beijing: Social Sciences Academic Press, 2005.

[2] Huang Ping. Some Strategic Thinking on the Issues of Migrant Labors in China, 2003.

[3] Zhang Zheng: "The Statistic Analysis on the Rural Migration", *Chinese Rural Economy*, 1 (2005).

[4] Jing Jiqiu and Chen Yongjun: "Research on the Rural Labor Transfer Mechanism within the Process of Chinese Industrialization and Urbanization", *DongNan Academics*, 4 (2004).

[5] Cai Fang and Wang Dewen: "The Migration as the Marketization", *Chinese Population Science*, 5 (2000).

[6] Institute of Industrial Economics of CASS. *The Report on Chinese Industry Development*. Beijing: Economy Management Publish House, 2003.

4

Establishing a Network Between the Migrants' Rural and Urban Homes

Dr. Ma Chunhua

4.1 Rural-Urban Labor Migration in China

The transfer of rural laborers to non-agricultural activities has significantly increased in recent years. The government also has explored the situation of rural migrants through survey, investigation and monitoring activities, and this has provided us with insight into the actual situation of rural migrants: There are about 120 million rural laborers who leave their hometowns for non-agricultural jobs. Among them, about 100 million rural laborers migrate to urban areas, and about 60 million are employed through cross-provincial mobility (Liu Jun and Chen Lan, 2005). Their average annual income was 6471 RMB (USD 798) in 2004 compared to 882 RMB in 2003; and the average growth of their income from 2001 to 2004 reached 8%. Rural-urban migration has become the most important channel for increasing the migrant's income.

4.1.1 Aggregation of origin and destination: Urban vs. Rural, Eastern/Coastal vs. Western and Central/ Interior

Research by different agencies in China shows that the main force behind the rural laborers intentions to pursue industrial work and non-agricultural activities is their economic poverty, although the laborers who do engage in this work are not usually the poorest in their hometown. As many find out, for poverty-stricken counties in central regions in China, the local strategy of poverty reduction is to encourage at least one member from each family to look for non-agricultural work, or in their words, " when one manages to go out, the whole family is able to rise out of poverty" (Huang, 1997). Because of uneven development between rural and urban areas, between eastern/coastal regions and western and central/interior regions, these rural laborers can only find the income-earning opportunities in urban areas or coastal regions with booming rural industries and services, and in either monthly salaries or daily payments.

1) Rural-Urban Uneven Development

During the planned-economy period (1953~1978), China was divided into two parts-rural and urban-through the *Hukou* system, grain rationing system and labor policies (Guang, 2001). The former provided the sources for capital accumulation, mainly through the so-called "price of scissors" learnt from the Soviet Union: a cheap labor force and cheap products from the rural areas supported the urban centers. As a consequence, rural people were organized in the Commune, where there was a low cash return because of low production, low productivity, and even more, an unfair exchange with urban industrial sectors.

During the first period of the reform (1978~1985), the rural populations gained direct benefits from the Household Responsibility System, which was based on individual households and their initiatives, encouraging higher rates of production among rural laborers. At the same time, there were cutbacks in state investment in the inland provinces and cutbacks in state subsidies to the poorer provinces-the two types of provinces that were disproportionately agricultural in orientation. But the impact of these policies on the agricultural provinces was positive from 1978-1985. The agricultural boom, plus increasing market activities of farmers, narrowed the urban-rural income gap: urban to rural income dropped from 2.36 times in 1978 to 1.72 times in 1985 (NBS, 1994).

By 1985, the agricultural sector was beginning to reach the limit to the benefits received by the substantial (but still partial) deregulation of agriculture from 1978-1982. The governmental program for reform and development has been an unbalanced, often urban-oriented and industrial biased approach, which believes the rural areas have already benefited from the early reform that re-allocated arable land to rural households, i. e, the household-based agriculture (Huang Ping, 2003). Consequently, the rural-urban gap widened again in the early 1990s, but especially after 1998. Income disparities between urban and rural areas did not exceed the national average in China's richest provinces: Shanghai reached 2.36:1; Beijing, 2.53:1; Tianjin, 2.28:1; Zhejiang, 2.44:1; and Jiangsu, 2.20:1. On the other hand, income disparities in the poorest provinces exceeded the national average. Guizhou reached 4.25:1' Gansu, 3.98:1; Yunnan, 4.76:1; and Guangxi, 3.77:1 (NBS, 2005).

2) Uneven Regional Development

Substantial disparity in regional incomes and development is a reality in every geographically large country. It is also true in China. One study on regional uneven development in China pointed out that "regional differences among China's thirty provinces are so large that they resemble the gaps between the advanced industrial countries and the poorest countries in the world; China's most developed province follows closely after high income economies, its least-developed province is hardly much better than low-income economies" (Wang & Hu, 1999). In 2004, for instance, Shanghai and Beijing reported GDP per capita levels of USD 5273 and USD 3538 respectively, and the lowest per capita GDP in China's Guizhou Province was only USD 503 (NBS, 2005).

Table 4-1 in the appendix also shows the ranking of China's provinces by per capita GDP (1995 prices) in key years of China's economic history. The data indicate that there have been little changes at the very top and the very bottom of the scale. The three metropolises were in the top throughout the whole period, and Yunnan, Shaanxi, Gansu, and Guizhou in the western region remained the poorest provinces. The provinces that improved their ranking most significantly during the reform period were the coastal/eastern provinces, especially Fujian, Shandong, and Hainan. In 1999, the five richest provinces were Shanghai, Beijing, Tianjin, Zhejiang and Guangdong, which are located in coastal/eastern region; and the five poorest provinces were Sichuan, Yunnan, Shaanxi, Gansu and Guizhou, which are all located in the western/interior region. In 2004, the scale remained approximately the same. Table 4-2 gives a much clearer idea of the regional disparity.

Table 4-1 Ranking of Chinese Provinces by GDP per capita

Region	1952	1958	1965	1978	1984	1991	1998	2002
Shanghai	1	1	1	1	1	1	1	1
Beijing	9	5	4	2	2	2	2	2
Tianjin	4	3	2	3	3	3	3	3
Zhejiang	7	11	9	7	6	6	4	4
Guangdong	8	9	8	9	8	5	5	5
Jiangsu	12	22	16	8	7	8	6	6
Fujian	11	13	12	16	10	10	7	7
Liaoning	5	4	7	5	4	4	8	8
Shandong	22	24	24	17	11	11	9	9
Heilongjiang	2	2	3	4	5	7	10	10
Hebei	6	16	19	11	16	15	11	11
Hainan				21	19	13	12	15

Continued

Region	1952	1958	1965	1978	1984	1991	1998	2002
Xinjiang	10	6	5	14	13	9	13	12
Jilin	3	10	10	10	12	12	14	13
Hubei	18	12	15	18	15	18	15	14
Inner Mongolia	15	7	13	19	18	16	16	16
Shanxi	17	8	11	13	14	19	17	17
Hunan	13	15	18	15	20	20	18	20
Anhui	19	18	17	23	21	27	19	22
Henan	23	26	27	26	24	24	20	18
Qinghai	16	14	6	6	9	14	21	19
Ningxia	20	19	14	12	17	17	22	23
Guangxi	25	23	23	20	23	25	23	27
Jiangxi	14	17	20	25	27	26	24	21
Sichuan	21	20	21	22	22	21	25	24
Yunnan	26	27	22	24	25	22	26	26
Shanxi	27	25	26	27	26	23	27	25
Gansu	28	28	28	28	29	28	28	28
Guizhou	24	21	25	29	28	29	29	29

Note: Tibet is not included due to missing data for GDP components. 2002 figures are not measured at the constant prices in 1995.

Sources: Demurger, Sachs, Woo, Bao, Gang, and Mellinger, 2002, p. 51; 2002 figures came from NBS, 2003, p. 63.

Table 4-2 GDP Per Capita Level between the top-5 and bottom-5 Provinces

	1952	1958	1965	1978	1985	1992	1998
Top-5	1028	1650	1445	2500	3797	5607	12759
Bottom-5	403	583	543	746	1157	1770	3557
National Mean	616	838	780	1143	1849	2929	6400
Absolute Income Gap	625	1067	901	1754	2641	3837	9202
Relative Income Gap	1.01	1.27	1.16	1.54	1.43	1.31	1.44
Income Ratio Between the top 5 richest provinces and the 5 poorest provinces	2.55	2.83	2.66	3.35	3.28	3.17	3.59

Note: GDP per capita is measured according to the 1995 calculated prices. The average GDP per capita level is computed as the weighted sum of per capita provincial GDP levels, the weights being the provincial share in total population of the group (top-5, bottom-5 or all provinces). The top-5 are the five richest provinces in a particular year and the bottom-5 are the five poorest provinces in a particular year. The relative gap is the difference between the top-5 and bottom-5 divided by the national mean.

Sources: Demurger, Sachs, Woo, Bao, Gang, and Mellinger, 2002, p. 52.

An increasingly widespread concern since 1992 has been the growing divergence between coastal and non-coastal provinces, in both per capita growth rates and levels. The distribution of per capita GDP growth rates in China is given in tables 4-3 and 4-4. Table 4-3 reported that the gap in the growth rate between highest (coast) and the lowest (Northwest) regions climb the second peak 5.1% during 1992~1998, a little lower than that of 5.9% from 1959~1965 (the Great Leap Forward, economic collapse, and recovery). The gap between the highest and lowest from 1966~1978 was 4.8%, but kept increasing to 5.1% from 1992~1998; and the coastal provinces were always the regions with highest growth rate. Table 4-4 also shows a similar outcome: from 1992~1998, Fujian Province had the highest annual growth rates of GDP per capita (14.6%), more than two times of that of the lowest province (Qinghai, 6.4%).

Table 4-3 Growth Episodes by Region

	1953~1998	1953~1978	1953~1958	1959~1965	1966~1978	1979~1998	1979~1984	1985~1991	1992~1998
			Medium Growth	No Growth	Low Growth		Med-High Growth	Medium Growth	High Growth
Metropolises	5.6	3.3	5.4	−4.6	6.5	7.9	6.8	5.5	11.4
Northeast	4.2	1.7	5.4	−6.8	3.6	7.3	6.4	6.2	8.7
Coast	5.5	1.8	2.8	−1.0	2.9	10.3	8.8	7.7	13.1
Center	4.2	1.5	5.2	−3.0	2.0	7.8	7.7	4.9	11.2
Northwest	4.3	1.6	7.1	−2.8	2.5	7.7	7.1	6.9	7.9
Southwest	4.2	1.0	5.8	−0.9	1.7	7.4	6.7	5.4	9.1
National Mean	4.8	1.7	4.9	−2.6	2.7	8.6	7.6	6.3	11.2
Gap Between Highest and Lowest (%)	1.5	2.3	4.3	5.9	4.8	3.0	2.4	2.8	5.1

Note: Average annual growth rates are calculated by regressing the logarithm of per capita GDP on a time trend. GDP per capita is measured at the constant prices in 1995. Tibet is not included due to missing data for GDP components.

Sources: Demurger, Sachs, Woo, Bao, Gang, and Mellinger, 2002, p49.

Table 4-4 Average Annual GDP Per Capita Growth Rates

	1953~1998	1953~1978	1953~1958	1959~1965	1966~1978	1979~1998	1979~1984	1985~1991	1992~1998
			Medium Growth	No Growth	Low Growth		Med-High Growth	Medium Growth	High Growth
Metropolis									
Shanghai	5.7	3.4	5.1	−4.3	6.4	8.2	6.6	5.5	12.7
Beijing	5.8	3.0	7.3	−5.9	8.1	8.0	7.8	6.5	9.3
Tianjin	5.5	3.8	7.5	−5.0	5.8	7.5	6.3	4.4	11.9

Continued

	1953~1998	1953~1978	1953~1958	1959~1965	1966~1978	1979~1998	1979~1984	1985~1991	1992~1998
Northeast									
Jilin	4.0	0.8	0.8	−3.0	1.8	8.3	8.5	6.5	10.0
Liaoning	4.9	2.6	7.4	−7.6	5.5	7.8	6.2	6.6	8.9
Heilongjiang	3.5	1.0	5.3	−7.9	2.4	6.3	5.7	5.5	7.9
Coast									
Guangdong	5.4	1.5	4.5	0.8	1.7	11.5	8.9	11.0	12.2
Fujian	5.1	0.9	5.2	−2.2	1.6	10.8	9.8	7.9	14.6
Zhejiang	5.5	1.5	3.3	−0.1	2.3	10.5	9.7	6.6	13.8
Jiangsu	5.9	2.3	0.5	1.6	3.6	10.3	8.6	7.6	13.5
Hainan						10.0	9.0	7.7	9.0
Shandong	5.9	2.5	−2.0	−2.0	4.0	10.0	10.0	6.5	13.0
Hebei	4.5	1.2	−5.5	−5.5	2.9	8.4	6.1	6.0	12.1
Central									
Henan	4.9	1.8	3.1	−4.9	2.8	8.4	9.2	5.7	11.5
Hubei	4.4	1.4	8.1	−2.1	2.0	8.1	7.7	5.0	11.6
Anhui	4.0	1.6	4.3	−1.0	1.6	8.0	8.6	3.4	13.3
Jiangxi	3.5	0.8	3.8	−3.0	0.4	8.0	6.6	6.0	11.3
Hunan	4.0	1.5	5.7	−3.8	2.3	7.0	5.8	5.0	9.8
Shanxi	3.9	1.5	6.2	−4.0	2.1	6.9	7.8	3.8	9.1
Northwest									
Xinjiang	4.1	0.2	7.4	−1.8	0.6	8.7	8.5	8.0	7.5
Inner Mongolia	3.9	0.7	7.7	−5.3	1.9	7.8	8.5	6.0	8.7
Shaanxi	4.6	1.9	6.8	−3.9	3.0	7.8	7.4	7.4	7.7
Gansu	4.5	2.2	5.6	−2.4	5.3	7.4	3.8	7.4	8.4
Ningxia	4.3	2.8	5.2	0.5	3.1	6.5	6.2	5.6	6.8
Qinghai	3.6	2.6	7.1	3.0	2.2	5.3	5.9	3.5	6.4
Southwest									
Yunnan	4.4	1.7	5.9	0.7	2.0	8.0	7.7	7.3	8.8
Sichuan	4.3	0.6	5.3	−0.4	1.0	7.5	6.3	5.4	9.2
Guangxi	4.5	2.6	7.1	−1.4	4.2	7.2	6.2	4.5	10.3
Guizhou	3.1	−0.4	6.5	−3.5	0.1	6.5	8.6	4.6	6.5

Note: The per capita GDP is calculated according to prices in 1995. Annual growth rates are calculated by regressing the logarithm of per capita GDP on a time trend. Tibet is not included due to missing data for GDP components.

Source: Demurger, Sachs, Woo, Bao, Gang, and Mellinger, 2002, p 50.

3) Aggregation of Sending and Receiving Places of Rural Migrants

International experiences indicate that labor tends to flow from the poor regions to the rich regions. Although the concern for social equity and social stability has led China's top leaders to commit themselves to accelerating the economic growth of the interior provinces, and subsequently increasing budgets for infrastructure investments in the poor provinces every year[16], the urban-rural/coast-interior/rich-poor/developed-underdeveloped dichotomy cannot be altered in the short term. When agricultural productivity and growth has reached its limit in the interior provinces, and when the rural enterprise sector fails to perform as profitable and efficient as the coastal provinces because it lacks the same linkage opportunities to foreign-funded enterprises and because it faces higher costs in transporting goods to foreign markets, the "pull factor" (cash earning opportunities) in urban areas and coastal regions pulls rural laborers to leave their hometown for non-agricultural jobs and activities.[17]

The urban-rural/coast-interior/rich-poor/developed-underdeveloped dichotomy is transferred into the sending/receiving places duality of distribution. This is viewed from the national level: The more developed/richer areas experienced the highest reception of rural migrants, while the poorer areas experienced very little influx of migrants.

In 2000, most cross-provincial rural migrants came from central and western regions, accounting for 90% of total rural migrants. Of the cross-provincial rural migrants, 83% concentrated in the eastern region. Guangdong Province alone absorbed 52% of total cross-provincial rural migrants. Provinces in which most rural migrants searched for non-agricultural jobs include Jiangxi (71.5%), Chongqing (64.4%), Anhui (58.5%), Guizhou (53.4%), and Hubei (52.0%). The proportion of cross-provincial rural migrants in these provinces is much higher than the national average (24.9%). The top provinces where cross-provincial rural migrants come from include Sichuan and Chongqing (18.7%), Jiangxi (13.9%), Hunan (10.7%), and Anhui (10.5%) (MOLSS & NBS, 2003).

In 2004, 67% of the rural migrants came from central and western regions, and 70% of rural laborers migrated to eastern regions, a 2% increase from 2003. From the MOLSS survey in 2005, it is estimated that 62% of rural migrants found their jobs in the eastern region, 20% in the central region, and 18% in the western region. If we divide rural migrants in terms of their sending places, 97% of rural migrants from the eastern region

16 The state's investment in infrastructure of western regions kept increasing every year, from 9,522 billion RMB in 1990 to 49,785 billion in 1997 and to 103,092 billion in 2002 [NBS, http: //www.cei.gov.cn, based on China Statistics Yearbook 2003 and China Infrastructure Investment Statistics Yearbook (1990~1994)].

17 The study argues that when China's metropolises and other large coastal cities develop into endogenous growth centers, labor mobility is the only easy solution to slow (or reverse) the increase in urban-rural regional inequality (Demurger, Sachs, Woo, Bao, Gang, and Mellinger, 2002).

also found jobs in the same region, and almost none of them found jobs in central and western regions; 65% of rural migrants from the central region found jobs in the eastern region, opposed to the central region, and few found jobs in the western region; and 56% of rural migrants from the western region found jobs in the same region, 41% in the eastern region, and few in the central region (Liu Jun and Chen Lan, 2005).

4.2 Rural migrants: floating between sending and receiving places

When the Spring Festival approaches, a most important traditional holiday with the implication of family reunion, similar episodes of migration are witnessed, such as crowded waiting rooms at railway stations with large numbers of anxious and excited rural migrants waiting to migrate home to rural areas. This is one of major reasons why the state wants to control and even stop rural urban migration: the current transportation system cannot support the needs of rural migrants during these special festivals. And urban residents complain these rural migrants wreck their typically harmonious holidays. In fact, these rural migrants have to remain adrift between sending and receiving places because they cannot settle down in the receiving places. It is more impossible for them to bring their children and parents to live with them in receiving places. They miss their children and parents, and therefore go home every Spring Festival. But they are poor, and therefore they have to leave their hometown for cash-earning in other places.

According to Chinese understanding, these rural migrants have in fact not "migrated", officially speaking. Instead, in Chinese parlance, their chief characteristic is that "they float and move", implying that they are not a permanently settled group. It is why in some articles these rural laborers are called the "floating population" or "flowing population" (Liudong Renkou)[18] to stress they cannot settle down in receiving places, have to float between sending and receiving places, and keep peasant-worker identity at the same time. Rural-urban labor migration has occurred in every industrialized and developed country, and mainly as a result of industrialization and urbanization. But they have been very different in nature.

"Floating" between sending and receiving places is an important characteristic of these rural migrants. They consist of persons who, without local registration, are by official

18 In this paper, the author uses "rural labor migrants", in accordance with common English parlance, and in order to keep the terms consistent in the whole paper.

definition "engaged in partial temporary relocation." Furthermore, they are characterized as people who "maintain their ties with their original place of inhabitance, where their permanent residence registration remains" (Wu, 1990). These rural migrants have met three conditions: they have crossed over some territorial and administrative boundary; they have not altered their permanent registration; and, at least in theory, they "flow in and out" of sending and receiving places. That being said, beginning with the 1982 census, all those who had been living in a location different from that of their places of permanent registration for a year or more were counted as migrants, that is, as residents of their new locations; but they were still perceived and treated as outsiders in their actual daily lives. Under Chinese current institutional arrangements, most of these rural laborers cannot transfer from "floating" to "migrating."

Integrated with employment, education and the social welfare system, the permanent residence registration system (Hukou system) has prevented the transfer of these rural laborers from "floaters" to "legal migrants." In the Chinese case, changing the place of inhabitance alone cannot alter registration status from rural to urban, since, the urban Hukou is linked with a large amount of benefits and privileges; rather, an individual migrant can change his residence registration only with the consent or at the order of government officials. At present, richer rural migrants can purchase, and skilled rural migrant workers can get so-called "blue-sealed Hukou" (Lanyin Hukou) in urban areas.[19]

Conveniently for the regime, this system limited at least to some degree an unplanned increase in the numbers of persons permanently residing in urban areas. By enabling the regime to treat rural laborers who had reached the cities as outsiders or non-citizens, the residence registration system legitimated its policy of exclusive expenditure. This classification scheme for decades found its justification in the planned economy: "at all levels and in all localities, administrative management agencies plan their work and projects in accordance with the size of the registered permanent population within their respective jurisdictions" (Wu, 1990).

Large scale rural-urban migration and its huge impacts on social institutions and systems compelled the Chinese government to launch the reform of the permanent residence registration system. But the old permanent residence registration system is entangled with education, employment and social welfare system. If the latter is not

19 City dwellers with blue-sealed Hukou enjoy more benefits than temporary residents, but fewer than the permanent city population. If they choose to leave the location of their blue-sealed Hukou residency, migrants must return to the site of their original permanent household registration.

reformed, the reform of the former cannot take effect. Moreover, one of serious problems with the Chinese administrative system is "the problem of the matrix of authority lines." The reform of the residence registration system will be launched through the vertical bureaucracies, but without coordination between horizontal bodies organized on the basis of territorial units – and therefore the reform cannot be successfully implemented. Up until now, it has been difficult for rural migrants to become "migrants", and instead had to float between sending and receiving places.

4.3 The Predicament: Government Considerations of Sending and Receiving Places Exists Simultaneously

In the past, it was very important to have household registration coincide with the place of residence. Administrative management agencies at all levels are only concerned with the population that possesses local permanent *Hukou* within their respective jurisdictions. This *Hukou* system plans their work and projects for them, and provides certain jobs, housing, grain, education, medical treatment and other services (Cheng and Selden, 1994). Urban Hukou have become the *minggenzi* (lifeblood) of the Chinese people because they are used to obtain welfare rights (housing subsidies) and children's education for urban residence.

When the rural migrants are wandering nomadically between sending and receiving places, they are confronted with a serious dilemma: on the one hand, they are unable to obtain urban Hukou through transferring their place of residence and remaining there for a specified time, and therefore they cannot enjoy the benefits and privileges linked to the local *Hukou*; on the other hand, though their *Hukou* are kept at their original home, they cannot enjoy some of the benefits linked to their *Hukou* at their hometown because they are not physically present.

Within the destination areas of migrants, they are "outsiders" and "strangers"; in reference to their original home areas, they are "floaters" and "wanderers". In China, the jurisdictional system, administrational system and even educational system and health care systems are all designed according to the household registration system. Household registration residence is the passport for access to comprehensive resources and benefits. Rural migrants' Hukou is invalid in their places of destination, and therefore, and they cannot use their valid passport within environments outside their original place of residence. As a result, rural migrants' identity and status becomes ambiguous and uncertain.

4.3.1 Jobs

Without an urban *Hukou*, there are few eligible jobs in urban areas for rural migrants. In the process of the rural mobile labor force entering into the cities, some large cities in order to understand the employment problem of local inhabitants, are generally installing a series of policy barriers and implementing measures that restrict employment with regard to the rural labor force. As a result, migrants are relegated to low-skilled, low paying jobs that urban workers no longer want. Another consequence is that the jobs rural migrants find in cities are many times of a temporary capacity.

4.3.2 Skills Training

Both the public and the government at all levels failed to attach any importance to skill training for migrants until 1992, and no skill trainings were provided for migrants with the exception of a select few rural migrants who were able to afford training by themselves. Since 2000, in accordance with the pro-rural migrants' policies, ministries such as the MOA and MOLSS have launched some skill training programs for rural migrants. And, at local levels, government agencies of sending and receiving places, including mass organizations, such as the Women's Federation and Youth League, have started to provide training programs for rural migrants (Huang and Zhan, 2003). But one important issue which should be considered is how to make skill training a foundational component for helping rural laborers find employment in receiving places, or, in promoting their career development. From this viewpoint, the skill training, provided by the local government of destination, should be more efficient because they know more about the needs of labor markets.

4.3.3 Housing

Rural migrants are not allowed to build houses in the destinations (cities and coastal provinces). In China, only rural residents with local permanent *Hukou* can apply for a piece of land to build their own house. The state has historically provided the housing for urban residents, and they generally have no rights for applying for a piece of land to build their own housing. During the reform era, some villages in coastal provinces are becoming urban areas; and the local economy is booming in these areas. But the great number of rural migrants who come here for industrial-urban work have no rights to apply for land to build their own house because they are without local permanent agricultural *Hukou*. Only local peasants have the right to apply for a piece of land to build their own house. They have to rent rooms from residents, obtain them from their work unit, or even sleep in alleys, vacant lots or the waiting areas of train/bus stations. Due to the uncertainty of the future, these rural migrants have to invest in housing in their hometown, and in the meantime, tolerate adverse living conditions in receiving places.

4.3.4 Educational system

Children whose mothers do not have an urban *Hukou* are unable to receive free public education in urban areas. Rural migrants have to pay more tuition if their children want to attend a school, and for most, this is not a feasible option. While virtually 100% of city-born children, ages 5~12, were enrolled in school in 1995 (in Beijing), only 40% of the migrant children were enrolled (Solinger, 1999). In 1998, the Ministry of Education and Ministry of Public Security jointly issued a regulation requiring local governments to guarantee education for migrants' children between the ages of 6 and 14 if they had lived in the area for more than 6 months. Most cities handled this by opening separate schools for migrant children rather than allowing them to attend the same schools for children with local *Hukou*. Another important issue is that the education system in China is also designed in terms of household registration system. Local governments of sending places have been asked to take the majority of the responsibility for the compulsory education for children with local *Hukou*. As a result, this forced the migrant children to return their hometown to pass the entrance examination to junior middle school before attending middle schools in their hometown, even though they had lived in cities since birth.

4.3.5 Health care system

Since state funding for public health facilities, medications, and personnel continued into the reform era to be pegged to a planned level of urban population per city, arrangements for the health care of unattached newcomers from the outside appeared to bureaucrats to be out of the question. Therefore, rural migrants in receiving places lack access to the cities' hospitals, doctors, and pharmacies, though the situation is gradually changing. In 2004, in order to protect legal rights of rural migrant workers and make sure they can enjoy the social security system, Beijing government issued the "Temporary Regulations on Injury Insurance for Rural Migrant Workers in Beijing" and the "Temporary Regulations on Medical Insurance for Rural Migrant Workers" which ask work units to pay these insurance fees for rural migrant workers through a regulated percentage. As a result, these rural migrant workers can enjoy the equal rights local workers enjoy.

How are these problems resolved? Particularly, how does the government approach the issues of skill training and managing rural migrants? The state is concerned with these issues because they are relevant to social equity, social stability and social development. The process of dismantling the *Hukou* system, the most important structural barriers in the way of rural migrants, will likely be difficult and will be met with opposition by powerful stakeholders, including urban residents, local governments, the public security personnel and private business people (Mackenzie, 2002). A more applicable and realistic approach is to establish the network between sending and receiving places, and promote cooperation between local governments to provide service and support to rural migrants. But the more important issue is how to reach these achievements. Through the discussion about relationship between farmers, state and local governments, difficulties will be revealed. But the project "Urban Poverty Reduction among Young Migrants" have experienced cases of both success and failure. The author will discuss them in the following section of this paper.

4.4 Relationships: Peasants, the State and Local Governments

In this paper, the local governments refer to the governments of receiving places and sending places of rural migrants.

The relationships between peasants, the state and local governments, which are changing over time, are very complex. There are three relationships:

(1) Peasants and the state. Ash argued that the institutional framework of agriculture defines the context in which the relationship between the peasant and the state is conducted (Ash, 1996). Before reform, this was true to a great extent because most of the peasants were engaged in agricultural jobs. But since the early 1980s, the occupation and employment of peasants are differentiated while the state provides more space for the autonomy of peasants. Only the whole institutional framework in which peasants are involved, rather than that of agriculture itself, can define the context in which the relationship between the peasant and the state is established. In this paper, these relations define the context at the macro level in which the network between governments of sending and receiving places is set up to provide services and supports to the rural migrants.

(2) Local governments of sending and receiving places. In the late 1980s, rural-urban migration gradually became a new socioeconomic phenomenon, and dealing with its consequences has become a major policy challenge for authorities both at the national level

and locally in the sending and receiving places. However, local policy agendas do not always coincide because they are drafted and formulated according to their respective interests. As a result, whereas large cities on the whole wish to limit the inflow of migrant workers, national government and the local governments of the receiving places are keen to maximize the opportunities for local development through migration. The different policy agendas of major sending and receiving places are by no means easy to reconcile. The central government finds itself in the position of having to coordinate between different interest groups. The different agendas of sending and receiving places also have important implications for the situation and rights of rural migrants; and it is one of most important barriers for establishing the cooperative network between sending and receiving places. Just as discussed above, regional disparity, both in growth rate and income, is so huge that some scholars pointed out that the "First World and Third World coexist within China" (Wang & Hu, 1999). In general, the sending places of rural migrants are classified to "Third World" in China, and receiving places of rural migrants are classified to the "First World" in China. The power relations between the third world and first world in the international context are represented between the sending and receiving places, which significantly influences the efforts to establish the network between sending and receiving places.

(3) Peasants and local governments in sending and receiving places. The relationship between peasants and local governments, especially at receiving places, has been discussed above. Since the beginning of 21st century, the central government has paid much more attention to the rural migrants' interests and benefits, and thus has formulated a lots of policies, referring to children's education, skill training, work protection, health care, and assimilation into urban life, etc., in order to improve the working and living conditions in receiving places. But for the rural migrants, their living and working conditions depend on how local governments put these policies into practice. Recent studies on central-provincial relations have highlighted the growth of provincial power relative to that of China's central government in the reform era (Yang, 1997). Rural migrants, as second-class citizens, inferior citizens or non-citizens, are not considered to be the responsibility of local governments in the receiving places. As a consequence, the authorities from the migrants' hometowns often play an important role, including public order and compliance with family planning quotas (Huang and Pieke, 2003).

4.4.1 The Relationship Between the Peasants and the State

Since the economic reform starting in the late of 1970s, the Household Responsibility

System (HRS), or the practice of turning production over to the household, has been the key source of the most important transformation in rural China since 1978 (Zhou, 1996); and the land-bound peasants have been transformed into farmers as a result. Farmers obtained independent decision-making power of allocation of rural laborers and capital. These farmers did not make any attempts to seize control from the state, but they did inadvertently take away the state's control over farming, markets, industries, migration and even family production. The introduction of contractual arrangements between individual household and the economic representatives of the state pointed to a new production relationship between the state and the individual farmer (Ash, 1996).

The rising supply of rich and varied agricultural goods, after the implementation of the HRS, led to a rapid increase in markets in China. If HRS altered the relationship between the local government and the farmers within the collective structure, the development of markets altered the relationship between the state and farmers outside the villages (Zhou, 1996). When previously unavailable opportunities opened, farmers eagerly seized them to make money. They took the state by surprise through rapid increases in productivity and manipulation of the state plan. Farmers were far ahead of urban people in the market activities. As a result of market expansion and the hard work of rural merchants, a substantial portion of farmers' total economic activities were transferred to the market. In many ways, the farmers took over the market from the state.

The Chinese state's industrial development attempted to keep farmers away from industrialization. For a while, the state succeeded, binding the majority of the Chinese population to the collective land; but once the farmer reassumed family autonomy, the base of the former patterns was shaken. The rural population developed rural industries on a spontaneous, unorganized, leaderless, and non-ideological basis. Thus, farmers now lead Chinese industrial development (Zhou, 1996). The rapid growth of rural industry has constrained the state's two-tier price system practice. The growth of rural industries and the changes that accompanied it ahs made it impossible for the state to stop the growth of rural industry without also hurting itself.

The most important barrier blocking rural-urban migration has been the *Hukou* system, which in turn rested on the control of grain rationing. The system of rationing food and other consumer goods came to an end in 1992. This represents a watershed event in the evolution of a new peasant-state institutional relationship. In the 1980s, the state put aside *Hukou* considerations and opened up small towns to farmer's settlement. This document enlarged the hole in the Hukou dike, a hole already opened by farmers' market activities. After 1986, the *nongzhuanfei* (changing of farmers' *Hukou* from rural to non-rural) formally ended. In the 1990s, the Hukou system went through more drastic modification, and as a result, the *Hukou* is losing its importance in controlling rural-urban migration.

Large scale rural-urban migration has promoted the development and expansion of labor markets in China (Zhou, 1997). As a result of the legacy of "unified allocation" formulated in the 1950s, the *Hukou* system, and policies on labor markets, the labor market in China has been divided. In this labor market, and under the current institutional arrangements, the rural migrants are always in a disadvantageous position, though, the state has formulated some policies that promote the development of unified labor markets and improve the employment conditions of rural laborers in receiving areas.

4.4.2 Relationships Between the Local Governments of Sending and Receiving Areas

1) The Administrative system in China

Figure 1 in the Appendix shows the basic administrative system in China. There are two basic levels: central administrative system (central government) and local administrative system (local government). The latter is controlled under the former. The central administrative system includes the central administrative organs (Ministries, Commissions, the People's Bank of China and Administrations) under the system of the National People's Congress and the leadership of the central administrative organs over local administrative organs at various levels. The State Council is the executive body of the highest organ of state power and the highest organ of state administration. The State Council exercises unified leadership over local state administrative organs at various levels throughout the country, regulates the specific division of power and function of the state administrative organs at the central level and the provincial, autonomous regional and municipal level.

At the local governmental level, there are four sub-levels: (1) the province/autonomous regions/municipality, which are controlled by the central government directly; (2) the prefecture /prefectural-level city, which are responsible for reporting their work to provincial-level governments and who accept the leadership of the State Council at the same time; (3) the county/autonomous county/county-level city, with is a relatively strong rural administrative function, controlled by the provincial-level governments in Beijing, Tianjin, Shanghai and Chongqing, and prefectural-level governments in other areas; (4) and the township/ethnic township/town, the local governments in rural areas, which are controlled by county-level governments. Generally speaking, the higher level the local government in this bureaucratic hierarchy, the greater the authority it is able to enjoy. Their places determine the scope of their administrative powers, the degree of control they exercise over investment decisions (including foreign investment), their relative access to financial support from the state, their capacity to secure reliable food supplies from subordinate counties and, to a diminishing degree, the extent to which they qualify for subsidized food prices (Fitzgerald, 2002).

2) Problems with the Administrative System in China

At and above the county level, local governments at different levels are made up of bureaus and commissions that direct and administer the administrative affairs in their respective areas. These bureaus and commissions are controlled by the local government at the same level, and the next higher level of the corresponding area at the same time. For example, the Zhejiang Provincial government and the Ministry of Agriculture at the central level at the same time control the Bureau of Agriculture of Zhejiang Province. As a consequence, "the matrix of authority lines problem" (tiao/kuai issue) has emerged as a serious problem with the Chinese administrative system. "TiaoTiao" means vertical bureaucracies on the basis of specialized functions (showed through the vertical line in Appendix Figure 1): the lower bureaucracy is under the control of the next higher bureaucracy, for example, from the Ministry of Agriculture at the central level (*Nongye Bu*) to the Bureau of Agriculture at the provincial level (*nongye ting/ju*) to the Division of Agriculture (*nongye chu*) at the county level to the Section of Agriculture at the township level (*nongye ke*). "KuaiKuai" means horizontal-coordinating bodies organized on the basis of territorial units (showed by the square in Figure 1): no one has administrative power over the other, and they have to bargain in order to establish some connection. For example, the local governments in sending and receiving places are two units (*kuaikuai*), and they have no administrative relationship.

While vertical lines of authority run within bureaucracies, horizontal lines link different bureaucracies at the same administrative level. The relationship between "tiaotiao" and "kuaikuai" is the so-called "tiao/kuai guanxi" or the "tiao/kuai issue." It indicates a fragmented authority in the administrative system. This makes it very difficult for an individual or a group to attempt to bargain or negotiate with the local government. For example, the project of "Urban Poverty Reduction among Rural Young Migrants" attempts to establish a network between sending and receiving areas, but in the process it encounters great difficulty and confusion. They don't know which bureau they should contact first because there are many bureaus or divisions that are involved in monitoring, regulating or administering rural-labor migration. If the project has established relations with one of the bureaus or divisions in sending places, they then must attempt to establish a relationship with the corresponding bureau or division in receiving places because these bureaus or divisions are included in the same vertical line (*tiao*), though they are included in different horizontal lines (*kuai*). Consequently, it increases the difficulties in establishing a network between sending and receiving areas.

This fragmented authority posits a huge impact on the policies related to rural-urban migration. Different local governments (*kuaikuai*) are trying to promote their own interests. If their common interests cannot be aligned, it is be very difficult to establish a network between receiving and sending areas for providing services and support to rural migrants. Conflicts and tensions between different ministries/bureaus/divisions (*tiaotiao*) exacerbate the problem, even causing fragmentation among the central government. The Ministry of Public Security, in charge of registering and controlling migratory flows, for instance, has very different priorities compared with those of the Ministry of Labor and Social Security or the Ministry of Agriculture. These divisions are one of the main reasons that attempts at more radical reform have been repeatedly watered down or stalled. At the local level, a similar situation emerges, and these have important implications for the status and rights of rural migrants.

3) The Possibility for Coordination Between Local Governments

In China, the central government is indeed becoming less interventionist, and provincial power and influence is increasing. At the same time, the exercise of economic control by a provincial leadership might be undermined by the power of sub-provincial economic regions where economic activities are concentrated, for example, Dongguan, Panyu, Zhongshan, and Shunde in Guangdong Province.

(Hendrischke, 1999). Further details regarding the relationships between the central government and the local government of receiving and sending areas will define the context in which the network between sending and receiving areas will be established, and will provide opportunities to explore why some cases related to the Project "Urban Poverty Reduction among Rural Young Migrants" are less successful, and some cases are more successful.

During the ten-year period from 1981 to 1990, a whole array of economic and political incentives including centrally funded investment, fiscal support and preferential policies were directed towards the coastal provinces. While the coastal region (receiving ares of rural migrants) prospered in overall terms, the inland regions (sending areas of rural migrants) suffered a relative decline in income, living standards and economic growth. In the central government's long-term economic planning, inland provinces were to provide raw materials, energy and cheap laborers to coastal provinces and in turn receive industrial products, technologies and capital. They were to benefit eventually from a "trickle down effect" radiating from the coastal regions into the inland and gradually integrating the inland with coastal economies. However, this effect has not worked. The relative economic disadvantage of the inland provinces prevailed over its rise to socioeconomic prosperity.

As the central government no longer has the previous mechanism of income redistribution at its disposal, it has turned to other forms of regional policy to redress regional disparities. The focus of central-regional policy shifted from the coastal/inland/western divide to the importance of the previous Great Regions, most of which include coastal as well as inland provinces. These regions were expected to provide the coordination between richer and poorer provinces by facilitating horizontal links, division of labor and overall superior linkage between the provinces (Cannon, 1990). This demand for coordination and equalization was a major readjustment from encouraging unequal development during the earlier reform period. Without administrative power, this policy showed little effect in practice. It certainly did not reduce the differences in the economic development between coastal and inland areas (Lu, 1996).

In 1996, the regional policy was shifted towards an emphasis that major economic regions should concentrate on developing their comparative advantages rather than pursuing regional equalization. This was a return to the original coastal development strategy under which the coastal provinces continued to develop their fast growing manufacturing, information and service sectors while the inland provinces concentrated on providing agricultural products and raw materials. The inability of the center to dictate regional economic policies and the strong economic role of provinces is reflected in a new type of regional planning which focuses on smaller trans-provincial regions with specific economic advantages. The central government's role in this degree is only one of setting the macro-economic parameters, including large-scale planning to facilitate such synergies (Hendrichke, 1999).

Due to the status of various provinces, whether or not they accept the central authority's "policy", depends upon whether or not the central authority's investment is capable of bringing about benefits for the particular province, such as, balancing provincial budget deficits, guaranteeing the flow of raw materials and state's purchase of products. Thos that are cut off from central supports become economically self-reliant, and thus, they have no choice but to pursue their own interest. That means the local governments of coastal areas have more capacity to bargain with the central government. While these local governments in receiving areas are considering the content of local interests, they always exclude the interests of rural migrants. Some of the inland provinces seem to have less capacity to bargain with the central government because they have to depend on central supports through industrial investment and infrastructure, or preferential policies similar to those enjoyed by the coastal provinces.

4.4.3 The Relationships Between Peasants and Local Governments

1) The Relationship between peasants and local government in sending places

The unprecedented scale of rural-urban migration in China is simultaneously a spontaneous response to, or consequence of, economic reform and increasingly a component of government policy. But at the beginning of the "Migration Wave", while facing the large-scale rural labor migration, all levels of government were not concerned, nor did the government formulate laws or regulations to control the situation. In fact, the governments in sending areas first paid attention to these rural labor migrations, especially in poorer areas where there exists large population levels and comparatively little arable land and other resources. When local governments discovered that rural labor migration can act to relieve local pressure related to resources and poverty, and facilitate remuneration from urban to local areas, they encouraged migration and its effects in promoting local development.

Sichuan Province is a good example. Sichuan is the largest province in terms of its population, the number of laborers and rural-urban migration. The official statistics show that the number of rural migrants in this province was near 100 thousand in 1983. In the middle of the 1980s, the number increased to one million. From 1989 to 1994, the number was as high as ten million each year, on average. In 1986, Sichuan Provincial Government regarded "the rational transformation of rural laborers to non-agricultural sectors and sending rural laborers" as a strategy for promoting the local economy in Sichuan, where "sending rural laborers" becomes an industry, so to speak. The local government set up about 1700 Laborer Service Stations in townships. They also established offices (Laborer Services and Management Stations) in receiving area, such as Shenzhen and Guangzhou (with a total number of 28 offices).

The provincial government of Sichuan continued to encourage the rural laborer's migration through different policies in order to develop the local economy and reduce the local poverty. But there have been some adjustments in their strategies in recent years:

(1) to help more rural laborers seek non-farming employment in their hometown through industrializing local agriculture; (2) to develop local industry and service sectors to provide more non-agricultural opportunities for rural laborers; (3) to promote the urbanization and establishment of a city network in Sichuan so as to provide the opportunities for rural laborers to settle down in urban areas; (4) to industrialize "sending rural laborers", and help it become the pillar industry of the rural economy; (5) to provide skill training opportunities to rural migrants; (6) to establish the unified labor market between rural and urban areas, and eliminate the institutional barriers that block rural laborers from seeking non-farming employment; (7) to set up the employment security system for rural laborers, and protect their rights and benefits (Sichuansheng Laowu Kaifa Bangongshi, 2001).

Although Sichuan Province as a whole is taken as a sending area of rural migrants, some relatively developed urban areas within Sichuan Province are also regarded as receiving areas when compared to other poorer areas, for example Chengdu city compared to Jintang County. That is why the Sichuan Provincial Government has begun to pay attention to the rights and statuses of rural migrants in urban areas within Sichuan Province as the local government of receiving areas. It is more difficult to establish a network of sending and receiving areas when they are in different provinces, and much easier when they are within the same province.

In general, the local governments always encourage rural laborers to leave their hometown for non-farming employment or non-agricultural opportunities in urban areas since it is proven an efficient approach for reducing local poverty or balancing uneven development between coast and inland provinces. In 2000, it was estimated that the remittance of rural migrants in Sichuan Province reached 21 billion RMB, and the income of rural laborers who found non-farming employment officially rose to 880 million. In some areas of Sichuan Province, income from non-farming employment contributed to more than half of the income of rural people (Sichuansheng Laowu Kaifa Bangongshi, 2001).

Though these rural laborers physically leave their hometown, they have to retain their origin *Hukou* status and therefore they are still under the jurisdiction of the home governments. The governmental offices of sending areas not only protects the rights of rural migrants, negotiates with the local governments, and helps rural migrants find jobs in receiving areas, but they also monitor rural migrants and force them to follow the policy on family planning. Due to unbalanced economic power, the local government of sending areas is always in the disadvantageous position when they attempt to establish connections, and bargain or negotiate with local governments in receiving areas for rural migrants. But the "Mingong Huang" (shortage of rural migrant workers) in 2004 changed their position to some extent. Without enough rural laborers from inland provinces, it was difficult for coastal areas, with Guangdong as an example, to maintain its high rates of economic growth.

2) The Relationship Between Peasants and Local Governments in Receiving Places

While the local governments of sending areas have paid attention to rural-labor migration since the middle of 1980s, the local governments of receiving areas failed to recognize their future influence. Just as noted above, the policy agendas in these areas are very different from those in sending areas. When local governments formulate policies, they keep in mind are the interests of local residents with permanent *Hukou* registration. For local governments and residents, rural migrant workers are "strangers", "outsiders" and even "invaders", even though the local industrial takeoff and the economy development depended upon on these rural migrant workers. The everyday life of local governments and residents came to depend on these rural migrant workers; in fact, local dwellers become affluent as a result of close relations with these rural migrants. When the state-owned enterprises were reformed, and a great number of urban workers were laid off, these rural migrants become the scapegoat, even "enemy" of local residents because they believed that the rural migrants has deprived them of their job opportunities.

Since 1995, local governments in receiving areas have formulated a series of policies and regulations on rural migrants. These policies and regulations have mostly been concerned with the constraints and requirements of rural migrants, rather than their rights and status. Nonetheless, there is no doubt that that these regulations and policies addressed the rights of rural migrants to a certain extent. For instance, the government required employers to sign a labor contract with rural migrant workers, provide them with necessary working and living conditions and rest time, and pay them on time. Related bureaus should focus on the protection and cure of occupational diseases of migrant workers, and provide relevant safety training. When migrant workers are injured during work, the employers should rectify the situation in an efficient manner, and compensate injured workers and their families. Furthermore, rural migrant workers have recently been able to participate in social security programs, and enjoy the benefits of the social security system. In recent years, no longer able to deny the privileges of urban residency to migrants, many city governments that are already running steep deficits will have to increase funding for services such as education, health care and public security. To some extent, these are the unintended consequences of rural migrants' actions. The migrants in the cities themselves-along with the market-have had a major influence on the unfolding policy, on the style of administration, and on the behavior of the managers, even as their presence and praxis contributed to refashioning the modes of distribution in the city (Solinger, 1999).

Recent regulations and policies reveal that rural migrant workers are treated more equally in receiving areas. But some scholars point out that there are huge gaps between government formulation and implementation of policy. Guangdong Province is an example. As foreign investors increasingly inserted themselves into the economy as bosses in place of state managers and began to mistreat their employees, it began to look as if at least the local government had become, like that in India, the maid of capital in "a common front against the fragmented and defenseless proletariat." A tacit alliance developed between local officials and overseas entrepreneurs operating on their soil, wishing to attract and hold onto foreign investment (Solinger, 1999). Two Chinese Reporters interviewing in Guangdong Province relayed the typical words of one of these officials: "Everyone knows what they have, so no one wants to offend him. In labor capital disputes, our management personnel often stand on the boss' sides, and rarely say an impartial word for the migrant workers" (Ge and Qu, 1990).

4.5 Establishing a Network Between Sending and Receiving Places

4.5.1 The Central Government's Efforts

The uneven development and widening gap between coastal and interior regions posits significant implications for future economic and social development. They compel the central government to explore possible approaches to balance the development and narrow the gap. One important approach of the central government has been to promote the cooperation between coastal and inland provinces.

Establishing a network between sending and receiving areas and promoting the rural-urban and cross-regional migration are the other approaches that the central government emphasizes in its strategy. Similar to local governments in sending areas, the central government believes that rural-urban migration is an important and efficient approach for reducing poverty and narrowing regional and rural-urban gaps. This is why the central government's policies are always coinciding with those of local governments in sending areas, but not consistent with those of local governments in receiving areas.

1) Related Policies

(1) On November 3, 1993, the Ministry of Labor issued the *Publishing and Distributing Plan on Promoting Employment in Urban and Rural Areas: "Re-employment Project" and "Orderly Cross-provincial Migration of Rural Laborers*." This document was created in order to facilitate the "orderly migration" between sending and receiving areas. It emphasizes that related departments should provide management, supervision, rights protection and services to rural migrants, and regional coordination should be strengthened.

(2) On August 8, 1994, the Ministry of Labor issued *The Practical Plan on Promoting the Development of the Labor Market and Establishing Measures to Improve the Employment Service System.*

(3) On November 17, 1994, the Ministry of Labor formulated a comprehensive national policy, the *Provisional Regulation regarding the cross-provincial employment of rural laborers: how to Apply for Temporary Residence Cards and Regulations on Renting for Rural Migrants*. These documents, along with a variety of regional regulations on various aspects of rural labor migration and employment (ranging from birth control to housing), constituted the documentary basis of the "orderly migration" framework that is still evolving.

(4) On November 25, 1997, the State Council issued the document *Guidelines on Organizing the Orderly Migration of Rural Laborers*. The document has different requirements for local governments in receiving and sending areas: (1) The former should prepare plans on recruiting rural migrant laborers and establish corresponding management systems according to the local urban planning, infrastructure, and labor demands; and they should ask the employers to sign work contracts with rural laborers and help migrants protect their rights, as well as provide skill and non-skill training for migrants. (2) The latter should prepare a plan for sending rural laborers in terms of local circumstances, provide accurate information and services, establish a stable connection between employers and organizations responsible for sending rural laborers, and provide primary vocational skill training for rural laborers. More importantly, the coordination and communication system should be established between sending and receiving areas in order to provide better services and management for rural migrants.

(5) On January 17, 2000, the Ministry of Labor and Social Security promulgated *Opinions on Employment of Rural Surplus Laborers*. The document asks the local governments of sending and receiving areas to formulate together the overall plan on employment and training of rural laborers.

(6) On January 5, 2003, the State Council issued the first document *Improving Management and Services for Rural Labor Migrants*. It is a very important document for improving the living and working conditions of rural migrant workers in receiving areas. The details will be discussed below.

(7) On July 22, 2004, the Ministry of Labor and Social Security issued an announcement on *Strengthening the Partnership of Cross-Provincial Labor Service*. This document reviews the history of the partnership of cross-provincial labor service. It points out that most local governments of sending provinces have established official offices for laborer services in most of the major receiving provinces, which play an important role in promoting orderly migration and protecting the rights of rural migrants. The local governments of sending provinces should accredit those official offices for laborer services, which should be included in the local administrative system in the major receiving areas, to cooperate with receiving provinces to manage and protect the rights of their own rural migrants; and the local governments of receiving provinces should support those official offices for laborer services, and provide some new policies and labor market information.

(8) On October 26, 2004, in the national tele-conference on promoting rural laborer's cross-regional employment, Mr. Zhang Xiaojian, the Deputy Minister of Labor and Social Security, reported that the main tasks related to promoting cross-regional rural labor employment are improving the employment conditions of rural migrants, insisting on training and employment in sending areas, providing more public employment services and protecting the rights of rural migrant laborers in receiving areas. Through establishing an efficient work network between sending and receiving areas, rural laborer's cross-provincial employment will gradually become "Shuchu You Zuzhi, Qiuzhi You Fuwu, Jiuye You Jineng, Quanyi You Baozhang" (the local governments of sending and receiving areas will be responsible for organizing and sending rural laborers, helping them seek jobs, providing vocational skills training for them, and protecting their interests and benefits). In order to improve employment conditions and eliminate discriminatory policies and regulations, Zhang said the policy, which has controlled the rural-urban migration for "Waichu Renyuan Dengji Ka" and "Wailai Renyu an Jiuye Zheng" about ten years, will be abolished, and rural laborers will enjoy the same rights that urban laborers have, both of which will be included in a unified employment management system (Xinhua News Agency, 2004).

2) Case Study of Policies

In order to learn more about how the local governments in receiving and sending areas draft policies in terms of policies corresponding with the central government, the document *Improving the Management and Service for Rural Labor Migrants* is used as a case study. This can provide more ideas regarding the relationship between central and local governments, the different standpoints of local governments in sending and receiving provinces, and even how the their respective power works.

On January 5, 2003, the State Council issued the document *Improving Management and Service for Rural Labor Migrants*. It stipulates that:

"When local governments in sending areas are organizing and sending rural laborers to urban areas for non-farming employment, they should provide necessary training, referring to rights protection, laws, policies and regulations, common sense for living in urban areas, and knowledge on how to find jobs, before they leave the sending places in order to establish their capacity to comply with laws and regulations and protect their rights. Local governments in sending and receiving places should mobilize all educational resources, and entrust some qualified vocational skills training organizations to provide diversified training."

3) Receiving Areas

Beijing:

On July 30, 2003, the Beijing Bureau of Labor and Social Security issued an announcement on *Promoting the Vocational Skill Training and Labor Service for Rural Migrant Laborers*. In this document, it was stipulated that in terms of the State Council's first document in 2003, "local governments in sending areas should provide necessary training to rural migrants before they leave." Consequently, the Beijing Government would not provide similar training. At the same time, these trainings were no longer a precondition for rural migrants to apply for a "Work Permit in Beijing."

4) Sending Areas

Sichuan:

On November 25, 2003, the Sichuan Provincial Governmental Office issued the document *Sichuan Provincial Announcement on Promoting the Employment Service and Management for Rural Migrants,* which insisted on paying equal attention to training and certificate. Bureaus of Labor and Social Security should endow the corresponding Skill Grade Certificate and Vocational Qualification Certificate to rural migrants if they accept training and pass the examination. Bureaus should reduce the fee of certificates, and help more rural migrants acquire these certificates.

5) Comments

The local governments in sending and receiving areas interpret these policies from their individual perspective. The local governments of receiving areas pass the responsibility of providing knowledge training to local governments of sending areas since this is a central policy mandate. The local governments of sending areas pay more attention to skill training because they believe it will help rural laborers more efficiently find jobs in receiving areas. Unfortunately, the central government is only capable of planning macroscopic policy, and is without the strength to intervene in how these measures are being implemented in various government localities.

"The rural migrant children's rights of compulsory education should be ensured. Local governments of receiving areas should permit migrant children to enroll in public primary and middle schools, ensure they have the same rights urban children have, and subsidize the tuition of poorer children. Local governments of receiving areas should support "Migrant Children Schools", and other poor school conditions, and include them in the local educational development system and planning. Local governments of sending areas should cooperate with local governments in receiving areas, and require local primary school and middle schools to accept these returned migrant children without any additional requirements. And it should be prohibited to ask rural migrants to pay more for their children's education."

6) Receiving Areas

Beijing:

On March 30, 2003, the Beijing Bureau of Education promulgated the *Provisional Regulations on Conducting Compulsory Education among the School-Aged Rural Migrant Children in Beijing*. (1) If migrant children are under the conditions of guardianship in the place where they have permanent *Hukou* then they should return to receive compulsory education. (2) If migrant children have no guardianship in the place where they have permanent *Hukou*, and their parents have Temporary Residence Cards and live in Beijing for more than half a year, then they can "jiedu"[20] in Beijing's primary and public schools. (3) The qualified migrant children should apply for the authorization to attend schools in Beijing in the place where their parents retain their Temporary Residence Cards with their

20 This is a special Chinese term, which emphasizes that these rural migrant children don't have urban permanent *Hukou* registration, and therefore, they have to borrow schooling opportunities. In this case they are required to pay more money for their education compared with their urban counterparts.

parents ID, Temporary Residence Card, Work Permit for Beijing and relevant certificates before they "jiedu" in Beijing's public schools.

7) Sending places

Sichuan:

On November 25, 2003, Sichuan Provincial Governmental Office issued the document *Sichuan Provincial Announcement on Promoting Employment Services and Management for Rural Migrants*. It put Law on Compulsory Education into practice, and ensures that the rural migrant children's right to compulsory education. Local governments should try their best to make sure these children can go to school. These children should have the same rights as urban children.

8) Comments

It is evident that the related policies of receiving areas still discriminate against rural migrant children. They set many obstacles for migrant children who should be able to enroll in public schools. If these non-farming parents think that in terms of the economic conditions the children should be brought nearby, why does the receiving area's government demand that the parents keep their children in their hometown? (Ma, 2003). In addition, one stipulation of Beijing's law is that in order for migrants' children to have the opportunity of studying in Beijing schools, their parents must live in Beijing for more than half a year and acquire a temporary residence permit. But why are migrant children not allowed to enroll in public schools if their parents live in Beijing less than half a year? That means if a child of school age migrates with his parent to Beijing, he must wait for more than half a year before obtaining the right to enroll in a local public school? If an urban child has to move to the new place because his father or mother shifts to a new job, his school will be arranged before he arrives in the city. Why are the rural and urban children treated so differently?

9) Results

From the policy mentioned above, the central government has paid attention to coordination between sending and receiving areas for a long time, and therefore have issued a series of policies. More recently, the content of these policies has focused on rural migrants' rights. Despite these efforts, it seems these policies have yielded little effect, or, that these policies do not play a very important role in improving living and working conditions of rural migrants and protecting their interests as the central government has envisioned. The causes for this are as follows:

- Due to decentralization, the central government gradually releases some power to local governments. It plays the role of a macro-policy decision-maker, rather than an interventionist as before. Consequently, provincial power and influences are increasing. If the local government believes central policy conflicts with local interests, it resists the policy, or deals with it courteously but without sincerity.
- The fragmentation of the administrative system is another important obstacle in putting these polices into practice efficiently. The so-called "tiaotiao" (ministries/departments) and "kuaikuai" (regions) all represents different interest groups. Even if one ministry issues the policy, it still needs the support from other ministries/departments. When other ministries/departments believe it conflicts with their own interests, they will resist the policy or disregard it altogether.
- During the reform era, the influence of the *Hukou* system has gradually declined, but there are still many obstacles in the way of implementing *Hukou* reform. At present, the *Hukou* system still has a great impact on dividing rural-urban regions. Local governments still determine who are under their jurisdiction and who can enjoy public goods in light of their *Hukou* status. The *Hukou* system becomes a legal and efficient measure for local governments in receiving places to refuse equal treatment of rural migrants, and therefore, prevents them from public goods and social security – even though these governments must tolerate rural-urban migration in order to develop local economies.
- At the macro level, the central government's policies give direction to local policies, but these policies are relatively abstract. Without details and operational guidelines, local governments can interpret these policies in terms of their demands and interests. Consequently, the one particular central policy produce diversified local policies. It becomes difficult for central ministries to supervise the practice of these policies, and it is impossible to compare the results of the same policy in different areas.

4.5.2 Local Government Efforts in Sending and Receiving Places

At the end of the 1980s, and as an initiative to facilitate "orderly migration", Guangdong Province took steps to organize the Southern China Labor Service Partnership. It represents the earliest cooperation between sending and receiving areas. Later on, the central government extended this model of regional partnership to northern (led by Beijing) and eastern China (led by Shanghai).

1) Earlier efforts

In 1991, provincial Bureaus of Labor in Guangdong, Sichuan, Hunan and Guangxi jointly issued Setting up Partnership of Cross-Provincial Labor Service, and Strengthening Management of Rural Migrant Laborers in Guangdong. This included: (1) Setting up a cross-provincial labor service partnership center, the administrative office of which is located in the Guangdong Labor Service Company. Every sending area (Sichuan, Hunan and Guangxi) can accredit an Official Office for Labor Services in Guangdong; (2) Every Official Office for Labor Services should supervise their local migrant laborers in Guangdong, help local governments, and ensure that each employer signs work contracts with rural migrants. In order to guarantee that these provisions are successfully implemented, every provincial government should publish corresponding views.

2) Recent Efforts: Pan-Pearl River Delta Region Labor Service Partnership Network

It is reported that Guangdong continues to strengthen its interaction with neighboring provinces in terms of labor service. In order to lead a "win-win" game within the "Pan-Pearl River Delta Region" (PPRDR), Pan-Pearl Delta Region (9+2) Labor Service Partnership Network (PPRDR-LSPN) was introduced in 2004. PPRDR includes Fujian, Jiangxi, Guangdong, Guangxi, Hainan, Sichuan, Guizhou, Yunnan and Hong Kong, Macao (9+2), whose area accounts for more than 1/5 of the national total, population more than 1/3 of the national total, and total economic output exceeds 1/3 of the national total (excluding Hong Kong and Macao). There are more than ten million migrant laborers from the other eight provinces in the PPRDR region who are working in Guangdong, and there are 200 thousand migrant laborers from Hong Kong and Macao who are working in Guangdong.

On July 13, 2004, the first joint conference on PPRDRLSPN was held in Guangzhou. "Agreement of the PPRDR-LSPN", [21] and the "Joint Conference Constitute on PPRDR-LSPN" was promulgated in the conference. In terms of the former, PPRDR-LSPN will focus on coordinating policies on labor services and employment among the "9+2" provinces, exploring informational exchange mechanisms, strengthening the formation of cross-provincial employment service systems, providing more help for poorer province in labor services, promoting vocational skill training and vocational assessment, pushing the

21 Hong Kong and Macao are Excluded

establishment of laborers' rights protection system, and driving labor service partnership between nine provinces in Mainland China and Hong Kong and Macao. The Joint Conference will be held every year. It is reported that a unified, open and orderly labor market will be established in PPRDR, which includes unified policies on labor services and employment, a unified employment service system, unified vocational skill training and vocational assessment system, unified laborers' rights protection system, and a social security system (Nanfang Daily, July 14, 2004).

On July 15, 2004, Sichuan and Jiangxi declared the corresponding policies to promote the formation of a unified labor market within PPRDR. It is reported there are about 1.49 million rural laborers from Sichuan, and 0.84 million from Jiangxi, who are currently working in Guangdong Province (Xinkuai Newspaper, 2004).

3) Comments

The efforts of local governments to establishing cross-provincial labor service partnerships indicates that local governments of receiving areas recognize that the rural-urban migration can become a "win-win" game, rather than a "zero-sum" game, between receiving and sending areas, receiving areas and rural migrants. But earlier efforts seem to have less impact, and it is too early to assess recent efforts. As one rural migrant said: "If there is an actual unified and open labor market which is presented in PPRDR, it will mean we are treated more equally, that the Hukou and languages are no longer obstacles, and that we can integrate with the cities."

4.6 Practices of "Urban Poverty Reduction Among Young Rural Migrants"

"Urban Poverty Reduction Among Young Rural Migrants" is a crosscutting project on poverty reduction implemented, and the project was implemented through the Huamnities sector of UNESCO. This research-action project tests solutions on integration of young female migrants in 7 pilot sites throughout China: Chengdu, Dalian, Shanghai, Beijing, Chifeng, Kunming and Diqing,[22] which include large, middle, and small cities. Far from being isolated, they form a comprehensive partnership network, through which the experiences in different situations should be shared and linked (sending-receiving areas).

---

22 At the beginning of the project, there were eight pilot sites: Jintang-Houjie, Chengdu, Dalian, Shanghai, Beijing, Chifeng, Kunming, and Diqing. In addition to seven of these, there was also Jintang-Houjie, but afterwards this was cancelled.

The project's main partner is the Institute of Sociology, Chinese Academy of Social Sciences. Its approach is the so-called participatory approach: the involvement of migrants themselves in order to build a bottom-up approach to address the problem of poverty among young migrants. It attempts to establish partnership networks with social science researchers, NGOs (local women federations), local authorities, officials and policy-makers at municipal and national levels.

Objectives of the project include: (1) To address the problems of urban poverty among internal migrants (young and especially female migrants) and improve their living conditions through social services and activities that can empower them and strengthen their capabilities and development; (2) To reduce migrant's social and economic exclusion by reinforcing solidarity networks, enhancing their knowledge about socio-economic rights, their awareness of urban problems and a better mutual understanding and social cohesion within the neighborhood; (3) To facilitate social and professional integration of young female migrants; (4) To capitalize on knowledge and values acquired in urban areas in order to participate in the modernization and development of their native rural villages if they return home. (5) To capitalize on lessons learnt through these actions in order to enrich policies addressing social exclusion and to influence policy-makers.

Establishing networks between sending and receiving areas is one of the most important approaches in attempting to achieve these objectives. While the efforts of the central government and local government do not have the intended effects, the project has provided some alternatives and more efficient approaches to establishing a network between the sending and receiving areas of rural migrants. Some cases are more successful, and some are less successful. These models intend to answer the following question: how do we establish a network between receiving and sending areas that acts to help rural migrants improve their living and working conditions, enjoy the same rights and benefits as urban people, and reduce their poverty in urban areas?

4.6.1 More Successful Cases[23]

Model 1: The Chifeng Case-Establishing Service Organizations for Rural Migrants Between Sending and Receiving Places

The Chifeng sub-project's partner is the Chifeng Prefectural Women's Federation (CPWF). In 1998, CPWF became involved in sending rural laborers to urban areas for

23 Mr. Zhan Shaohua, one of the core members of the CASS team, mainly summarizes models 1 and 2 and is responsible for communication with the Chifeng, Kunming and Diqing sub-projects.

seeking non-farming employment and non-agricultural opportunities. It was one of the first organizations that organized and sent rural laborers. Its experiences show that rural laborers migrate not only to the big cities, such as Beijing, Tianjin and Dalian, but also to the middle cities, such as Chifeng Prefectural City. in this way, Chifeng is not only a sending area, but also a receiving area. In order to protect rural migrants' rights, especially female rural migrants, and in order to meet their needs, CPWF, under the support of Oxfam Hong Kong and UNESCO, established the Beijing Migrant's Club and the Chifeng Migrant's Center. At the same time, CPWF makes use of the current hierarchy within the women's federation system[24] to establish a network between Chifeng (receiving area) and counties/towns/townships/villages (sending area). Figure 4-1 shows thatCPWF has established a three-level network, which connects the rural areas (sending areas), middle cities (sending/receiving areas) and municipalities (receiving areas).

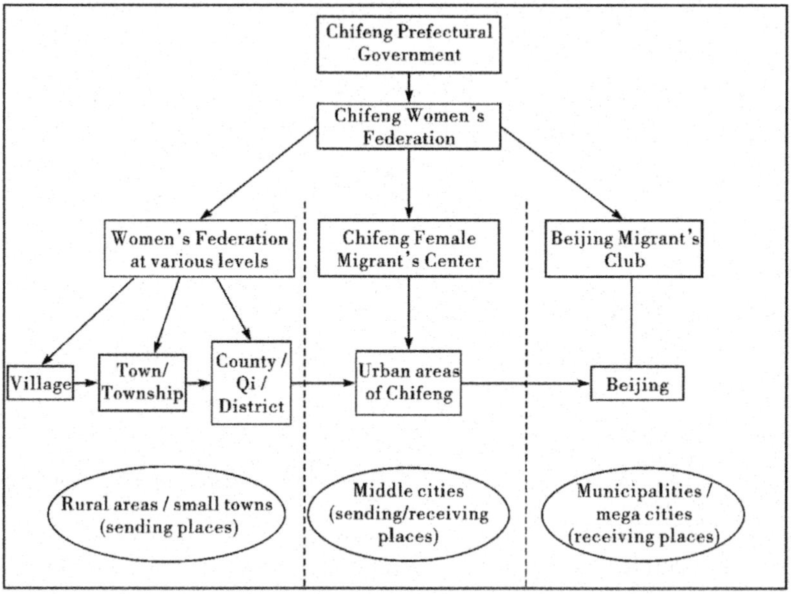

Figure 4-1 The Network Organization Between Receiving and Sending Areas (The Case of Chifeng)

24 Though Women's Federation is called non-governmental organization in the Chinese context, it is actually part of the Chinese administration system. It is also one of the "tiaotiaos." It has its own vertical system, ranging from central to province to prefecture to county to town/township. Higher levels within the women's federation control those levels directly below them. At the same time, local governments control the corresponding levels with the Women's Federation. The organ is always marginalized in the local administration system and therefore they have less power and resources. Consequently, when the women's Federation becomes in partnership with the project, it is difficult for the organ to involve other organs of the local government. This situation is disadvantageous for development of the project.

Through the Beijing Migrant's Club and Chifeng Migrant's Center, CPWF uses a participatory approach to provide knowledge training, such as law, health, social protection, and how to live in the urban community. Community-based training for female laborers as well as weekly self-improving activities is organized in order to broaden and strengthen the network among female migrants in Beijing and Chifeng. CPWF communicates information about labor demands through the three-level network from top to bottom, before the lower level women's federation organizes qualified rural laborers, provides necessary trainings, and sends them to receiving areas. When a migrant girl has an accident, the Beijing Migrant's club will convey this information to the Chifeng Migrant's Center, will which then convey this information to CPWF, to the women's federation at the town/township level, and finally, to her family. They also work together to explore how to deal with the issue. This pathway is demonstrated in Figure 4-2.

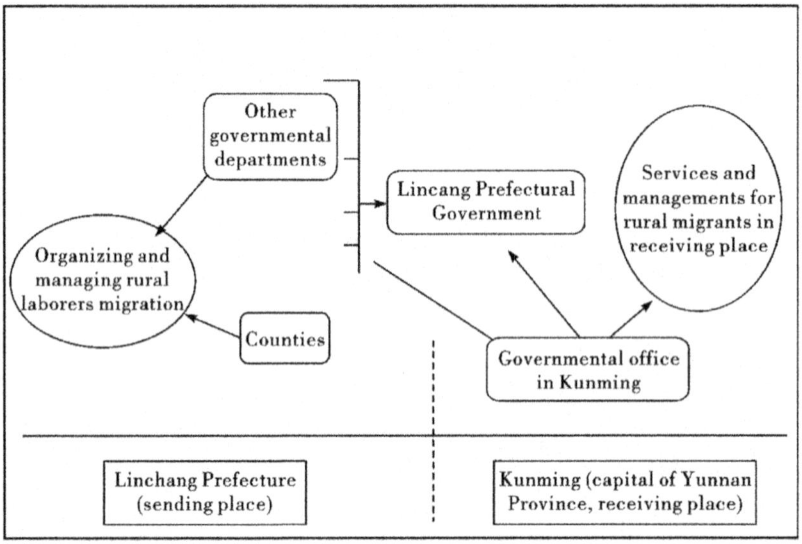

Figure 4-2 The Network Organization Between Receiving and Sending Places (the Kunming Case)

It is without doubt that the service organizations for rural migrants (Beijing Migrant's Club and Chifeng Migrant's center) play an important role in the operation of the network. They are the nodes of the network, which not only provide necessary training and activities for rural migrants in receiving places to meet their basic needs (social interaction, skill training, knowledge training, rights protection, and some other related issues), but also exchange important information through the whole network, and very quickly. Because these organizations are not included in the local administration system, the latter's segmented control cannot have a great impact on the former. And it is easy to adjust these organizations at any time.

But it is also double-edged sword. Because these organizations and the network are not included in the local administration system, the funding which is necessary for supporting them is not included in the annual administrative budget of local governments. They have to depend on the funding from other resources, such as Hong Kong Oxfam and UNESCO. As soon as they are unable to obtain these funds, it becomes very difficult to maintain the organization and the network. Thus, CPWF is marginalized in the local administration system. It has few resources and little power to support the organization and the network by itself; and it has less capacity to involve other governmental departments in the project. The other weakness of this model is that CPWF cannot establish a partnership between the labor service and any departments of the Beijing Government, including the Beijing Women's Federation. From the discussion above, we know that there are significant obstacles in the way of achieving this objective. This weakness makes it difficult to protect the rights of rural migrants or improve their living and working conditions in Beijing.

1) Model 2: The Kunming Case-Making Use of Existing Governmental Resources to Establish the Network

Most of the prefectural-level and above cities in inland provinces establish their governmental working offices in either Beijing, the provincial capital or other developed areas of the coastal provinces (always the receiving places of rural migrants). These working offices are included in their original local administrative system. As a result, there are full-time officials, housing, telephone, and other necessary working conditions. Some of these offices are also managing enterprises. One of the most important functions is to establish a connection between the destination and their origin. Though promoting rural-labor migration is not included in their tasks, the working offices and their resources can be used to establish a network and provide services and trainings for rural migrants.

The Kunming sub-project's partner is the Institute of Philosophy of Yunnan Academy of Social Sciences (YASS). As an academic institute, the partner is without administrative and organizational resources. But it has its own strengths, such as extensive social relations and membership within governmental think tanks. In 2003, YASS cooperated with the Lincang Prefecture Working Office in Kunming (LPWOK) to provide training and services for rural migrants. Through the Lincang working office, the network between Lincang (sending place) and Kunming (receiving place) was established, as revealed in Figure 4-2. By way of the network, Lincang prefectural-level and lower governmental departments recruited rural laborers and sent them to Kunming, and then LPWOK provided necessary training, including vocational skill training, rights protection, salary management, and employment in Kunming.

Similar to the Chifeng case, the Kunming sub-project did not establish a network between local governments of sending and receiving places. In fact, the Kunming sub-project has worked with local governments in Kunming, such as the Jinniu Street Office and the Kunming Commission of Ethnic Affairs, in 2004. But it seemed very difficult for the Kunming sub-project to connect Lincang Prefecture with the Kunming local governments (Zhan, 2004). It should be noted here that the Kunming sub-project has solved the problem related to the sustainability of the network Chifeng network. LPWOK is included in the administrative system of their origin. As a result, its funding can be included in the annual administrative budget of the local government. It is not necessary for them to depend on funding from other resources. And while this model has involved the Lincang Prefectural Government in the project, it means they have a greater capacity to mobilize resources and provide services and assistance to rural migrants.

2) Model 3: The Shanghai Case-the Four-Section Employment Chain

The Shanghai sub-project's partner is East China Normal University. The same as that of the Kunming sub-project's partner, it is also an academic organization; the difference is that it has established close connections with enterprises, especially employment agencies. One of the important local partners of the Shanghai sub-project is the Shanghai Star International Corporation. The corporation is transferring their focus from only high-level skill training, such as English training for managers in the foreign corporations, to both high-level and low-level skill training. The Shanghai sub-project believes that through the market perspective, it is feasible to provide skill trainings for rural migrants and protect their economic, social and political rights. It emphasizes that it is powerless in helping the rural migrants protect their rights without enough money. Through the market, it is possible to achieve the "win-win" game for both the corporation and rural migrants. At the same time, the network established by the Shanghai sub-project can maintain its survival.

The principles of Shanghai's sub-project include government instruction through its issuing of related policies; enterprise participation in the establishment of four-section employment chain and the network; and the sub-project's implementation in agreement with market principles. The sub-project also believes that employment is essential and indispensable for rural migrants. It also continues to pay attention to the establishing the four-section employment chain: recruitment, training, recommendation and management. This means that when there are some vacant positions, the Shanghai sub-project will recruit rural laborers in their hometown (sending place), send them to Shanghai (receiving place), train them for vacant positions, help them obtain these vacant positions, and provide services and management when they are working in Shanghai. Through establishing the four-section employment chain, the Shanghai sub-project will have established the network between sending and receiving places, shown in Figure 4-3.

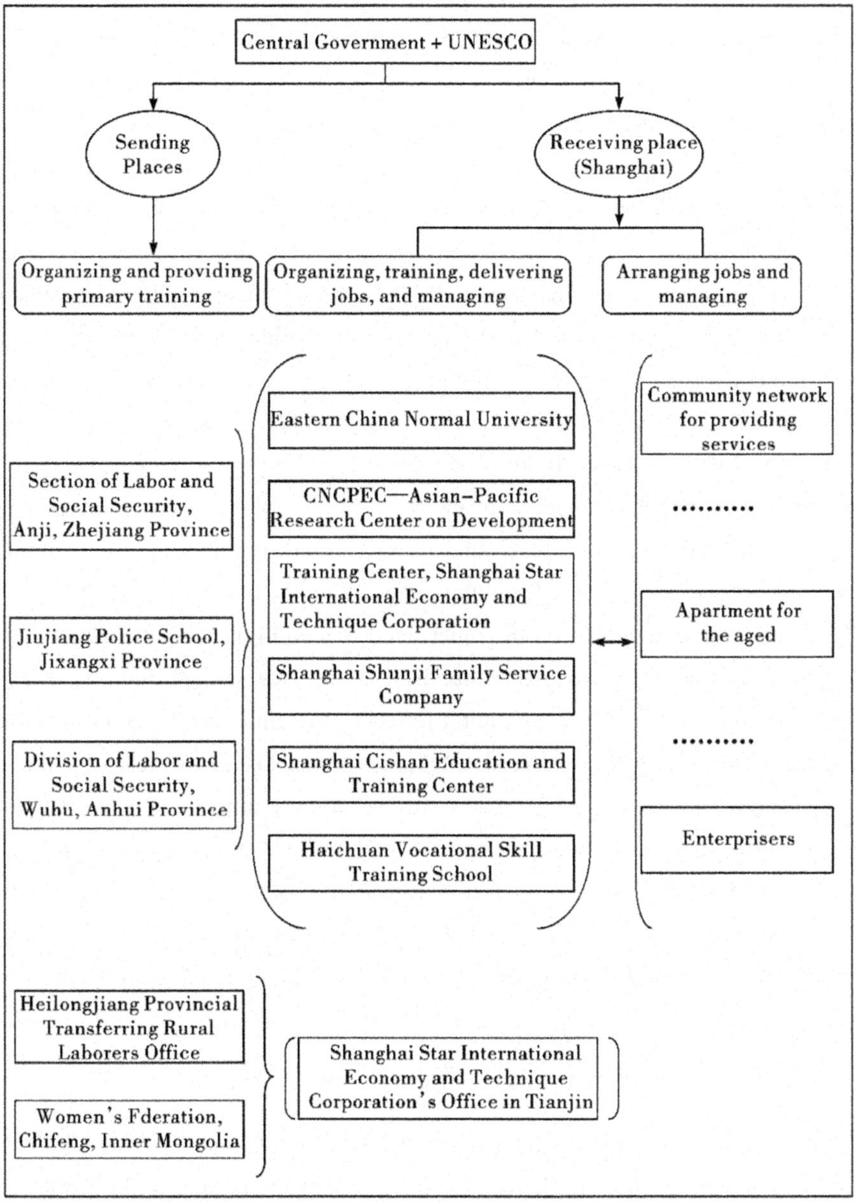

Figure 4-3 The Network Organization Between Receiving and Sending Places (Shanghai case)

As a rapidly developing mega-city, Shanghai provides a large number of non-farming jobs and non-agricultural opportunities for rural laborers. It is an important reason as to why the Shanghai sub-project can establish the employment chain. The other important reason is that they have enough resources and can integrate all resources, including governments, enterprises, academic institutions and other social resources, which have been presented in Figure 4-3. It may not be easy for other projects to copy this model. But it indeed provides an alternative approach for establishing a network between sending and receiving places. The efficiency and feasibility of the approach is important, and its sustainability is equally important.

In the Shanghai sub-project, the enterprises play an important role. An enterprise is firstly an economic body, and profit maximization is what it pursues. It is why persons are worried about whether or not the enterprise can insist on providing services and management for rural migrants. Just as noted above, the sub-project will be implemented in agreement with market principles. This means it is impossible for the enterprise to provide free skill training for rural migrants. Another potential problem is how the rural laborers pay for the training. Furthermore, how do the enterprises determine tuition amounts for the training? How do they factor in the rural migrant's capability of accepting the price? How do the enterprises balance their own interests and rural migrants' interests? Local governments, especially those of receiving places, should play an important role. On the one hand, local governments of receiving places should supervise enterprise behavior through administrative methods; on the other hand, it should use economic methods, such as tax reduction and subsidies, to ensure that these enterprises will provide, for a reasonable price, qualified skill and knowledge training for rural migrants. For the latter approach, the central government should be involved since part of the tax is extracted by the central government. Furthermore, it is unrealistic to ask local governments of receiving places to provide subsides for rural migrants because it conflicts with local interests. Local governments prefer to provide subsidies for training local laid-off workers and local farmers whose land has been confiscated for the development of urban areas. The combination of market and government could very well be a realistic approach in solving the problem.

4.6.2 A Less Successful Case: The Jintang Case

The previous Jintang sub-project's partner is the Jintang County Women's Federation (JCWF). Jintang is one county in Sichuan province. Since the middle of the 1980s, Zhugao Township Government (ZTG), which is under the administration of Jintang County, began to organize labor exportation and built a stable relationship with the Houjie Township of Guangdong for labor supply. In 2001, Jintang exported 160 thousand workers and half of them worked in Houjie Township, Dongguan of Guangdong. There were around 30 thousand workers from Jintang.

While the ZTG established a working office in Houjie in 1988, Jintang County Government (JCG) has yet to establish its own office. For some time, the office has played a positive role in exporting migrant workers from Zhugao and Jintang (sending places) to Houjie (receiving place). And it also plays an important role in protecting rural migrant's rights. JCG did so while it realized the importance of trainings and services in exporting laborers and the government's role in the whole mobility process.

This means that ZTG and JCG established a network between receiving and sending places before the Jintang sub-project was initiated in 2002. The Jintang sub-project took advantage of and expanded the existed network (shown in Figure 4-4) to provide services and training for rural migrants. Compared with Model 1, there are some obvious similarities: Local governments of sending places initiated and controlled the network, operated the Women's Federation, and few departments of local governments were involved

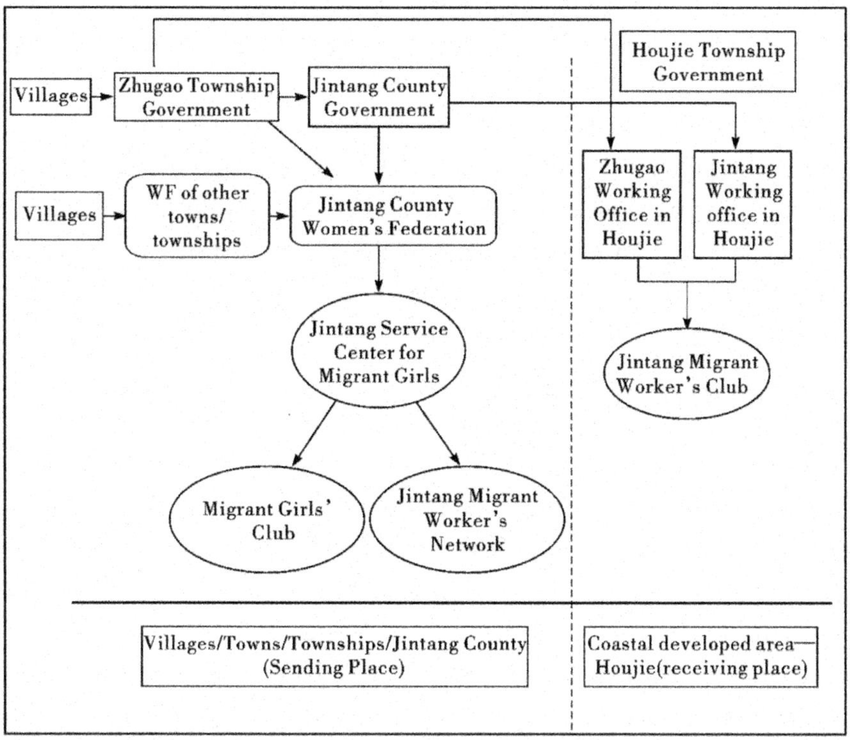

Figure 4-4 Sketch on network between receiving and sending places, Jintang case

in it, at least at the beginning. And they did not establish relationships with local governments of receiving places. This is an important reason as to why Jintang case was not successful. Another important reason was the long distance between sending and receiving places. The cost of JCWF to maintain the network operation was much higher than that of CPWF. Though the sub-project was included in the regular jobs of JCWF, the network could not be maintained without enough funding. Jintang is a poor county and cannot afford it, though JCG was planning to strengthen its management and services for its migrant workers in Houjie. The UNESCO project also could not afford it, and this was an important reason as to why the UNESCO project excluded this pilot site and the sub-project in 2003.

Recently, the Zhugao and the Jintang Working Office in Houjie were all withdrawn. Due to the increase in the number of private labor service companies, the labor export of Jintang and Zhugao began to transition from government behavior to market behavior. The Zhugao Township Government stationed outside of the Houjie Working Office was unable to compete with them; in relying on the intermediary they were unable to maintain their own operations, and once again they were incapable of establishing relations with the Houjie Government (Xu, 2001). The policy of Guangdong Province forced the withdrawal of the Jintang Working Office. Guangdong Provincial Government issued a document which did not permit the governments at counties and below to set up working offices in Guangdong. This demonstrates the huge impact of local government policies of receiving places. Even if the governments of sending and receiving places are in the same administrative level, it is very difficult for the former to negotiate and bargain with the latter. Even if the government of sending places has a higher administrative level, the result is the same. The relationship between them is unequal: the more resources, the more power.

4.6.3 Policy Recommendations

(1) While the central government is formulating policy to promote the partnership between sending and receiving places, it should take into consideration the interests of different stakeholders, especially powerful stakeholders. The interests and benefits of disadvantageous groups are certainly the first issue the central government should consider. But it is important to balance the interests among different stakeholders. If the government attempts to protect rural migrants' rights at the expense of the powerful stakeholders' interests, the latter are more likely to either resist policy implementation. In this case, attempts at policy formulation have little effect, and rural migrants' rights cannot be

protected. It is a fact that local governments of receiving and sending places have different resources and therefore different views towards rural migrants. Policy formulation should use different provisions in relation to the sending and receiving places, and should consider their different positions.

(2) In order to maximize the effects of the policy, policy should be formulated with detail and with attention to its operational items. If the policy is of an abstract quality, then local governments are able to interpret policy to fit its own agenda and interests. These detailed and operational items of corresponding policies should include how to supervise the practice of policies, how to appraise the result, and what responsibility every department of local administrations should bear. The final point is very important because the administrative system in China is very divided. Establishing the so-called "Bumen Wenze Zhi" (system of departmental responsibility) would ensure that the appropriate policy measures are put into practice. In particular, "Bumen Wenze Zhi" means after the policy is implemented, the central government appraises whether every department has completed their corresponding responsibilities. If not, the department would be fined via administrative or economic methods. Results should also be included in the "political achievements" (Zhengji), which posits major effects on the promotion of officials.

(3) The central government and local governments should integrated all resources, including governments, enterprises, and academic institutions, etc., to establish the network between sending and receiving places and to provide services and managements for rural migrants to improve their living and working conditions in receiving places. The governments should consider administrative as well as market methods. For example, in order to encourage private agencies to provide qualified and cheap skill training for rural migrants, the government should provide subsides or tax reduction for these private agencies. The government should consider how to integrate with the market.

(4) The central government and local governments should promote *Hukou* reform and initiate "unified urban-rural household registration system." Without the *Hukou* system, the receiving government has no legal methods to exclude rural migrants from the local social security and welfare system. Without the *Hukou* system, rural migrant workers have greater capacity to negotiate and bargain with governments and enterprises.

(5) The central government should explore how to establish a mechanism where rural migrants' voices can be heard, and where they can express their opinions freely.

1) Appendix

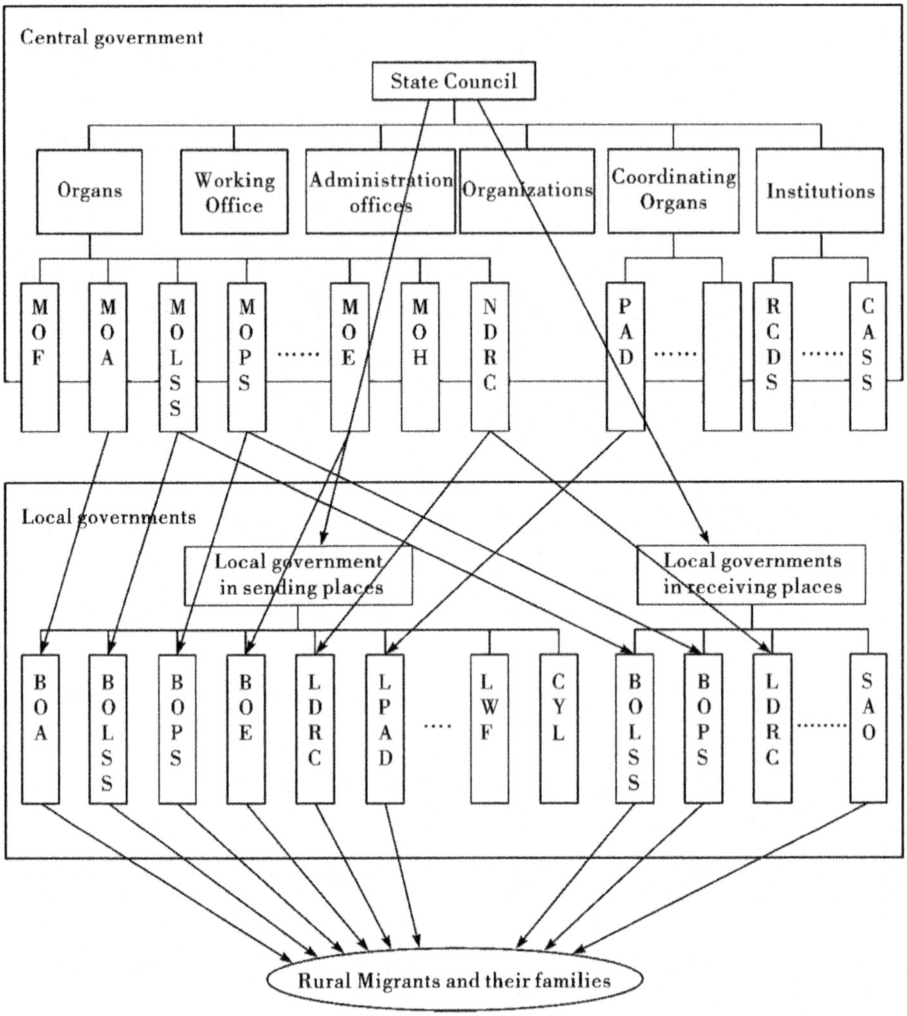

Figure 1 The Administration System in China

2) Note:

(1) Central government:

State Council: Main responsibilities include policymaking, and supervising and monitoring policy implementation at the central and local levels.

Organs: Under the unified leadership of the State Council, they are in charge of directing and administering the administrative affairs in their respective areas and exercising prescribed state administrative powers. There are 28 organs altogether.

- MOF: Ministry of Finance
- MOA: Ministry of Agriculture
- MOLSS: Ministry of Labor and Social Security
- MOPS: Ministry of Public Security
- MOE: Ministry of Education
- MOH: Ministry of Health
- NDRC: National Development and Reform Commission

Working office: General Affairs Office of the State Council.

Administrative Offices: These are offices set up within the State Council to assist the Premier in dealing with matters in special areas. There are 8 administrative offices.

Organizations: These are organs that are in charge of administrative affairs in special areas, under the unified leadership of the State Council. They are lower than the organs listed in the administrative ranking. There are 18 organizations altogether.

Coordinating Organs: These are set up by the State Council in order to deal with special affairs.

- PAD: Poverty Alleviation and Development, State Council Leading Group

Institutions: Directly under the direction of the State Council. There are 14 institutions altogether.

- CASS: Chinese Academy of Social Sciences
- RCDS: Research Center for Development Studies

(2) Local Governments

Abbreviations:

- BOA: Bureau of Agriculture
- BOLSS: Bureau of Labor and Social Security
- BOPS: Bureau of Public Security
- BOE: Bureau of Education
- LWF: Local Women's Federation
- LDRC: Local Development and Reform Commission
- LPAD: Local Poverty Alleviation and Development
- CYL: Communist Youth League
- SAO: Street Administration Office (jiedao)

(3) Arrows: "from a to b" means a controls b.

3) Source:

"The Local Administrative System" and "The Central Administration System", in

China Internet Information Center, http: //www.China.org.cn; and Huang and Pieke, 2003.

References

[1] Ash, Robert F., 1996, "The Peasants and the State." In *The Individual and the State in China*, ed. Brian Hook. Oxford University Press, 1996.

[2] Bao, Shuming and Woo, Wing Thye. "Geographic Factors and China's Regional Development Under Market Reforms, 1979~1998." *China Economic Review*, 13 (2002): 89-111.

[3] Burds, Jeffery. *Peasant Dreams and Market Politics: Labor Migration and the Russian Village 1861~1905*. Pittsburgh: University of Pittsburgh Press, 1998.

[4] Cannon, Terry. "Regions: Spatial Inequality and Regional Policy." In *The Geography of Contemporary China-the Impact of Deng Xiaoping's Decade*, ed. Cannon, Terry and Jenkins, Alan. London and NY: Routledge, 1990.

[5] Chan, Anita. "Regimented Workers in China's Free Labor Market", *China Perspectives*, no. 9 (1997): 12-16.

[6] Chan, K.W. and Li Z. "The Hukou System and Rural-Urban Migration in China: Processes and Changes", *The China Quarterly* 160 (1999): 818-855.

[7] Chen, Ping. "China's Challenge to Economic Orthodoxy", *China Economic Review* 4, no. 2 (1993): 139.

[8] Cheng, Gang and Lin, Jie. "Rural Migrant Workers are Insufficient in Guangdong Province, and the Bureau of Labor and Social Security Advises the Entrepreneurs to Improve the Working and Living Conditions of Rural Migrant Workers", *China Youth Daily*, 13 August, 2004.

[9] Cheng, Tiejun and Selden, Mark. "The Origins and Social Consequences of China's Hukou System", *The China Quarterly*, 139 (1994): 644~668.

[10] Cheung, Peter. "Guangdong under Reform: Social and Political Trends and Challenges" In Rethinking China's Provinces, ed. Fitzgerald, John. London and New York: Routledge, 2002.

[11] Demurger, Sylvie; Woo, Wing Thye; Bao, Shuming; Chang, Gene; and Mellinger, Andrew. "Geography, Economic Policy, and Regional Development in China", Working Paper, National Bureau of Economic Research, Series 8897, http: //www.nber.org/papers/w8897, 2002.

[12] Du, Yang. "Changing the Situation of Dividing between Rural and Urban Areas, Establish the Unified Labor Market", *Chinese Information Newspaper*, January 13, 2005.

[13] Duara, Prasenjit. *Culture, Power and the State: Rural North China, 1900~1942*. Stanford: Stanford University Press, 1998.

[14] Feng, Wang; Zuo, Xuejun; and Ruan, Danching. "Rural Migrants in Shanghai: Living under the Shadow of Socialism", *International Migration Review*, 36, no. 2 (2002): 520~545.

[15] Fitzgerald, John. "Introduction." In Rethinkging China's Provinces, ed. Fitzgerald, John. London and New York: Routledge, 2002.

[16] Goodkind, Daniel and West, Loraine A. "China's Floating Population: Definitions, Data and Recent Findings", *Urban Studies*, 39, no.12 (2002): 2237~2250.

[17] Goodman, Davis S.G. (eds.). *China's Provinces in Reform: Class, Community and Political*

Culture. London and New York: Routledge, 1997.

[18] Guangdong Provincial Bureau of Statistics. "Understanding the Shortage of Rural Migrant Workers in Zhujiang Pearl Delta in 2004", http: //www.stats.gov. cn/tjfx/fxbg/t20050128_402227245.htm, 2005.

[19] Guangdong Provincial Bureau of Statistics. *Guangdong Statistical Yearbook 2000*, Statistical Press, 2000.

[20] Guang, Lei. "Reconstituting the Rural-Urban Divide: Peasant Migration and the Rise of 'Orderly Migration' in Contemporary China", *Journal of Contemporary China*, 10, no. 28 (2001): 471~493.

[21] Hendrischke, Hans. "Provinces in Competition: Region, Identity and Cultural Construction", In The Political Economy of China's Provinces: Comparative and Competitive Advantage, ed. Hendrischke, Hans and Feng, Chongyi. London and New York: Routledge, 1999.

[22] Huang Ping,. *China Country Report for Project on Urban Poverty Alleviation among Young Migrants in East Asia*. UNESCO, 2003.

[23] Huang, Ping and Pieke, Frank N. China Migration Country Study, presented at the Conference on Migration, Development and Pro-Poor Policy Choices in Asia, Dhaka, 22~24 June, 2003.

[24] Huang Ping. *Seeking Survival*. Kunming: Yunnan People's Press, 1997.

[25] Huang Ping and Zhan Shaohua. *Capacity Analysis of Skills Training System for Migrant Labors in China*, Canadian International Development Agency, 2003.

[26] Lu, Xueyi. *Chinese Society in the 21st Century*, Yunnan Renmin Publishing House, 1996.

[27] Kelliher, Daniel. *Peasant Power in China: the Era of Rural Reform 1979~1988*. New Haven: Yale University Press, 1992.

[28] Knight, John; Song, Lina; and Jia, Huaibin. "Chinese Rural Migrants in Urban Enterprises: Three Perspectives.", *The Journal of Development Studies*, 35, no. 3 (1999): 73~104.

[29] Ma, Chunhua. "Marketization and Gender Relation in Rural Families of China", dissertation, Institute of Sociology, Chinese Academy of Social Science, 2003.

[30] Mackenzie, Peter W. "Strangers in the City: the Hukou and Urban Citizenship in China", *Journal of International Affairs* 56, no.1 (2002): 305~319.

[31] Ministry of Labor and Social Security, *China Labor Statistical Yearbook 2003*, China Statistics Press.

[32] MOLSS and NBS. "Situation of Employment and Migration of Rural laborers in 2000", http: //www.lm.gov.cn, June 1, 2003.

[33] "PPRDR-LSPN Promote the Labor Service Partnership", *Nanfang Daily*, July 14, 2004.

[34] National Bureau of Statistics, *China Rural Statistical Yearbook 2003*, Statistics Press, 2003.

[35] National Bureau of Statistics, *China Statistical Yearbook 1994*, Statistical Press, 1994.

[36] Sichuan Provincial Labor Development Office. "Research on How to Transfer the Rural Labor in Sichuan in the New Century", http: //report.drc.gov.cn, 2001.

[37] Siu, Helen. Agents and Victims in South China: Accomplices in Rural Revolution. Yale: Yale University Press, 1989.

[38] Solinger, Dorothy J. *Contesting Citizenship in Urban China: Peasant Migrants, the State and the Logic of the Market*. Regent: University of California Press, 1999.

[39] Tan, Shen. "Feasibility Report of the Sichuan Sub-Project", In *Poverty Reduction among Rural Young Migrants, project*. UNESCO, 2002.

[40] Tan, Shen, "The Relationship between Foreign Enterprises, Local Governments and Women Migrant Workers in the Pearl River Delta." In Women and Gender Research in China 1987~2003, ed. Du, Fangqin. Tianjin Renmin Publishing House, 2003.

[41] Wang, Wuding. *Shanghai's Floating Population in the 1990s*. Eastern China Normal University Press, 1995.

[42] Wu, Ruijun. "Defining the Floating Population". *Population and Economy* 3 (1990): 53~55.

[43] "The Ministry of Public Security: Dismantling Hukou System Gradually", January 5, 2003, http: //www.xinhuanet.com.

[44] "Sichuan and Jiangxi Establish Partnership with PPRDR in Labor Service without Any Obstacles", *Xinkuai Newspaper*, July 17, 2004, http: //www.southcn.com.

[45] "Beijing Regulations on Migrant Laborers and Businessmen will be Abolished, and the Temporary Residence Card System will be Kept ", *Xinjing Newspaper*, January 16, 2005.

[46] Xu Ping "From Governmental to Market Behavior: Study on Rural-Urban Migration in Zhu Township", paper, International Forum on Chinese Rural-Urban Migration 2001, Beijing.

[47] Yang, Dali. *Beyond Beijing: Liberalization and the Regions in China*. London and New York: Routledge, 1997.

[48] Zhou, Kate Xiao. *How the Farmers Changed China: Power of the People*. Boulder, Co: Westernview Press, 1996.

[49] Zhou, Lanchun. *Beijing's Migrant Population*. Chinese Population Publishing House, 1996.

[50] Zhou, Qiren. "Opportunities and Capacities: Employment and Migration of Rural Laborers in China", *Management World*, no. 5 (1997).

5

Possibilities and Limitations of Female Migrants' Informal Employment in China*

Pan Jie

5.1 Background

The problem of informal employment arose along with China's reform and opening-up policy. In the era of the planned economy, under the policy of "high employment but low income", about 80% of urban laborers were employed in government and state-owned enterprises, and the rest were employed mostly in the collective economy (Cai Fang, 2004). At the same time, all the rural labor force participated in collective production, such as agricultural production, poultry and livestock industry and other sideline production. This was under the control and management of People's Commune, which conducted labor management, protected laborer's rights and ensured reasonable income. In this way, nearly all the laborers were employed in these two systems, although there was the existence of informal employment, such as domestic workers, part-time jobs, etc.

This employment situation did not change much until the 1990s and with the growth of the non state-owned economy. The percentage of labor employment in the state-owned economy declined from 78.3% in 1978 to 31.9% in 2001, and urban collective unit employment declined from 21.5% to 5.4%, while other new and developing city employment rose to 24.4%. Meanwhile, informal employment kept growing, increasing to 91.59 million in 2001, and consisting of up to 38% of all employed laborers (Cai Fang, 2004).

The changes above were due to the policy adjustment on employment. Employment was no longer solely a national responsibility, but now also the responsibility of market's

* This paper was drafted and finished by Pan Jie, thanks to many valuable suggestions from Prof. Huang Ping, Dr. Chen Xin, Mr. Zhan Shaohua, Dr. Ma Chunhua and other team members of the CASS-UNESCO project team; and equal thanks to Dr. Sit Tsui, who helped with English editing of this paper.

and laborers. Different kinds of labor markets flourished, and the multifarious economy began to develop. On the other hand, in rural areas, the household took over agricultural production as a result of the disintegration of the People's Commune. In this sense, rural labor became free to job-hunt, and thereby, making rural migration possible. The rural labor migration was pushed also by poverty, the gap in income between the eastern and the western areas, and between city and countryside. Due to the lack of education, skill training, household registration, etc., most rural migrants, especially female workers, could not find formal employment in the cities. They largely poured into the informal economy. This represents the social background of informal employment, together with the striking problems faced by female migrants in terms of political, economic, social and legal aspects.

5.2 The Definition and Development of Informal Employment

5.2.1 The Definition of Informal Employment

Informal sector (economy) is a special concept, first used in 1971, and proposed by the International Labor Organization (ILO) and the United Nations Development Bureau (UNDP) in the report on employment in Kenya. The term refers to small-scale economic activities, commodity production, circulation and services, and those non full-time jobs, temporary jobs and so on in the formal economy. In recent years, according to the Chinese Ministry of Labor and Security, informal employment has been defined as employment in small-scale enterprises, satellite enterprises, family enterprises, the household economy, independent services, social services and self-employment practices.[25]

In this paper, informal employment generally refers to the working conditions or working relations of employment that are not stated in any legal document. The term includes employment in the informal economy and those temporary jobs, seasonal work, part-time jobs, dispatching services, and subcontracts in the formal economy, for example, domestic workers, peddlers, etc. However, it does not include illegal economic activities, such as crime, begging, bawdry, and the drug trade.

This paper will focus on informal employment in community services industry, in which the rural female migrants have become the majority. Furthermore, this paper will use

25 Guo Huiling: "The rights protection of the female migrants in informal employment" (Feizhenggui Jiuye Dagongmei de Quanyi Baohu), Informal Employment Forum: The Third Workshop on the Female Migrants' Rights Protection (Feizhenggui Jiuye Luntan:Disanjie Dagongmei Quanyi Baohu Yantaohui Lunwenji), p. 31,October 2004.

domestic workers for further discussions.

5.2.2 The Development of Informal Employment

Research in 2004 revealed that after 1996, China's employment witnessed a shift from a dual focus to a single focus, particularly emphasizing informal employment. In the period from 1996-2-1, China's national informal employment realized a new increase totaling 81.28 million, which represented an average annual increase of 16.26 million per year. During the same period, the sum of formal employment was 40.53 million, which saw a decrease of 8.11 million per year. The principal reason for the decrease in the employment rate was the drop in formal employment. There were two main sources behind employment growth from 1978 to 1996. The first was formal employment, where from 1978 to 1996, the national employment net increase in formal employment was 53.46 million, representing an average increase of 2.97 million per year, and occupying a new national increase in employment of 18.6%; and a new national increase in cities and towns of 51.4%. The second was informal employment, where the net increase in informal employment was 50.62 million, representing an average increase of 2.79 million per year, and accounting for 81.4% of the new national increase; and 48.6% of the new employment increase in urban areas (Hu Angang, 2004).

The flourishing development of informal employment is a universal phenomenon. In the developed countries, the continued increase in global competition and the strengthening of enterprise uncertainty, as well as considering the construction of the small family household, forced nations to utilize a flexible economic and employment form as its response. In turn, they decreased the full system of work and regularized positions, and increasingly adopted temporary employment, contract systems, and self-employment in order to resolve in part the employment problem (Cai Fang, 2005).

Meanwhile, a similar phenomenon is found popular in developing countries. "From 1990 to 1994, informal employment provided 80% of new jobs in Latin America; in Africa, 93% of new jobs were also a result of the informal economy. The percentage of informal employment was 57.2% in Africa, 36.2% in Latin America, and 32.8% in Pacific Asia."[26] There is no doubt that this phenomenon has an indirect relationship with the social problems in Latin America and the underdevelopment of Africa. But generally speaking, the experiences in many countries proved that informal employment contributed

---

26 Cai Fang: "Exploring Thoughts on Developing Employment Opportunities" (Tanshuo Kuoda Jiuye de Xin Silu), QIANXIAN, No. 5, 2005.

significantly in solving the unemployment problem.

As one study revealed, there are mainly two groups that form the informal employment in China: rural migrants (54.6%), and laid-off workers in urban areas (29.8%) (Xue Shaojun, 2004). Informal employment has not only developed at a rapid rate, but even more so it has become the most important sphere for the rural laborers as they enter the cities. In other words, it has become the most important source of non-agricultural income for the rural labor force entering the cities. In this way, informal employment is significant not only in solving unemployment problems, and poverty alleviation, but also in providing social services in cities.

5.2.3 The Advantages of Informal Employment

In China, the ratio of informal employment to formal employment grew from 1:4 in 1996 to 1:2 in 2001 (Cai Fang, 2004). Why did informal employment grow so fast in such a short time? What are its advantages?

- The First and most prominent advantage of informal employment is low cost requirement, flexibility, and greater adaptability to the changing labor market, as well as less risk in the market. Small enterprises in informal employment have the advantages of flexibility, small-scale nature, quick reaction to market demands, small capital amounts and low technical requirement, and therefore, it is easier to adjust to the changes of the market and to have more competitiveness.
- The second advantage is that unit capital produces an abundance of employment. Since most employment in the informal economy is labor-intensive industry, it needs small capital to start businesses and requires minimal skills, and therefore, more employment can be provided. On one hand, these small factories or businesses can provide jobs for female migrants who have lower education levels or working skills in the cities. Furthermore, the flexible working schedule also allows the migrants to work and therefore choose to avoid the busy farming season. On the other hand, the informal employment can absorb cheap labor force, and spend less on social security expenditure, management cost and wages.
- The third advantage is stability. As most informal employment is in social services and traditional sectors, it is able to avoid the pressure and risk of the global market and therefore obtain more stability than those in modern sectors. That is also why informal employment frequently becomes the first priority when a rural woman migrates to the city to work (Pan Jie, 2003).
- The fourth one is that some informal employment is in new industries and services.

Taking the social services industry as an example, "according to the survey of social services in four cities (Shenyang, Qingdao, Changsha, and Chengdu), co-organized by MOLSS and UNDP, 34.1% of families in the four cities have the needs of family services, such as housework, but only 16.7% of families are able to obtain these services, and 17.4% of families are still in need of these services. Thus, we can calculate that there are roughly about two million employees needed in this respect in these four cities, but there are still one million job vacancies. By this calculation, there would be over fifteen million new job opportunities provided by 32 big cities with a population of over 1,000,000, and 43 cities with a population of over 500,000population, not to mention 192 medium cities and more than 400 small towns. Hence, potential employment of family services is very high."[27]

According to sampling investigation carried out by the National Statistical Bureau, in seven cities such as Beijing, Shanghai, Chengdu, Xi'an and so on, 70% of families have the needs of community services, household electrical appliances maintenance, document delivery, household maintenance and cleaning, baby sitting, and taking care of the elderly among others, equating to roughly 7.07 million employment opportunities.[28]

5.3 Gender Characteristics and Analysis

We can easily figure out the gender characteristics of informal employment in China from Table 5-1, based upon the Second Statistics of Chinese Women's Social Status Survey, conducted by the All-China Women's Federation, in 2000.

Table 5-1 Data on Sector-Based Employment According to Sex (%)

	Male	Female	Total
Employment	57.5	42.5	100.0
Employment in Formal Sectors	60.2	39.8	100.0
Employment in Informal Sectors	52.9	47.1	100.0
Percentage of Employment in the Informal Sectors	34.0	41.0	37.0

27 Huang Ping and Frank N. Pieke: China Migration Country Study, presented at the Development and Pro-Poor Policy Choices in Asia, Dhaka, 22~24,June 2003.

28 The Domestic Service Industry has become one of the main fields providing new employment, Hebei Labor and Security Website, 2002-06-18 (Hebei Laodong Baozhang Wang: Jiazheng Fuwuye Zheng Chengwei Woguo Xina Laodongli de Zhongyao Qudao).

From looking at Table 5-1, we can see that the total male employment is 15% higher than that of female employees, and there is 6% more male employment in the informal sectors; and the number of male migrants employed in the formal sector is 20.4% higher compared to the number of female employees.

By examining the occupational composition of the migrants engaged in informal employment, we can discover that the male migrants engaged in comprehensive jobs, apart from physical laborers such as guards and deliverymen, are mainly engaged in primary technical jobs, such as builders, repairmen, drivers, retail sellers, computer services providers, automobile repairmen, and so on, covering all services in social production and daily life. Furthermore, not only do these jobs offer relatively higher income, but also greater possibilities for self-development and transforming into formal employment, compared with the jobs that female migrants are engaged in.

In view of the female migrants in informal employment, their jobs are relatively focused on two areas: the community services industry and family services, such as working in restaurants, entertainment industries, beauty salons, domestic workers, cleaners, nursemaids, representing relatively simple working skills and lower incomes. Thus, the female migrants have fewer possibilities for self-development and transformation into formal employment in the future, when compared with the jobs that male migrants pursue.

This division of labor (between the male and female) reveals the characteristics of the traditional sexual division of labor. Certain jobs have become specially "designed" for female migrants, such as nursemaids, hospital attendants, cleaners, domestic workers, etc. That is why in terms of the total output of the rural surplus labor force the male population is much larger[29], but why female migrant workers have a higher rate of informal employment than male workers.

In this way, we can conclude that the fields in which the male migrants work are mainly modern industries or other industries providing comprehensive jobs, relatively higher incomes and better futures. On the other hand, the fields in which the female migrants work are relatively concentrated on traditional sectors with gender characteristics. It is very difficult for the female migrants to find permanent jobs in modern fields, because of their low education level. According to Arthur Lewis' classification of "good job" and

29 Among the rural migrants, about 65% are male, 34% female, according to the data from the survey on the rural labor employment and migration status in China in 2000, conducted by the research team of the National Statistic Bureau and the Ministry of Labor and Social Security of China.

"bad job"[30], the gender characteristics of rural migrants' employment reveal that female migrants are more likely to obtain a "bad job" than the male. Although informal employment creates many job opportunities for the rural female migrants and improves their economic status, it enlarges the gap between female and male from the perspective of long-term development.

5.3.1 Reasons Why Female Migrants Pursue Informal Employment

The UNESCO-CASS project took domestic workers as an example, and carried out the following questionnaire in 2002[31]:

Table 5-2 Reasons to Seek Non-Agricultural Jobs in Beijing

Questionnaire		Frequency	Percent	Valid Percent	Cumulative Percent
Effective	Earn money and escape poverty	68	62.4	64.2	64.2
	Experience work in non-agricultural sectors	30	27.5	28.3	92.5
	Acquire an urban lifestyle	1	0.9	0.9	93.4
	Visit Beijing	3	2.8	2.8	96.2
	Other	4	3.7	3.8	100.0
	Total	106	97.2	100.0	
Ineffective		3	2.8		
Total		109	100.0		

Data: Based on 109 questionnaires with domestic workers.

According to Table 5-2, 64.2% of the 109 domestic workers responded that poverty is the main reason for migrating to Beijing for employment. As a result of rural poverty, as well as their own limited working skills, they are forced to accept the unsatisfactory, or even unfair working conditions in the labor market and informal employment. Moreover, 28.3% of female migrants choosing to experience work in non-agricultural sectors reflects that they have considerable self-development consciousness.

30 Arthur Lewis: *Dualism Economics.* Beijing: Beijing Institute of Economics Press, 1989.

31 This is a non-random small-scale survey, conducted by the Beijing Migrant Girls' Club in 2002, with 109 efficient questionnaires. The interviews were conducted at six domestic workers' agencies in Beijing, and the interviewees are female rural labor migrants who just arrived in Beijing to do as domestic workers, some of them come out for job seeking for the first time.

Table 5-3 Reasons for Choosing the Domestic Worker Occupation

Questionnaire		Number	Percent	Valid Percent	Cumulative Percent
Effective	Easier to earn money	6	5.5	5.6	5.6
	Suitable	32	29.4	29.9	35.5
	Lack of skills	45	41.3	42.1	77.6
	Interest	15	13.8	14.0	91.6
	Other	9	8.3	8.4	100.0
	Total	107	98.2	100.0	
Missing		2	1.8		
Total		109	100.0		

Data: Based on 109 questionnaires with domestic workers, Beijing, 2002.

The largest percentage of respondents (42.1%) chose the occupation of domestic worker due to their lack of skills. There is no evidence proving that the male has more skills than the female when initially migrating to the cities. However, since the males are apt to learn skills during work, they have an easier time obtaining a "good job" in the future. Discrimination against females in employment becomes worse in the labor market. Male migrants' working ability and self-development are strengthened, but female migrants' social status remains unchanged, or they are marginalized after working in non-agricultural sectors in the cities. As women migrants age, they also face a more disadvantageous job market. The employment discrimination against female migrants over 25 years old in the labor-intensive manufacturing industries and assembly line have become more or less a "rule" in Southeast China.[32], indicating the problems of female employment in modern industries.

In summary, the above circumstances illustrate that on the one hand this reflects that the traditional nature of the division of labor structure is still the occupational basis for the woman in entering the urban labor market; in other words, working as domestic workers does not change the woman's social status, but rather reinforces the woman's traditional role in the gender biased labor-division structure. On the other hand, some argue that working skills can lead to vocational change; in this sense, female migrants can obtain higher economic status through learning working skills. But it does not mean that working skills can change the female's disadvantageous status in the labor market in terms of gender bias. Does a discriminatory gender market make it difficult for female migrants to acquire

32 Tan Shen: "The Security and Health of Female Rural Migrant Laborers" (Wailainvgong de Anquan yu Jiankang), Chinese Women in the Transforming Society (Zhuanxing Shehui Zhong de Zhongguo Funv), Beijing: China Social Sciences Press, 2004.

certain working skills? Or is it the female's lack of working skills that causes the discrimination against female migrants in the labor market? There is still much to be studied on that issue. An alternative way to tackle this issue is to examine the gender status in the labor market of women with significant working skills, though the result is not so encouraging. Although working skills can improve the female's economic status, it seems to have little impact on the gendered labor market.[33]

Out of 109 questionnaires, 29.9 % of female migrants selected that "this type of work is suitable for me"; and 14% selected that "it stemmed from the fact that it was interesting", which reflects that 43.9% of 109 domestic workers have an understanding of their own traditional role with regard to the work of home management service. But further study is required to understand the reasons behind this identification Therefore, we can make the following inference: regardless of how much the female migrants like or dislike this occupation, combined with the above domestic service narration, their dissatisfaction is even more concentrated in the their discriminatory treatment.

Moreover, we learn from some interviews that employment as a domestic worker is not a completely forced choice. In recent years, the factories in the coastal areas and Southeast China have a massive shortage of young female workers, and the working conditions have been relatively improved under the pressure, but many female migrants are still reluctant to work in those factories because of expensive living costs in coastal areas, laborious working conditions, hardships related to the living environment, and little developmental opportunities.

5.3.2 Anticipated Analyses of Female Migrants in Informal Employment

Female migrants' decision to engage in informal employment is, on the one hand, a historically multi-faceted choice. "At the beginning of the rural-urban labor migration in the 1980s of China, most of the rural migrants were male, working as construction workers. There were very few families willing to let women, especially the unmarried girls, migrate into the cities to work. But as more and more rural laborers rushed into the cities to work as construction workers, salary payments have increased. In this context, some female employment, such as a domestic worker, was not only encouraged by the Women's

33 Pan Jintang: "Gender Discrimination to the Graduate in the Labor Market and Countermeasures: A Research on Labor Demand and Supply of Female Graduate's Employment" (Daxuesheng Jiuye Shichang Shang de Xingbie Qishi Yuxingbie Zhengshi), Chinese Women in the Transforming Society (Zhuanxing Shehui Zhong de Zhongguo Funv). Beijing: China Social Sciences Press, 2004.

Federation, but also appeared to be a desirable job with a stable income and cheap living costs. Thus, there is an increasing number of rural women migrating to the cities for non-agricultural employment."[34]

On the other hand, urbanization has caused a fundamental transformation in the Chinese family structure change, from an expanded family to a nuclear family, with baby-sitting or elderly nursing absent from the nuclear family. In addition, the large-scale enterprise transformation has caused the state to retreat from this type of service, and therefore, these problems have to be resolved within the market. Capable of enduring hardships and working hard, the female migrants become those laborers working in the informal employment in order to provide such social services.

As a result of urban demands and choosing to evade risks, the female migrants seem to emerge in large numbers in the informal sector of employment. Thus, the questionnaire also addresses the following questions: "Is this a willing choice for the female migrants"? And "Do the female migrants have their own expectation or plan in view of working in the informal employment."

Table 5-4 Female Migrants' Motivation for Working: Settling down in Beijing

Response	Frequency	Percent
No	101	92.7
Yes	8	7.3
Total	109	100.0

Data: Based on 109 questionnaires with Domestic Workers, Beijing, 2003.

Table 5-5 Female Migrants' Motivation for Working: Learning Working Skills

Response	Frequency	Percent
No	63	57.8
Yes	46	42.2
Total	109	100.0

Data: Based on 109 questionnaires with Domestic Workers, Beijing, 2003.

Table 5-6 Female Migrants' Motivation for Working: Earning Money

Response	Frequency	Percent
No	80	73.4
Yes	29	26.6
Total	109	100.0

Data: Based on the 109 questionnaires with Domestic Workers, Beijing, 2003.

34 Interview with the leader of Zhaoping's villager, L County, by Pan Jie, in September 2003.

Table 5-7 Female Migrants' Motivation for Working: Setting up a Small Business at Home after Capital Accumulation

Response	Frequency	Percent
No	65	59/6
Yes	44	40.4
Total	109	100.0

Data: Based on 109 questionnaires with Domestic Workers, Beijing, 2003.

Table 5-8 Female Migrants' Motivation for Working: Acquiring a Decent Job in Beijing

Response	Frequency	Percent
No	99	90.8
Yes	10	9.2
Total	109	100.0

Data: Based on 109 questionnaires with Domestic Workers, Beijing, 2003.

Table 5-9 Female Migrants' Motivation for Working: Returning Home for Marriage after Capital Accumulation

Response	Frequency	Percent
No	108	99.1
Yes	1	0.9
Total	109	100.0

Data: Based on 109 questionnaires with Domestic Workers, Beijing, 2003.

Table 5-10 Female Migrants' Motivation for Working: Other

Response	Frequency	Percent
No	104	95.4
Yes	5	4.6
Total	109	100.0

Data: Based on 109 questionnaires with Domestic Workers, Beijing, 2003.

The survey reveals that the answers with the highest frequency are "learning working skills" (42.2%) and "Setting up a small business at home after accumulating capital" (40.4%). This proves that personal development is still the most important concern for female labor migrants, or in other words, the female migrants in this survey have a high expectation when they leave their home villages for urban areas for the purpose of seeking for non-agricultural job opportunities.

But there is a major discrepancy between the high expectations of the female migrants and the actual reality, in terms of informal employment. Although the female migrant laborer's economic status is improved and their working fields are further explored, they have little opportunities to obtain skill training or to achieve upward social mobility under the domination of capitalist market and urbanization. Although working in the informal employment improves their economic situation, a portion of them have become a new type of "family servants" in the cities.

Case 1: The following is from a letter by one rural migrant laborer: "I felt insulted and was overcome by despair. I paid a heavy price to come to Beijing for non-agricultural work. The road is not as smooth as I expected. With insufficient working skills and experience, the only job I could find was employment as a domestic worker. I came to a family to engage in housework and to take care of a spoiled girl, who would always get me into trouble, and who would even vituperate me. Furthermore, I have little time to rest and have no private space in that family. The girl destroyed my books and dairy, and broke my glasses in order to express her defiance towards me. I tried to ask her parents for help, but they took her as a hoyden, giving no intervention, worse still, her grandma even blamed me as a dishonest person and rumormonger and she treated me with disesteem. I felt most insulted and lost all my hope."[35]

The case above reveals plainly the discrepancy between expectations (a certain prosperous future) and reality (the broken city dream). Neither does the rural female migrant laborer's employment in the cities break the gendered labor division and gender discriminations that exist in the rural communities, nor does it achieve women's liberation as a result of leaving from the traditional rural communities and entering into the labor market.

The investigation also demonstrates that more than 90% of interviewees do not plan to remain rural-urban migrant laborers in the future (Table 5-9), and 92% of interviewees do not want to settle down in Beijing (Table 5-4). This challenges the optimistic hypothesis that migrating to the cities to work in the non-agricultural sectors is not only the first step for the realization of rural women's' liberation, but also an important advancement of rural women's development. Simultaneously, this survey reveals that about 73.4% of interviewees do not regard "making money" as their aim for migrating to the cities (Table 5-6), and 44% of interviewees' future plan is to open their own business at their home place after earning money in the cities (Table 5-7).

We obtained similar results from another investigative interview on a trained group of female migrant laborers from Northwest China. Starting with the most coveted position, they listed in descending order their choice of occupation with hairdressing at the top,

---

35 http://www.nongjianv.org/wenku/xie/cwenku03_1995_01.htm.

followed by waitress, domestic worker, and finally, factory worker. In the meantime, most of them don't plan on settling down in Beijing in the future. Though some prefer to return to their original home, the rest prefer to return home and open their own business.

In summary, the survey reveals that female migrant laborers encounter a dilemma; that is, they neither wish to settle down in cities nor are willing to return to their home place, primarily for two reasons. Firstly, the rural women's migrating to cities as short-term laborers does not lead to be long-term settlers. It is very hard for them to become integrated into city life, as a result of their disadvantageous labor capital in the labor market. Secondly, leaving their home environment also means the discontinuation of their social security network as a result of their employment in informal sectors, and with little chance to build a new one in the city. In this way, they are likely to experience circumstances of dual impoverishment both in the economic sense and the social sense.

Furthermore, 99.1% of interviewees indicated little desire to go home and marry after earning money in the cities (Table 5-9), which is very different from that of the male migrant laborers, who are willing to marry a rural girl and who the vast majority of in fact find rural spouses. But the female migrant laborers are reluctant to choose a rural man to marry, especially one who has little experience with migrants working in cities; however, even in the case of interest in an urban spouse, the chances of marrying an urban man are limited.

The discrepancy between expectation and reality for the female migrant laborers working in the informal employment questions the hypothesis that rural women's migrating as informal employment laborers in cities is not only helpful in poverty alleviation, but also meaningful in the improvement of the women's social status, the women's liberation, and transition from the traditional gendered labor division. On the contrary, female migrant laborer's working in informal employment actually enlarges the difference between male and the female both in the economic sense and in the social sense and creates new spaces of gender isolation in the labor market. In this way, it challenges the "big narration" that rural women's migrating into cities and into labor markets as laborers results in the women's liberation both in the economic sense and in the social sense.

5.3.3 Analysis of the Problems of Female Migrant Laborers in Informal Employment

1) Lack of protection and regulations relating to informal employment

There is little effective protection for the informal employment worker's rights and interests. Informal employment behaves according to loose working relations (temporary and seasonal employment in formal sectors), where most fail to sign contracts with the employers, or, when signing a contract forming one that is unrelated to labor. In this case, it is difficult to protect the labor relationship through the legal system, and therefore, when the salary is in arrears, or the laborers are injured during working, their rights are not sufficiently protected by law.

2) Immature employment standards in the informally employed labor market

The female rural laborers' high working risk in informal employment stems in part from the disorder of the labor market. In the initial period of Chinese informal employment, the laborers suffered from the problems of illegal charges, malignant competition, the cheating behavior, etc. The immature status of the labor market increases the danger of their working environment.

3) Lack of Protection from Social Welfare

As a migrating laborer from rural areas to urban areas, the female rural laborer steps out of the social security network in the village, and at the same time, is excluded from the social welfare system in the city. Without inclusion in a social security network, they face insufficient working safety, instability of employment, and lack of hospitalization insurance or endowment insurance.

4) Female migrant laborers' beauty (even sex as merchandise in the market)

In migrating into cities as laborers in informal employment, the rural women sometimes turn to their beauty for income. Sex with migrants becomes a commodity in the modern market, a phenomenon coined as the "Beauty Economy."

In summary, female migrant laborer's employed in informal employment can represent a positive function in view of economic development, but its significance for women's liberation and for the rural women's development is very limited. It does not act to transform the traditional gendered labor division; on the contrary, it enlarges the gendered gap between the male and the female, and brings a new inequality between genders. Although the rural women leave their internal working environment within the home and move into the external working environment of society, the jobs are still mainly in traditional fields and only an extension of the traditional household role.This in turn causes new problems for the rural migrant, particularly, loss of self-identity both in the sense of rural life and in the sense of urban life.

5.4 Discussion Regarding the Improvement of the laborer's Conditions Within Informal Employment

In the last few years, there have been a lot of practices intending to improve the economic and social status of the rural-urban migrating laborers, especially the female migrant laborers' working conditions in informal employment, and with series of perspectives. Below this author discusses these practices and perspectives.

5.4.1 Practices to Perfect the Standing Laws and Regulations

On June 16th, 2005, the Chinese Ministry of Labor and Social Security announced an amendment of the regulation on the cognizance of labor relations. Through the existence of the laborer's working unit, the new law would publicly give labor relations legal authority, and thereby provide simplified labor relations, easy operation and extensive safeguarding of the laborer's rights and interests.[36] Cai Jian.

In recent years, both the central government and local governments have made significant efforts towards the protection of migrant laborer's rights and interests through the improvement of laws and regulations, based on the validation of labor relations.

5.4.2 Practices to Formalize Informal Employment

In taking the domestic service industry as an example, there have been many attempts in the past twenty years (through guild regulations, industry standards, legislation and so forth) to formalize informal employment. Examples include the first industry regulation of domestic workers in Shenzhen city; the discussion on service standards of domestic service at the national level; and the regulation on management of the domestic service agencies in Shanghai.

Despite these attempts, there has been much doubt associated with the practice of formalizing informal employment. In fact, on July 3, 2000, the labor and social security department publicized a national standard for domestic workers. But it was canceled two years later in reference to a dispute claiming that the national standard negatively impacted the development of the domestic service industry and the employment of female rural laborers, although it regulated the industry order and improved the service quality. The

36 "Policy Analysis: The View Regarding the New Labor Welfare Laws' 'economical use of the temporary worker' is already out of date" (Zhengce Jiedu: Laobao Xingui 'Yong Linshigong Shengqian' Xiangfa Yi Guoshi), Beijing Yule Xinbao, 2005-6-24.

standard not only raised the threshold of those engaging in employment, but it also reduced the competition ability of the informal employment in the market. Overall, it produced a negative impact on the development of this profession. A strong point is that it was too early to talk about formalization of informal employment (Xue Shaojun, 2004). Nonetheless, there is need for further discussion on the advantages of informal employment while fundamentally ensuring protection of the laborer's rights and benefits.

5.4.3 Rectifying the Labor Order

The reason for the disorder in the labor export market is directly connected with the disorder of the labor import market. Ruling the labor import market, then, can solve this problem. For example, in the domestic industry, the Beijing Labor and Social Security Bureau publicly posted in 2004 the annual censorship on the career agencies which received licenses before Dec. 31, 2004. In the annual censorship there were 518 agencies that have joined and passed the censorship, and there were 8 agencies that experienced re-censorship, and there were 33 agencies that failed to join the re-censorship and therefore were deprived of a license.

Great expectations have been attributed to establishing a career association to rule the labor market and construct the career order; but it has limited effects on the industry in terms of self discipline, unified norms and harmonizing development. The main reason lies in the multi-membership institution in industry association, where this particular members' participation is very low in proportion to the whole industry, and therefore, they experience a lack of representation as well as various restrictions.

5.4.4 Government Intervention

1) Shanghai:

In 1996, the Shanghai government carried out a series of policies and measures to encourage the development of informal employment. This included forming the public welfare three-level service support system; channeling it into the basic scope of social insurance and encouraging its participation in employment risk insurance; and supplying various types of skills training opportunities. Unfortunately, the rural migrant laborers are excluded from all these policies and measures.

2) Dalian City:

Dalian City, representing 2.7 million residents and about 0.7 million migrant laborers, first launched the social/legal rights protection program for migrant laborers in 2000. In

Dalian, the Bureau of Public Security has been participating, coordinating, and supporting the establishment of apartments for migrant laborers, which they believe would function in meeting the basic requirement of the migrants of lower levels both socially and economically.[37] Based on the platform of the Migrants' apartment, Dalian Municipality supplies comprehensive assistance to migrants, and gradually enforces the management and control of the rural migrants.

3) Chifeng Migrants' Home in Beijing and the Female Migrants' Center in Chifeng

Chifeng City is a typical case of sending out a large quantity of rural surplus labor force and at the same time accepting those industrial workers entering the city. The government legislation and laws that establish informal employment are the platform for the female migrants entering the cities, and also expands the social safety net of the female migrants. Their network consists of all governmental agencies and other social actors at three different levels: those in rural areas, including village peoples' committees, the township government, and family-kinship relationships; those of Chifeng cities, including governmental agencies, Women's Federations at both the county and prefecture levels; and the Chifeng Migrants' Home in Beijing. The three-level network is effective in poverty alleviation and providing social and economic assistance to migrants, especially to female migrants.

Measures dominated by government through free trainings and building up a social security network, to support and push the development of informal employment, are encouraging and have proved helpful both to the protection of laborer' rights and benefits, and to the development of informal employment.

5.4.5 The CASS-UNESCO Project Intervention

(1) The key point of the project activities (through UNESCO, CASS, and the local government) is to create somehow a mechanism for combining organically the energetic competences attributed to non-government sectors, such as NGOs, research institutes, international organizations, with the overwhelming power or resources possessed by the government.

(2) Push the government to confront the migrant issues. In this way, we emphasize

37 Chen Xin: "How to Cooperate with Local Governments for Achieving Social/Legal Rights Protection for Migrant Laborers and Social Conflict Reduction", research paper for the CASS-UNESCO "Poverty Reduction among Young Migrants in East Asia" Project, 2004.

two relevant aspects: government awareness of reality; and its reaction to the reality by adopting new approaches in confronting the issues.

(3) Providing training to empower the rural migrants.

(4) Establishing a network between sending and receiving places. On the one hand, these programs' intervention enhanced the rural migrant laborer's knowledge and skills, and on the other hand it expanded the laborer's social safety net to some extent. These experiences also demonstrated that the key to the program's success lies in the synchronizing of different resources.

(5) A Short Conclusion and Policy Suggestions

Based on the above analysis, we can conclude that creating additional employment opportunities should be a priority as policy is formulated at both the central and local governmental levels. In this way, informal employment has great significance in solving the problem of unemployment and in alleviating rural poverty, due to its characteristics of low cost, flexibility and its advantage in creating a large number of employment opportunities. Furthermore, it is especially significant for those rural women with poor education and little skills receive employment opportunities in cities.

The female migrants entering the cities and entering the informal employment sectors are around 20 years old and are youth with low technical ability. As the above investigation revealed, they are demanding higher skills and wishing for further development; and they possess a very large potential for elevating their conditions and status. This is different from those of the female laborers (normally above the age of 30) working in community service and domestic service industries in other countries. The imbalanced nature (supply and demand) of China's labor market structure is very prominent, and therefore, improving their labor skills and changing the resources of the labor force, especially with regard to changing the impoverished nature of the female migrants, will be of great significance.

At present, "although informal employment faces many problems, such as the worker' low social status, instability of employment, poor working security, comparatively low salary level, little welfare, etc., this form of employment is helpful in solving the unemployment problem."[38] But the problems of high career risk, and poor legal and social protection of the female migrating laborers still remains a great challenge for China.

Is formalization of the informal employment sector a possible solution? What is the

38 Cai Fang: "Does the urban employment increase in China?" (Zhongguo Chengzhen You Meiyou Jiuye Zengzhang), http://www.macrochina.com.cn/zhtg/20040624065743.shtml, China macro economy and information Website (Zhongguo Hongguan Jingji Xinxi Wang), 2004-06-24.

practical solution for protecting the employee's basic labor rights? How can we ensure their working security? In view of this article's opinion, there is no necessary connection between informal employment and less protection of the employee's rights. The cooperation and intervention of the government and industry associations are essential in improving the employee's rights and working conditions, and at the same time, maintaining the informal economy's advantages in the market should be taken into account when formulating policy.

1) Below are several general policy suggestions:

(1) How to ensure the protection of both the employer's rights and the employee's rights is a key question that must be answered in attempting to manage the informal economy. Although normalization of the informal economy may be helpful to the management on informal economy, it will enhance the entrance requirement, increase the management cost, and eventually counteract the competitive advantage of informal economy in market, resulting in the failure of solving the problem of unemployment. An exception to this are those informal economies with large scale and stable market demands that demonstrate the ability to increase the labor price, and are easy to manage, partially normalized or gradually normalized management can be considered to practice, but cost is still one important factor we need to take into account, to maintain its competitive advantage in the market.

(2) Due to the comparative low-level of economic affordability of urban residents today, and due to the large demand for employment of uneducated female migrating laborers, it is still difficult to implement standardized management of the informal economy. In this way, reducing the probability of living and working dangers that migrant laborers may encounter, and extending their social safety network seems a practical way to protect their rights, on the one hand to enhance the workers' consciousness of self-protection through trainings on safe working and relevant laws, and on the other hand, to develop social aid and support for the migrating laborers. On one side, the Women's Federation and governmental local organizations (street affair office) should actively intervene in this aspect, especially with regard to assuming responsibility for the protection of the laborer's rights and interests, and in the context of a duty-bound governmental system. The government should also supply effective forms of public management and public service, intervening to ensure the rights and interests of employees, and thereby reducing the industry's risks. On the other side, social sectors (such as the resident's committee, owner's committee, etc.) should also play as coordinators and actors. In this way, the migrant

laborer's living condition and working condition could both be improved.

(3) An insurance program with a low entrance requirement will be very helpful in solving the problems in the informal economy, and in ensuring the rights protection both of workers and employers in these fields. The government should provide some support for this insurance program.

(4) Fourthly, we need to be prepared to face the problems that arise in the process of formalizing the informal economy. For instance, formalized management may possibly counteract the informal economy's original advantages, such as the low entrance requirement, the low negotiating cost in the market, and its flexibility and low cost on management. On the other hand, normalized management may also lead to an increased price of service, and then the effective demand will be decreased in the market. Eventually, normalized management will result in the enhancement of the entrance requirement, which may block the entrance of the poorest female migrating workers. Although the higher service quality from normalized management of the informal economy may benefit the urban families with high incomes, the majority of urban families with average or lower incomes may be unable to afford this service. Therefore, the informal economy's flexibility of employment and management should be maintained, especially in those industries with small-scale, large-demand, and low price requirements.

(5) Finally, as most rural migrating young women serving in informal economy are facing the problem of career transferring, educational opportunities are in great need. Because of marriage or birth, some of the rural migrating women have to return back to their home places, and then they may face the problem of living and development in their home areas. Some hope to get vocational training and working skills in order to get better jobs in the cities. Furthermore, educational opportunities are important in that they benefit the laborer under all circumstances. For whatever condition, there is a great need to create educational opportunities for them. The labor market should refrain from creating excuses that serve to exploit rural female migrants as cheap laborers; on the contrary, education and other new developmental opportunities (whether in countryside or in cities) should become their main equipment for realizing a path towards progress in society.

In conclusion, in the management of the informal economy its inherent advantages should not be sacrificed. We need to place priority on the tasks that extend legal service and social support to the informal economy, adjusting the management to an acceptable extent and helping it to develop properly.

References

[1] Jiang Yongping: "Informal Employment and the Sex-based Categories of Labor Market", paper, presented on the Informal Employment Forum, October 2004, Beijing.

[2] Tan Shen. "Study of the Female Rural-Urban Labor Migration from a Gender Perspective", Beijing TOT workshop, UNESCO-CASS Project: Poverty Reduction among Young Migrants in East Asia, November 2004.

[3] Jiang Yongping. "Main Findings and Suggestions on the Second Statistics of Chinese Women s Social Status Survey", China Employment Forum, 2004.

[4] Xue Shaojun. "Observing and Thinking on the Problem of Informal Employment in China", presented on the Informal Employment Forum in October, 2004, Beijing.

[5] Hu Angang. "The Biggest Warfare of Employment Began in China", 2004.

[6] White Paper of Employment Situation and Corresponding policies in China, 2004.

[7] Tan Shen. "A Summary of the Discussion on Rural-Urban Migrants Studies", paper, symposium in Guangzhou, 2000.

[8] Cai Fang. "Informal Employment: its Function in Labor Resource Allocating in the Market" (Feizhenggui Jiuye: Fahui Laodongli Shichang Peizhi Ziyuan Zuoyong), July 2005.

[9] Feng Xiaoshuang: "A Summary of the Workshop for the Studies on Rural Migrant Laborers in the Mainland China" (Zhongguo Dalu Nongmin Gong Yanjiu Zuotanhui Jiyao), December 23, 2000, Guangzhou.

[10] Li Qiang. "Rural Migrant Laborers and Informal Employment in Cities" (Chengshi Nongmin Gong yu Chengshi de Feizhenggui Jiuye), *Sociological research*, no. 6 (2002).

[11] Huang Ping and Frank N. Pieke. "China Migration Country Study", presented at the Conference on Migration, Development and Pro-Poor Policy Choices in Asia, Dhaka,
June 22~24, 2003.

[12] Cai Fang. "Do China's Urban Areas Experience Employment Increase?" (Zhongguo chengzhen you meiyou jiuye zengzhang), http:www.macrochina.com.cn/zhtg/20040624065743.shtml, China Macro-economy and Information Website, (Zhongguo Hongguan Jingji Xinxi Wang), 2004-06-24.

[13] Chinese Women in the Transforming Society (Zhuanxing Shehui Zhong de Zhongguo Funv), Beijing: China Social Sciences Press, 2004.

[14] Pan Jie. "A Discussion on the Problems in Domestic Service Industry", *Rural journal of China revolution*, 12 (2003).

6

Improving the Basic Rights of Migrant Workers

Wang Hongyan

6.1 Background

6.1.1 The Appearance of the Migrant Worker and Problems Regarding their Basic Rights

The appearance of the migrant worker is related to economic, institutional and social causes.[39] In the early 1980s in China, "the rural reform had released farmers to such an extent that it was possible for rural laborers to have more and more time to engage in various kinds of non-farming activities "(Huang Ping, 2004a). From the mid 1980s, "the government launched the urban reform, where an increase of construction projects demanded more manual laborers" (Huang Ping, 2004a). From then on, more and more farmers migrated to towns and cities to seek non-agricultural jobs. A scholar named Zhang Yuling from CASS calls the special group "Nongmin Gong" (migrant workers). This group is special in its "combined or confused" status, for members in this group are with agricultural *Hukou* but without agricultural jobs. In other words, they are different from farmers in their jobs but different from urban workers in their Hukou. At first, the Chinese government (especially local government) took some measures to limit this flow of farmer laborers. In the mid 1990s, the Chinese government changed its policies regarding this special group and decided to begin managing its labor flow. At the end of the 20th century,

39 The economic causes include: (a) that "Economic poverty is a key factor in producing migrants"; (b) "TVEs become less capable of absorbing rural labors"; (c) "the income increase from agriculture has decreased since the mid 1980s"; the reform of the *Hukou* system, the introduction of ID cards in the late 1980s and the abolishment of the Food Coupon System in the early 1990s are the institutional causes; and migration was an intended or unintended consequence of the attractive urban life, the decline of the rural community and the government programme "providing free TV sets to the countryside." See Huang Ping, "Urban Poverty among Young Migrants in China", Together with Migrants, UNESCO Beijing Office, pp. 85-187.

the Chinese government encouraged the "surplus" laborers from the countryside to move to the towns and cities and issued many policies to facilitate this labor flow. In short, governmental policies towards migrant workers changed "from prohibiting rural-urban migration to restricting, then to regulating, and finally to encouraging" (Luo Keren, Ma Chunhua, 2004).

The basic rights of migrants workers have become a problem and are therefore now given attention as a result of the following three points: first, migrant workers are a "special" group, as mentioned above; second, it is a group in large number which cannot be neglected by the government and society. In recent years, more and more rural laborers flow into towns and cities. In 2002, the total number of migrant workers was about 94 million. In 2003, the number leaped to as many as 114 million and they represent 23.2% of the total agricultural labor force (Xinhuanet.com, May 16, 2004); third, as time progresses, their rights are being improved.

6.1.2 Migrant Workers and Basic Rights

The migrant population is within a particular spotlight in China as a result of its unique characteristics and sheer size. It is reported in the media that migrant workers encounter discrimination of admittance into (certain) employment fields together with discrimination inside employment. The specific description of these encounters are (1) overwork; (2) no guarantee of payment; (3) bad working and living conditions; and (4) high risks related to work (Chinanews. net, October 29, 2004).

A survey conducted by our team shows the following: (a) Migrant workers are discriminated by city dwellers; (b) there is protectionism at the local level; (c) wages are sometimes reduced; and therefore (d) migrant workers need the safeguard of the law (Huang Ping, 2002).

6.1.3 New Governmental Actions and Policies

Although there are some unpleasant phenomena listed above, overall the basic rights of migrant workers have been improved. Furthermore, the Chinese government has positively intervened and is assisting in the protection and improvement of migrant workers' basic rights. At the end of 2003, Premier Wen Jiabao returned delayed payments to migrant workers in person. Up to December 3, 2004, 95.88% of the delayed payments of migrant workers have been returned nationwide (Xinhua.net, December 15, 2004.).

In addition, in order to provide better public surroundings to protect migrant workers and supervise the employers in this regard, in November of 2004 the Ministry of Labor and

Social Security of China organized a series of activities called "Safeguard Migrant Workers' Labor Rights." The main content and form for disseminating and popularizing the laws are as follows: Conducting legal policy counseling activities, conducting literature and art shows, touring exhibits, etc. (The Handbook of Rights Protection for Migrant Workers, *Nongmin Gong Weiquan Shouce*).

At the same time, the Central Government has issued many policies to protect and better migrant worker's basic rights, such as "Improving Management and Services for Rural Labor Migrants" (i. e, Document No. 1, 2003) issued by the State Council Office in January 5, 2003 and "Decisions to Accelerate the Increasing of Earnings for Rural Laborers" (i. e, Document No. 1, 2004) issued by the Central Committee of CCPC in January 2004.[40] Accordingly, all governments at lower levels followed suit.

6.1.4 On the Notion of Rights

Under this background, UNESCO's Social & Human Sciences Sector and CASS launched a project called Urban Poverty Reduction Among Migrant Youth in China in 2002. This project has been carried out for 5 years. The direct goal of this project is to safeguard and improve migrant workers' basic rights.

Rights, as a concept, have experienced a complicated development. From the Declaration of Human and Civic Rights (1789) to the Universal Declaration of Human Rights (1948), from the International Covenant on Civil and Political Rights (1966), the International Covenant on Economic, Social and Cultural Rights (1966) to the Declaration on the Granting of Independence to Colonial Countries and Peoples (1986), the concept of rights is identified as "3-generational": generation I, concerning political and civic rights; generation II, concerning economic, social and cultural rights, which pays much more attention to providing basic freedoms for individuals; generation III, concerning collective rights, including rights of self-determination, rights of development, etc.

Since rights are such a complex concept, much more attention should be paid to understanding and applying these rights. The following points should be emphasized:

Rights permit differences.

Differences internal and external to nations should be taken into consideration. Thus when making comments on the state of rights in China, Chinese characteristics (concerning history and reality) should be included.

The concept of rights has many dimensions, including political, economic and social

---

40 See Xinhua Monthly (volume XII), 2003: p. 9.

dimensions. This research paper stresses survival rights and development rights and posits that both of them are chief human rights, functioning as the base for all the others. Furthermore, this article focuses on migrant workers' basic rights and rights of employment, residence, education, and so forth.

6.2 Factors Impacting Migrant Workers' Basic Rights

6.2.1 The *Hukou* System

1) Change of functions

China implemented the *Hukou* System in the late 1950s. It should be noted that *Hukou* System is one of the uneven development strategies that the Chinese government adopted under certain circumstances and it has indeed reduced the pressure of cities, decreased the speed of urbanization and has kept a stable society during this time. Objectively speaking, the *Hukou* System has contributed much to the socialist construction with Chinese characteristics.

Principles and norms should be established in any society in order to arrange resources. The *Hukou* system belongs to such types of norms, which guarantees certain groups (city dwellers) some privileges but excludes other groups, i.e. the rural population. In this sense, the *Hukou* system is regarded as the basic cause for the creation of a dual social structure (LiQing, 2002).

Currently, the Chinese government keeps pace with time and has begun to conduct the reform of the *Hukou* system. In fact, March 2001 the Government decided to reform the *Hukou* System starting from small towns.[41] Such changes have been reflected in governmental policies. The Central Government proclaims that "farmers with stable vocation and residence can register their *Hukou* where they work or live and assume these rights together with the duties according to the local rules." (The Central Committee of the CPC. "Decision on Some Problems of Improving Socialist Market-Oriented Economy System", Xinhua Monthly (volume XII), 2003: p. 9).

Accordingly, governments at local levels, such as Shijiazhuang in Hebei province and Jiangsu province, have made rapid progress in the reform of the *Hukou*.

The *Hukou* System is only efficient and effective to part of the rural population; and it is not ascribed factors but achieved factors that are playing an increasingly important role

---

41 See Huang Ping: "Urban Poverty among Young Migrants in China", Together with Migrants, UNESCO Beijing Office, p. 188.

in deciding a person's social status. Some "capable" farmers can strive for resources and opportunities "monopolized" by urban dwellers, which was unthinkable 15 or 20 years ago. In addition, from a micro perspective, many powerful examples can be seen in pilot areas of the project. In Beijing, some female domestic workers have become entrepreneurs; they have their own houses and stores or companies in Beijing, and therefore, they are living more of an urban life.

2) The Path of *Hukou* Functions

Although the function of the *Hukou* System has changed, these changes have not impacted the basic rights of migrant workers. Two paths – the "hard way" and the "soft way" characterize the functioning of the *Hukou.* The "hard way", refers to policies, and the "soft way" which will be detailed below.

The *Hukou* System is regarded as an important distinguishing feature of ancient Chinese society. It originates from the Shang Dynasty, and the present *Hukou* system has been in effect since 1958.[42]

As time goes by, with the implementation of this system, all social members have accepted not only its literal meaning but also its symbolic meaning, namely, the social rank or difference associated with the *Hukou* System.

Even though the strength of the *Hukou* transformation is significant, the *Hukou* system is regarded as a kind of internal symbol that still more or less influences the center of every policy. This kind of influence, through the layers of the masses, manifests as the "urban people" and the "rural people" and is an inflexible impression that thereby brings about cultural and social exclusion. Thus, policy-makers tend to formulate policy in favor of developing the urban areas while at the same time producing policies that neglect development of the countryside. But things have changed significantly since the Chinese government advocated building a harmonious and cohesive society in 2003.

3) Difference in Functioning

Furthermore, the *Hukou* System affects the migrant workers' rights in different ways and to different degrees in different fields. These differences includes an individual- type, a district- type and a link type.

For individual type, the *Hukou* System plays different roles concerning different individuals. To some capable migrant workers, the *Hukou* is not a barrier any longer; to

---

42 Lu Yilong: Hukou System-Social Control and Social Discrepancy, Commercial Press, 2003, p. 231.

some migrant workers with low qualification, the *Hukou* is still an obstacle that cannot be overcome. Thus, certain safeguards protect the former group, while the latter is at much greater risk overall.

In regard to the District-type, the *Hukou* system exerts different functions in different provinces or districts. In some cities (e.g., Beijing and Shanghai), the Hukou System is more decisive for resources and opportunities; in the others (e.g., Diqing and Dalian), it exerts less influence upon migrant workers' basic rights.

The last type is that *Hukou* system exerts different influence upon migrant workers in different procedures of their employment. Generally speaking, in the link type of moving into cities and seeking non-agricultural jobs, the *Hukou* System isn't as beneficial or effective.[43] Thus, it is not enough to use the *Hukou* system to ensure that migrant workers' basic rights are upheld.

4) Should the Hukou system be cancelled?

Whether or not to cancel the *Hukou* System is of major debate among academic circles. Some scholars, such as Lu Xueyi, contend to cancel the *Hukou* system. In Lu's opinion, the issue of migrant workers should be tackled from the "root" and the *Hukou* system is certainly the "root." He asserts that canceling some illogical restrictions in the employment environment is a kind of ineffective remedy, but reforming the *Hukou* system is a sort of drastic and effect measure to deal with such the situation. Only in this way can migrant workers integrate into urban society. What is more is that millions of migrant workers are looking forward to the relinquishment of the *Hukou* (Lu Xueyi, 2003).

Some scholars argue that the *Hukou* System has done much to protect farmers including migrant workers' basic rights, arguing that, with the existence of the Hukou System, rural laborers keep a piece of arable land for making a living. Without this system, many rural laborers may drop into the trap of being landless, then jobless and finally homeless, and therefore are ultimately forced into the slums (which can be seen in some other developing countries). In some senses, the *Hukou* System serves as a safety net for peasants in China (Huang Ping, Frank Pieke, 2004).

Such arguments show that scholars adhere to different research hypotheses and different ideas of development. For the former, modernization and urbanization is the only way to solve all of the Chinese problems, including the migrant issue. In this context, villages are looked upon as unenlightened sections and the numbers of farmers or peasants

---

43 The increase of the number of rural labor migrants year by year is a telling one.

should be reduced (Lu Xueyi, 2002). From this point, it can be concluded that "development" has achieved a great success, as a research model or faith in modern society.

The latter stresses Chinese characteristics and opposes the blind absorption of western experience. In their opinion, modernization and urbanization is just a kind of remedy which is effective in certain spaces and certain historical situations. Thus they claim to emphasize alternative development.

Specifically, they stress village rebuilding under Chinese circumstances. Even when looking at the projected percentage of urbanization in 2020, at 60% (the total population reaching 1600 million at that time), there are still over 600 million rural inhabitants (Huang Ping, 2004b).

In fact, it is impossible for China to replicate the western model, such as accelerating centralization of land and implementing large-scale farming, or transferring the rural surplus labor to the urban areas. On the one hand, China has an extraordinarily limited per capita cultivated land area; and on the other hand, the 900 million peasant population has a labor force of over 500 millions. Taking the urban force into consideration (which totals 300 million), there is more than 800 million laborers altogether. Thus, if the "surplus" labor flows into the market, they inevitably become "rubbish" or "slaves" (Wen Tiejun, 2004).

In contrast to this hot argument within the academic community, the rural laborers are less concerned about this issue. Statistics derived from a sample survey conducted in Beijing shows that 56% "are unwilling to" or "show no interest in " reform of the *Hukou* System.[44] As a consequence, the research team concentrates more on the practice of improving migrant workers' basic rights.

6.2.2 Policy

1) Policy Gaps

Currently in China, projects on poverty reduction are designed for two different impoverished groups: (1) the 30 million population in the countryside who live under the official poverty line; and (2) the more than 20 million urban residents whose income is lower than official standard. Furthermore, such poverty reduction policies are not combined closely and harmoniously and the outlying group (migrant workers) is not covered. In another words, there is an obvious "gap" in the policies of Poverty Reduction (Huang Ping,

44 Agriculture Information Center of Zhuji City: "Farmers Show Cold Shoulder to the Reform of Hukou System", May 23, 2003.

2003, 2004).

But it is also very obvious that, as mentioned above, the Central Government has drawn and issued lots of laws and policies to protect and improve migrant workers' basic rights in recent years. Among them some are designed specifically for migrants. These laws and policies range widely, containing employment, vocational training, migrant children's education, social security and residence, etc. Therefore, this paper insists that although there are still policy gaps, the problem of deficiency of laws and policies is being settled step by step.

2) "Policy transformation" during implementation

The phenomenon of "policy transformation" during policy implementation should be taken into account. Taking vocational policy as an example, the Central Government stipulates that "all districts and departments should cancel any measures that restrict the admittance of migrant workers, and governments at all levels should refrain from interfering in the employment of migrant workers."[45] In addition, "the enterprise or corporation should maintain equal standards when employing migrants and urban residents, such as skill levels and health conditions."[46]

But at the end of 2004, and upon arriving in Shanghai to monitor the operation of the project, the CASS team saw a column piece in a village publication notice that stated the following: Any enterprise or corporation that is considering hiring migrant workers should submit to the village administrative department the proof of shortage of local laborers, and, hiring of the position should be conducted only after the "Wants Advertisement" has been issued and only after locals have been given one month to apply for the position. From this point, we can see that some Central Government policies were transformed to some extent at the local level. This is a hint of local protectionism.

6.2.3 Markets

1) The Market Mechanism

The market mechanism exerts an unavoidable influence upon migrant workers' basic rights. The *Hukou* System distributes rights and interests in a man-made way but the market allocates resources and opportunities through an "invisible hand." Within the market, the

---

45 General Office of the State Council: "Notice on Better Management and Service of Employment for Migrant Workers", Xinhua Digest (Volume XIII), 2003, p. 14.

46 Ibid

overwhelming majority of migrant workers' conditions tend to remain unchanged or even in a state of deterioration. Firstly, if arranged or distributed only by the market, migrant workers with poorer education and fewer skills compared with the urban workers certainly will flow into lower positions in the labor market. Secondly, in the next 5 to 10 years, about 23 million rural laborers will migrate to towns and cities to seek non-agricultural work, while the urban labor market only requires 8 to 12 million laborers, which means supply is greater than the demand (Huang Ping, 2003). Under this background, migrant workers are certainly in a disadvantaged position resulting in much lower pay and much worse living conditions unless the government intervenes. In this sense, governments have to regulate the operations and functions of the market.

2) Unlawful Behavior in the Market

Further more, in the current labor market, informal behaviors are "aimed at" migrant workers. Findings show the average percentage of contract signing across the country for 2003 is 57.1% and that in private enterprises is only 30.5%. Many private enterprises disregard the Labor Law and refuse to sign contracts with migrant workers. Some unregistered vocation agencies even joined hands with some private enterprises in infringing upon migrant workers' basic rights.[47] Why have migrant workers become the object of such informal actions?

- Most migrant workers stay in the informal sectors. As mentioned above, current policies have not covered every corner of the informal sectors. The government has not stretched out its management throughout the informal sectors. Thus migrant workers, who stay in such informal sectors, have a higher probability of encountering these violations.
- Migrant workers are kept beyond the mainstream of social networks when migrating to cities to seek jobs (Li Qiang, 2003). In reality, they seek jobs through "shuren guanxi" (acquaintances) and some unregistered labor service agencies, which also result in a high probability for encounters with local violations.
- Migrant workers have low rights protection consciousness and do not know how to protect their own rights through established laws or policies. According to these problems the research team has designed some project proposals.

---

47 See Chinanews com, "100 Millions Migrant Workers Have not Join the Labor Union and Encounter Violation of Rights in Four Aspects", October 29, 2004

3) Migrant Workers' Logic in the Market

For migrant workers themselves they have their own logic in the market and therefore give up certain "rights" as a result. They enter into towns and cities with a mentality of "earning money." In conducting research, team members noticed that they often stressed monetary motives for migrating and that they would do anything (within the law) that would bring them cash income. With this logic, they prefer income rather than the "right of rest" and the like; in another words, they prefer to overwork rather than the legal rights for rest. It is quite the dilemma.

6.2.4 International and Global Factors

1) Keeping China within limits

In the age of globalization, the issue of migrant worker rights is not just an issue within the border of China but it is also connected with some international factors. Although peace, development and cooperation are a common global goal, fuel ready for war never runs short. In this case, on one hand, China has met the great opportunities to renew itself; but on the other hand, some western powers have created many difficulties for China.

In the late 1940s, the western powers "needed" poverty, that is, they needed to create space to exert their power and make a kind of political and economic world order that catered to their benefits. Thus poverty has been an international issue and on a large scale. Thus the power has reason to intervene in other countries. The reason is well-known: poverty is an obstacle to both the poor and the rich. The prosperity of the world is inseparable (Escobar, 1995: p. 1).

For this same "reason", esp. with the acceleration of globalization, the western powers need the development of China as well as the development of other nations of the third world. But, these powers' design for third world development is different from the Chinese government's design for its future development. These powers need the development of China, but within their framework. In other words, China cannot be too poor to trade or to conduct dialogue with the west; nevertheless China cannot be so prosperous that it is incapable of being controlled. The strategy is to keep China within limits, both in the political and in the economic realm.

From the political perspective, the power finds ways to fault China, taking issues of human rights and so forth as an excuse, and neglecting the discrepancy or difference between the developed and the developing nations, using the "international standards" to evaluate the developing countries. Even worse, sometimes double standards arise in these cases.

From the economic perspective, they according to their own current needs adjust trade protectionism and free trade policies. Therefore, we can see that on the one hand, they attack the lack of strength in China's market growth, while on the other hand they implement a kind of sanctioning with regard to China' production. This international trade protectionism results in lower wages for migrants or even unemployment of countless migrants.

2) Seeking Development Strategies Under a Difficult Environment

Generally speaking, when we commence our development plan the unequal political and economic world order comes into being. What we can do is to obey the given "rules", and to realize our proposal as possible while appealing for fair and equal principles. If China wants to realize its development, it must foster its own core competitive power; and under the present circumstances, China's competitive power rests in the low net cost of its labor force. Only in maintaining this low cost labor force can China also maintain its competitive power. In this sense, the problem of salary or wages related to migrant workers is not only a problem of government policy but it is also a problem of global market and competition.

If we give up maintaining this core competitive advantage, and if we give up exporting commodities and other articles at "low" (because of the low cost of the labor force) prices, then it will certainly lead to the decrease in employment positions and rising loss of employment. Specifically speaking, it will result in large numbers of unemployment including the joblessness of the migrant workers. Furthermore, under these circumstances, the stability and harmony of our society will become a significant problem. Nonetheless, low-wage employment is better than unemployment; and stability is the precondition for further development.

It is clear that economic factors coupled with political factors influence the Chinese migrants' rights in the increasingly global world. Nevertheless we should take into consideration both internal and external factors. As Giovanni Arrighi suggests, if China accelerates its economic growth and neglects the social and ecological cost, the U.S.A may have more chances to arouse district or global forces to obstruct China from its development and its renewal (Giovanni Arrighi, 2004: p. 213).

6.2.5 A Brief Summary

Considering the above analysis, this paper makes the following conclusions:

(1) The *Hukou* System is changing its traits from "a collective screen" to "an individual screen." Even though this system is regarded as a "mark of transformation", it remains in their minds in a real and continuous way. That being said, we can say that it is not the only decisive factor influencing the migrants' rights.

(2) The market mechanism exerts unavoidable influence upon migrant workers' basic rights. Part of this influence can be observed as certain adverse behaviors in the current labor market that violate their rights. Furthermore, migrant workers have their own logic in the market, namely, that they relinquish certain rights willingly for various reasons (particularly because of their strong desire to work within the urban market at all costs).

(3) Furthermore, the issue of basic rights for migrant workers is also tied closely to current international/global circumstances.

In short, the *Hukou* System, government policies, market principles and international/global circumstances all influence migrant workers' basic rights. As a result, to improve migrant workers' basic rights, CASS and UNESCO have, together with local partners and migrants themselves, launched and constructed a systematic project.

6.3 Strategies for Improvement

The research team has designed a systematic proposal and carried it out in China. In this project, the team has chosen 8 pilot cities. These are Beijing, Shanghai, Dalian of Liaoning, Chifeng of Inner Mongolia, Sichuan in Chengdu, Diqing and Kunmin in Yunnan, and Zhuolu in Hebei. In these cites, the team is probing ways and methods to improve migrant workers' basic rights.

6.3.1 Main Principles of the Project

1) The Principle of People's Livelihood

Survival right is the chief right and serves as base for all other rights. In this project, the team emphasizes people's livelihood above all else and takes employment as the starting point.[48] The team supposes migrant workers move to protect themselves and ensure their rights through employment.

2) Principles of Livelihood and Participation

Migrant workers' rights are difficult to protect, primarily as a result of their own

48 See detailed analyses in other papers of the research team.

competence levels. In contemporary China, individual competence is playing an increasingly important role. In the project, the team emphasizes migrants' competence building and focuses on a series of training programs. These programs are wide ranging, including fostering their consciousness of legal and social rights, basic knowledge of living in urban areas as well as the development of various working skills. Such trainings aim at (1) increasing migrants' income by uplifting their competitive ability in the labor market and (2) reducing migrants' cost of consumption by advancing their self-protection ability, e.g., less medicine because of less sickness or less engagement in a lawsuit. Accordingly, the project regards migrant workers as active actors (not passive victims) and encourages them not only to participate in the project but also to be masters/actors in the practice. Only in this way can migrant workers be empowered, self-protected and self-supported.

3) Integration of Resources and Coalition of Departments

As a result of the "policy gaps" and the phenomenon of policy alteration in the implementation of policy, the team attempts to merge together various kinds of resources for the protection and improvement of the migrants' basic rights. These include effectively utilizing material and non-material, institutional and non-institutional resources, and governmental and non-governmental resources in existence. Furthermore, the team attempts to establish a special network between relevant governmental and non-governmental departments or for-profit organizations and non-profit organizations. Through conformity and coalition, the problem of "policy gaps" is settled to some extent and joint efforts come into being to improve migrant workers' basic rights.

4) Attention to Diversity

In facing a complicated reality, any program with single dimensionality will be ineffective or inefficient. The right way is to study and settle concrete problems according to their specific context. When choosing pilots in the project, the team took into consideration the ethnic areas and Han Chinese regions, developed and developing districts, as well as the metropolitan areas and smaller cities. Furthermore, it implemented proposals according to local characteristics and the corresponding policy environment, the migration destination and scale of migrant workers, and the distribution of resources, etc. As a consequence, the pertinence, feasibility and efficiency of the program have been strengthened.

5) Towards the Ultimate Goal of Policy Improvement

The direct object of the project is to help ameliorate the conditions of the migrant workers in general, and the team launches such a program to protect their basic rights. In specific terms, what the team attempts is far beyond helping hundreds or thousands of migrant workers, which in the end is only a tiny proportion of the total migrant laborers in China. Instead, it puts this program into practice to accelerate the improvement of policies in the end, and thereby, the totality of migrant workers. That is why the team seeks cooperation and coalition with the government at different levels and its relative departments, as well as other agencies and social actors.

6.3.2 Path of Action

The first is a direct path, that is, the action aims directly at protecting and improving migrant workers' basic rights. For example, the pilot in Beijing focuses on "helping enhance the rights of female migrants who come into Beijing and seek jobs."[49] The other route is the indirect path, namely, to better migrants' basic rights by helping them obtain employment. For example, the pilot in Shanghai attempts "to help migrants who enter into Shanghai seek jobs, help with training and employment...and help in protecting their basic rights."[50]

6.3.3 Practices and Experiences of the Projects

1) Improving Basic Rights→Employment

The team uses employment as the starting point and improves migrant workers' basic rights by helping them obtain employment. Thus, all pilots concentrate on this task. The pilot in Diqing has developed a variety of employment services. This pilot combines introducing or recommending employment with pre-trainings, mutually combining outside employment with local employment, and combining village employment with urban employment. Furthermore, since the majority of migrant workers are serving in the informal sector, all pilots emphasize the standardization of employment. The pilot in Beijing focuses on standardization of family management and services. They develop the management mechanism from "agency" style to "membership" style. The pilot in Shanghai has developed a relatively intact chain of employment to help migrant workers lower risk in market. Their experience is labeled the "four in one" model, that is, they have cultured a complete chain with links of organization, training, introduction and management. In other words, they managed to build up a green passage for protecting migrant workers' basic

---

49 Together with Migrants, UNESCO Office Beijing, p. 42.

50 Together with Migrants, UNESCO Office Beijing, p. 43.

rights. Theoretically speaking, it is a kind of win-win mechanism.

2) Improving Basic Rights→Training

The training process is in fact a kind of empowerment process. The team designs training programs, including knowledge of legal and social rights, in all the pilots. In addition to special training content, skills for making a living in cities and seeking jobs as well as common sense of health and sanitation are also taught. In addition, the pilots give migrant workers technical training according to the demand of the labor market. Among the lecturers, some are specialists, some are youth volunteers and some are migrant workers themselves.

3) Improving Basic Rights→Legal Aid

The team sets up special organs of rights protection, e.g, in Beijing and in Kunming, to offer legal aid for migrant workers. In the pilot of Beijing, there is a "rights-protection panel for migrant female workers", in which a secretary is in charge of the protection of rights. It is worthwhile mentioning that the secretary himself is a migrant worker. More than twenty volunteer lawyers and volunteer students from law schools serve in this special group. This group offers help and care for migrant female workers who experience sickness, unexpected termination of employment and who suffer from employer violations, etc. Recently, this group launched a series of counseling activities regarding the basic rights of migrant workers in Beijing. The pilot in Kunming of Yunnan particularly emphasizes mobilizing legal specialists and lawyers to offer legal aid for migrant workers serving in the local areas.

4) Improving Basic Rights→Publicity

Pilots publish and distribute special magazines and handbooks to keep and protect migrants' basic rights. The pilot in Chengdu in fact produces its own magazine which is called *Fenyou*. Furthermore, they established a new publication-A *Window into Jintang Migrant Workers* and a "hot line" for rights protection. The pilot in Beijing compiled a handbook of rights protection for female workers serving in Beijing at the end of 2003, which is more practical and specific than the handbook created by the Ministry of Labor and Social Security (MOLSS). The latter was issued in November 2004.

5) Improving Basic Rights→Flats

The pilot in Dalian began to build Migrant Workers' apartments 3 years ago. At the end of 2004, the number of migrant workers' apartments had already reached 52. With the construction of special boarding houses for migrant workers, migrants' basic rights have been strengthened. On one hand, concentration of migrant workers is helpful for migrants in fostering their sub-culture, from which migrants enjoy solidarity and mutual support among themselves.[51] On the other hand, the apartments-the concentration of migrant workers' living areas–are an effective platform for protecting and improving migrant workers' basic rights. This has also facilitated the joining of local governments in order to improve the basic rights of migrant workers. The Dalian Model presents creative approaches and it also contains win-win mechanisms.

6) Improving Basic Rights→ Network

The team explores network building in the project (see the following Figure 6-1). The principle of "Integration of Resources and Coalition of Departments" is successfully practiced in the pilot of Chengdu. This pilot targets building academic study networks of migrant workers and service networks for migrant worker, and thereby, promoting better communication and cooperation among the researchers, the actors (migrant workers) and the government. They began such building from 2002. At present, they own a network composed of news media, academic organs, lawyer offices, youth volunteers, enterprises or corporations and governmental departments. This social supporting network contributes greatly towards improving the migrant workers' basic rights. In deviating from Chengdu, the pilot in Chifeng of Inner Mongolia has established a supporting network based on a regional

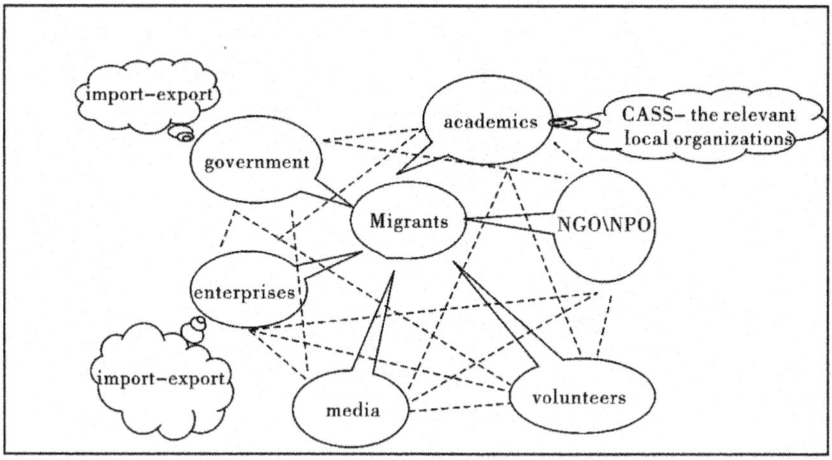

Figure 6-1 The Network of Improving Migrant Workers' Basic Rights

51 See detailed analysis in a separate paper from our research team.

link within and outside of the district. This pilot sets up one service institution in the city of Chifeng and another in Beijing. The former offers help to those living in the countryside of Chifeng but coming to the city of Chifeng and looking for jobs; the latter offers help to migrant workers in Beijing who come from Chifeng.

6.4 Discussions and Suggestions

6.4.1 How to Achieve a Shift from a "Small Goal" to "Seeing the Big Picture"

The direct object of the project is migrant workers and the team launches such a program to improve their basic rights. But, the team's vision digs deeper, and their ultimate goal is to improve the foundation from which the migrant workers' rights or lack of rights are derived. It puts this program into practice to ultimately accelerate the improvement of policies, and thereby, the totality of migrant workers, and even to the point where all social members can benefit. That is why the team seeks cooperation and coalition with the government at various levels and its relative departments, as well as other agencies and social actors.

One of the specific objectives of the project is to capitalize on experiences and lessons learnt through the research conducted in order to enrich policies addressing social inclusion and to influence policy-making. In the action research, the team attempted as best as it could to attract the (local) government's attention and participation. For example, the team invited officials to take part in activities and, when building social supporting networks, managed to mobilize some governmental departments to join in. Can the team achieve the former goal through those measures? Can the action research really influence policy-makers? How much has the team contributed to the improvement of policies concerned? What we want is to transfer a "small goal" into a "big picture goal." But can we achieve our proposed goal? These are questions that need to be further answered by continuing and deepening the research action.

In fact, through the research conducted we have acquired very many valuable experiences. The Dalian pilot has caused the local government to change its attitude toward the migrant workers and policies related to their basic rights, and thereby, significantly improving their rights. Experiences from Dalian have shown that the big picture of policy improvement can be achieved. In future action research, the team will further capitalize on lessons learnt from Dalian and probe more effective ways to further strengthen the cooperation between the government and the project. Following analysis of the Dalian model, the study group believes the following points deserve attention:

(1) Seek out "suitable" partners or co-workers. "Suitable" partners means that they show interest in protection for migrant worker rights as well as those partners that possess superior resources (being economic, political or cultural resources).

(2) Renew working methods and processes. Deviating from the training programs carried out in other pilots, Dalian has built special flats for migrant workers that have come to protect their rights.

(3) Emphasize the scale of the program. Create social benefits which can attract attention from all walks of life. Thus, improved surroundings will in turn realize improved working conditions.

In short, Dalian has done well in the reorganization or replacement of resources. Reorganization or replacement of resources is concerned with whether or not we can transfer "small goals" to "seeing the big picture." But many difficulties and problems have been experiences in these areas:

(1) Resources are reorganized or replaced within acquaintances or among friends.

(2) Resources are reorganized or replaced in non-institutionalized ways.

(3) The scale of reorganization or replacement is very limited.

In this way it seems that team research is in most cases developed in collaboration between friends. This does not mean that cooperation between friends precludes future success. But we are concerned with the relationship between specific efforts and policy improvement, and with the sustainability of our research.

6.4.2 The Basic Path for Resolving the Issue of Rights: surpass the Issue of Rights

In absolute terms, the team has significantly improved the migrant workers' rights. On the other hand, in relative terms, that is, compared with the complication of this issue and the large number migrant workers, the methods employed have experienced certain limitations. To better migrant workers' rights, specific action as well as policy reform is needed. Above all, in order to solve this problem, we need to ponder over exceeding the issue of rights.

The issue of rights reflects the large gap between the urban and the rural areas. Because of the large gap between the urban and the rural areas, namely, that the urban areas are "better" and more "developed" than the rural areas, the rural areas naturally flow into the urban areas on a large scale. But if the gap is bridged, if the difference between the urban and the rural areas becomes solely a geographical meaning, and without any social or cultural sense, the scale of migration will be decreased and in fact the migration from the urban to the rural areas would become a possibility.

In this sense, the objective behind the measures taken to solve the the issue of "san nong" and migrant workers in China, is threefold: to change our approach to decision-making (which tends to sacrifice the rural for the development of the urban); to provide conditions for the two sections to co-exist and develop in harmonious ways; and to rethink the modernization plan and its ongoing development.

It is reported that at the heart of 11th Five-Year Plan (2006~2010) lies China's ambition to build an overall well-off society. This plan emphasizes that the industrial sector should repay the agricultural sector and that the urban areas should sustain the rural areas. The carrying out of this plan is certainly to further the improvement of migrant workers' basic rights.

References

[1] Arrighi Giovanni. "Globalization from the Perspective of East Asia." Theoria 2004. China RenMin University Press, 2004.

[2] Escobar Arturo. *Encountering Development: The Making and Unmaking of the Third World.* Princeton: Princeton University Press, 1995.

[3] Huang Ping. "China: Rural Problems Under Uneven Development in Recent Years." In Lau Kin Chi, Huang Ping, 2003.

[4] Huang Ping and Peng Ke. "Laborer Migration in China." In Chinese Academic Reports, 2004.

[5] Li Qiang. *Structure of Social Stratification in Transitional China.* People's Publishing Company of Heilongjiang, 2002.

[6] Lu Xueyi. *Migrant Workers' Issues Should be Resolved from the Root*, 2002. www Weiquan.org.cn.

[7] Lu Yilong. *The Hukou System-Social Control and Social Discrepancy.* Commercial Press, 2003.

[8] *Xinhua Digest*, 2003~2004.

[9] *Xinhua Monthly*, 2003~2004.

[10] UNESCO Office Beijing. *Together with Migrants.*

7

Rural Labor Migration in China: Policy Challenges

Zhan Shaohua

Assistant professor, Institute of Sociology,
Chinese Academy of Social Sciences (CASS).

7.1 Introduction

7.1.1 Summary

Rural labor migration has become one of the most significant socioeconomic phenomena in China, the most populous country in the world. The number of rural migrant laborers has increased greatly since "reform and opening up" began in the late 1970s and early 1980s,but especially after Deng Xiaoping's speeches in southern coastal China in 1992, as well as the relaxation of the *Hukou* System (residence registration system), which no longer prohibits rural labor migration, but still restricts migrant laborers' access to public health care, the pension system, legal aid, social services, etc. In addition to the government's actions, other structural factors have also led to the large-scale rural labor migration in China (114 million in 2003) including numerous "surplus" rural laborers, growing income gap, regional disparity, etc. In recent years, the government has gradually come to appreciate rural migrant laborers and to a large extent has realized the importance of rural labor migration. However, even though many policies have been issued to protect rural migrant laborers and to promote rural labor migration, five challenges/problems have not been adequately addressed: first, the issues of poverty and poverty reduction among migrant laborers, especially in terms of the lack of competence and social exclusion of rural migrants, need to be taken more seriously by policy makers and social actors in the future;second, there is a policy gap between rural and urban poverty reduction, i.e., the current policies of poverty reduction do not address rural migrant laborers, who are working and living in urban areas but have no urban *Hukou*; third, government policy has not fully considered regional diversity in rural labor migration; fourth, few policies consider rural labor migration issues in terms of gender; and last, it is necessary and advantageous to forge a "win-win" relationship between rural migrant laborers and local developers. It is important to note that these challenges are not unrelated but rather intertwined. To confront these challenges, project or policy makers can find and utilize existing resources among NGOs, the government, academics, rural migrant laborers, and other social actors. Currently, agents involved in/affected by rural labor migration include: governmental agencies at both central and local levels (such as MOLSS, MOA, OPRD, etc., international organizations and local NGOs, academics, migrant laborers and their families, employers and volunteers.

1) Legal Framework

Since the early 1980s, governmental policies have gradually come to allow rural laborers the freedom to migrate to urban areas. Within the framework of current policies, rural (migrant) laborers can (1) move into cities and obtain permanent residency in small cities and townships; (2) seek nonagricultural jobs in urban areas; (3) appeal to urban authorities such as labor agencies for help and protection; and (4) enjoy more social services than before, such as training programs, children's education, health care, etc. Moreover, the Chinese Government has employed a comprehensive approach towards development rather than focusing solely on GDP growth. This so-called "New Paradigm for Development", launched by the Chinese Government in October 2003, aims for a more balanced, comprehensive and sustainable development. Under this new strategy, policies concerning rural labor migration can be expected to undergo more positive changes in the coming years. However, despite the positive effects of these new governmental policies, a large number of rural migrant laborers are living and working in poverty in terms of an observable lack of competence and social exclusion, and especially within the female migrant population, a particularly vulnerable population that has not been specifically addressed within the existing policy framework. Moreover, thus far governmental policy-making has not adequately taken into account that on the one hand, there is abundant social capital among migrant laborers, and on the other, that migrant laborers have different needs in different areas and at different times. To solve the problems, the policies concerning rural labor migration should, first, focus on poverty reduction among migrants and local development; second, address the needs of female migrants; third, take into account social capital among rural migrant laborers and integrate it into or link it with policies; last, take regional diversity into consideration and encourage local autonomy and creativity in policy-making and policy implementation.

2) Project Practices

To explore practical solutions to the above challenges, UNESCO, in cooperation with the Chinese Academy of Social Sciences, launched a six-year project (2002~2007) entitled *Urban Poverty Reduction among Young Migrants* (subtitled *Together with Migrants* in 2003). The project is action research, involving social science researchers in designing, monitoring and evaluating the actions, which include skill training, practical education (such as law, health awareness, etc.), network building, social capital promoting, etc., and was executed in eight selected pilot sites. Generally, the project advocates and examines more positive and practical policy changes to reduce poverty among rural labor migrants in terms of their lack of competence and social exclusion, especially from a gender perspective; it promotes local development through rural labor migration, and establishes "win-win" partnerships between different regions (sending and receiving areas; western, central and eastern regions; underdeveloped and developed regions). To reach its goals, the project has adopted the following measures/strategies during project implementation: first, to select a single local agency as the main local partner in each pilot site to take charge of policy implementation; second, to forge a triangular partnership network consisting of governmental agencies (officials), academic institutions (researchers) and NGOs/NPOs at both national and local levels; third, to publicize and promote the project in a comprehensive way, utilizing publications, media, academic seminars, art events, etc.; fourth, to draft policy papers/reports on the findings of the pilot sites, which will be published and also discussed with policy makers at both national and local levels.

3) Proposed Policy Implications

In drawing lessons from past policies concerning rural labor migration, it was found that the causes for ineffective policy are related to three possible factors: (1) they are without specific departments responsible for carrying out the project's policy requirements; (2) specific departments are incapable of or unwilling to collaborate with other relevant departments; or (3) in this process they don't consider the participation of the migrants. Concerning the new policies recommended by the UNESCO project in particular, two obstacles can be foreseen: one is that local governments, especially those approached by the project, may regard the new policies as unfavourable or unrelated to local development, and the other is that local governments may not understand the new policies correctly and thus be unable to implement them effectively. Moreover, the proposed polices could have a potentially harmful effect on local development and add to the burden on migrant laborers if they are misunderstood or implemented inappropriately. To avoid these negative ramifications, the policy-makers can first integrate the proposed policies into the new development paradigm and identify them as indispensable components in building a harmonious society; second, before and during policy implementation, projects can be launched to train the officials or other actors in order to facilitate an understanding of the new policies; third, one specific governmental agency should be designated to be responsible for the new policies, and in the meantime, it may be required that the policies be implemented jointly with other related agencies; fourth, academic institutions or research teams can be selected to monitor and assess the implementation of new policies; finally, during policy implementation/monitoring and assessment, beneficiaries' (rural migrant laborers) opinions and feedback should be seriously considered.

4) Monitoring and Evaluation During Implementation

The proposed policies possess three strengths (a strong duplicability or transferability, a focus on local development, and rural laborers' participation), two weaknesses (inadequate attention to class stratification of rural migrant laborers and on the needs of migrant laborers upon returning home), two opportunities (realization of the value of migrant laborers' contributions, new development paradigm) and two threats (income gap and regional disparity, "brain drain"). The proposed policies can be assessed according to both qualitative and quantitative indicators. Qualitative indicators include the policies' contributions to local development and gender equity, and various stakeholders' responses to the policies, such as local governmental agencies, NGOs/NPOs and rural migrant laborers. Quantitative indicators can be set up in terms of flow of financial resources, administrative resources and beneficiaries during policy implementation.

While evaluating, monitoring and assessing the policies, to receive and collect feedback, the policy-makers or experts can hold meetings, discussions, interviews and surveys to collect feedback from governmental officials, NGOs, local researchers, migrant laborers (especially female migrant laborers), and other stakeholders such as urban residents, potential rural migrant laborers, employers, etc. To regulate the process of policy implementation, the policy makers or experts can experiment and examine the policies in limited areas at first. After assessment and adjustment, the improved policies can be applied to a wider area. Moreover, to guarantee their flexibility and adjustability, the policy makers should make it possible for some parts of the policies to (1) be designed and adjusted by local governments and authorities, (2) be adjusted according to stakeholders' suggestions, especially migrant laborers; and (3) be in accordance with the strategies of local development.

7.1.2 Key facts

1) Facts about Rural Migrant Laborers in China

- In 2003, the number of rural migrant laborers reached 114 million, accounting for around 20 percent of rural laborers.
- The principal reason for migration from primarily rural to urban areas is to seek non agricultural work opportunities and escape poverty.
- Migrant laborers mostly come from China's underdeveloped western and central provinces such as Sichuan, Anhui, Henan, Gansu, and mainly head to urban areas, southeastern coastal locations and metropolises like Beijing, Shanghai, as well as nearby townships, surrounding counties, small cities and provincial capitals.
- By 2020, it is estimated that another 100 to 150 million "surplus" rural laborers will join the rural labor migration.
- Labor migration from rural to urban areas has contributed about 16 per cent of the total growth of China's GDP over the past 20 years.
- Since China's entry into the WTO, rural-urban migration has expanded significantly. In 2001, the rate of urbanization was 37 percent. It is expected to reach 50 per cent in 2030 and 70 per cent in 2050.
- 70 percent of migrant laborers are between 16 and 35 years old, and most have received up to a junior middle school level of education (9 years in school). Most migrant laborers earn a monthly income from 300 RMB (36 USD) to 600RMB (72 USD). About one third of migrant laborers are female.
- Most migrant laborers are employed in jobs which are generally considered dirty, dangerous and difficult, and which local inhabitants are unwilling to take. Today, migrant laborers in China significantly contribute to the development of industries, such as construction, commerce, food, services and sanitation. They play a chief role in the general improvement of life for urban residents.

(*Quoted from Together with Migrants, p. 36, partly revised by the author*).

2) A Historical Review on Policies Concerning Rural Labor Migration: 1949~2000

- 1949~1958: Planning rural labor migration. In this period, rural laborers were encouraged to participate in urban development. As a result, about 40 million rural laborers were recruited for the urban industrial sectors.

- 1958~1983: Prohibiting rural labor migration. Under the systems of *Hukou*, purchase and sale of food products, food coupons, and the People's Commune, rural laborers were prohibited to leave their home villages with the intention of seeking employment or running businesses without official permission.
- 1984~1988: Allowing rural labor migration. In 1984, an official document was issued to allow rural laborers to enter cities for employment. This "big" change was closely related to other socioeconomic and institutional changes, such as continuous harvest and agricultural production, the collapse of the People's Commune System, and the reform of the system of purchase and sale of food products.
- 1989~1991: Restricting rural labor migration. During this time, the central government regulated the national economy to combat inflation. Policies were issued at central and local levels to restrict rural labor migration.
- 1992~2000: Regulating rural labor migration. The policies at central level allowed, regulated, and even encouraged orderly rural labor migration, but some local policy-makers of large cities and coastal areas imposed regulations to restrict rural migrant laborers in flow and job seeking.
- After 2000: see below (Section 3).

7.2 Context

7.2.1 The Country

China is the third largest country in the world, covering 9.6 million square kilometers and located in East Asia. China has 22800 km of land borders and is contiguous to another 15 countries. Its topography can be described as generally high in elevation in the west and low in the east.

The country is geographically comprised of: mountainous terrain (33.3 percent), plateau (26 percent), basins (18.8 percent), plains (12 percent), and hills (9.9 percent).

By the end of 2004, China's population reached 1.3 billion, the largest in the world. Noticeably, in the last two decades, the proportion of rural inhabitants has decreased greatly from 82.1 per cent in 1978 to 59.5 per cent in 2003 due to rapid urbanization. However, with the growth of the population, China's rural population remains large, 768.5 millions in 2003. Therefore, per capita arable land has diminished, with only 0.1 hectares on average in 2003, representing less than half of the average in the world.

In the late 1970s, China began its transition from a planned system to a market economy. Concerning rural reform, the System of Household Responsibility has replaced that of the People's Commune. As a result, the collective owned farmland has been allocated to and cultivated by household units. After the success of rural reform, the government began urban reform in the mid 1980s covering the systems and policies of employment, finance, tax, etc.. Meanwhile, the central government instituted policies geared toward "opening up" to the international market and attracting foreign investment, especially in the eastern and coastal regions. As a result of the reform and opening up, China has seen record economic growth. The GDP growth rate has remained above 8 percent for more than 25 years on average since 1978 (NSB, 2004).

7.2.2 Rural Labor Migration[52] and Policy Challenges

When the Hukou System[53] was introduced in China in the late 1950s, China had yet to experience any large-scale voluntary rural-urban labor migration for almost two decades. In the early 1980s, rural labor migration remained relatively low with an estimated "floating population" of around 2 million (Zhao Shukai, 2003).

The year of 1984 represents a milestone in the history of rural labor migration in China. Rural laborers were officially permitted to move to cities to seek jobs or run small businesses. Consequently, rural laborers were highly motivated and the number of migrants reached 26 million by 1988.

Mr. Deng Xiaoping's speeches in southern coastal China in 1992 gave rise to another wave of investment and rapid development in China, especially in southern coastal areas. This generated a great number of employment opportunities and brought a great increase of rural labor migration so that the population of rural laborers reached 62 million in 1993 and 70 million in 1994.

In the late 1990s, the "Three Rural Problems" (rural production, rural community and

---

52 In this paper rural labor migration primarily refers to the voluntary movement of rural laborers, who leave their home villages for urban areas (ranging from township towns, county towns and other small cities within or outside the province of original residence, provincial capitals and the metropolis), seeking non-agricultural work opportunities, usually temporary or seasonal, at least three months a year, sometimes together with their family members.

53 The *Hukou* System is one of the social control/administration systems set up on the basis of households, whose members, either in rural or urban areas, must register at the local public security office as a legal resident. After registration, the households are issued a *Hukou* certificate, in which all members of the family are listed in detail as legal residents, and they are thereby more closely controlled by the local street office in urban, or village committees in rural areas (Huang Ping, 2000). Noticeably, the *Hukou* System, which was established in 1958, has been adjusted and reformed step-by-step in the last two decades and has less control over residents than before, even though it has not been eliminated yet.

rural people) reached a point of severity in China, especially in central and western regions. As a consequence of these problems, as well as the pro-urban, pro-eastern governmental policies, the income gap further widened between rural and urban residents, as did regional economic disparity between western, central and eastern regions. In this situation, many rural laborers, even those not considered "surplus", had to seek non-agricultural activities in cities (Huang Ping and Frank Pieke, 2003). As a result, ever since the number of rural migrants has risen: 94 million in 2002, and 114 million in 2003.

Rural-urban labor migration has become a significant socioeconomic phenomenon, and rural migrants have accounted for more than 10 per cent of China's total population. The central government has attached much importance to it, and especially since 2000, many policies have been formulated to protect the rights of rural migrants and even promote rural labor migration. However, some challenges or problems, especially that of poverty reduction among migrants, have not been adequately addressed or even neglected entirely. They include:

1) Poverty among migrants

Migrants are more vulnerable than permanent residents. In China, migrant laborers can earn more cash than those who stay in their home village and work on the farm, but they encounter more difficulties in cities in terms of legal rights, health care, lifestyle change, skill training, housing, social integration, etc.. Research shows that many migrants fall into poverty after moving into the cities (Wang Fenyu and Li Lulu, 2001; Zhan Shaohua, 2004). Poverty among migrants must necessarily be regarded as a multidimensional issue rather than simply economic poverty. In the future, the issues of limited rights and social exclusion of rural migrants needs to be taken into consideration more seriously by policy makers and social actors (Zhan Shaohua, 2005).

2) Policy gaps in poverty reduction

In China, poverty is categorized as rural poverty or urban poverty. Remarkably, the Chinese Government has made significant progress in rural poverty reduction: the number of people in rural poverty has decreased from 250 million in 1978 to around 30 million in 2000.[54]

Those living in urban poverty are officially defined as urban residents whose income is below the official minimal standard of living. Most of them are laid-off workers from

54 The White Book on China Poverty Reduction and Development, released by the central government in 2000.

State-owned Enterprises (SOEs), which have been reformed in the name of "increasing efficiency" since the mid-1990s (Tang Jun et al, 2003). To reduce urban poverty, the Ministry of Labor and Social Security and the Ministry of Civil Affairs have issued policies to provide training programs, employment, relief, etc., for the urban poor. However, these policies neglect the rural migrant laborers who are living and working in cities. Some scholars argue that there is a policy gap between rural and urban poverty reduction (Huang Ping, 2004a). Indeed, rural migrant laborers have less access to public health care, pension systems, legal aid, social services, etc. than do urban residents because they lack an urban *Hukou*, thereby making them more vulnerable and likely to fall into poverty. As rural migrants living in poverty in urban regions, they are reached by neither rural nor urban poverty reduction programs.

3) Regional diversity

Chinese migrant laborers disperse from the countryside in a variety of ways. They move from rural to urban areas, from interior to coastal areas, and from western and central to eastern regions. However, within this general trend, there is much variation in terms of places of origin and destination. For instance, among the receiving urban areas, rural labor migrants can move into small, medium-sized as well as large cities, which can have an impact on rural migrants in different ways. As for rural places of origin, there exists remarkable disparity between provinces in central and western regions. In provinces like Anhui, Sichuan, etc, large-scale rural labor migration started in the early 1980s, while in some provinces, especially ethnically diverse regions, labor migration began relatively late or has yet to occur (Huang Ping and Zhan Shaohua, 2004). Furthermore, research shows that rural labor migration facilitates a mixture of social, economic and cultural phenomena: the features of regions where rural migrants come and go. However, so far these regional diversities have not been fully considered by governmental policy makers.

4) Gender issues

Women account for about one-third of China's rural migrants and this proportion has maintained a rising trend (Li Yinhe, et al, 2000). Research shows that on the one hand, in comparison with male migrants, they may face greater adversity in the process of migration, and thus become more vulnerable (Tang Can, 1996), and on the other hand, female migrants make valuable contributions to their families and local development, and sometimes their migration experiences help to improve their social status and promote gender equality. However, the current policies concerning rural labor migration have not adequately taken gender issues into account.

5) Local development

The central government has acknowledged that rural labor migration can make a valuable contribution to both rural and urban development. However, despite the positive effects of labor migration, it has its negative impacts, such as "brain drain" in rural areas of origin and "over urbanization" in receiving urban areas. Therefore, it is important to forge a "win-win" relationship between rural labor migrants and local urban development. Considering the regional diversity mentioned above, policy-makers and projects must make local-specific strategies for local development in terms of labor migration. Therefore, it is important to select pilot sites in different regions when a project is designed to monitor/assist the process of local development with respect to labor migration.

It is important to note that these challenges are not unrelated but rather intertwined. Central and local governments have begun to focus on rural labor migration, and many policies have been issued to deal with its adverse ramifications, including those mentioned above. Stronger efforts are needed, however, especially in light of the new development paradigm (see below), and because China's development process faces new complications, such as the rural-urban gap, regional disparity, demand for employment, need for poverty reduction, etc. Therefore, concerning rural labor migration, more policy initiatives are needed to adjust China's approach to development in the coming 10 to 20 years.

7.2.3 Agents and Stakeholders

1) Governmental agencies

- The Ministry of Agriculture (MOA). MOA can be responsible for rural labor skill training and data collection and statistics. In 2004, MOA launched a project named the "Sunshine Project" to provide non-agricultural skill training programs for rural migrant laborers before they leave their rural home areas.
- Ministry of Labor and Social Security (MOLSS). MOLSS is responsible for monitoring the labor market, especially the urban labor market. Concerning rural laborers in urban areas, MOLSS can provide employment services and reform the system of social security to cover migrant laborers.
- The Office of Poverty Reduction and Development (OPRD). In 1986, the central government established the OPRD under the State Council to take charge of rural poverty reduction. Since the late 1990s, the OPRD has begun to provide rural laborers with non-agricultural skill training programs in impoverished rural areas

as well as help them find jobs in urban areas as migrant laborers.

- Others: The Ministry of Construction (MOC), the National Development and Reform Commission (NDRC), the Ministry of Finance (MOF), the Ministry of Health (MOH), etc., must also consider rural labor migration when they are involved in the issues of labor migration. For example, the MOC must take migrant workers into consideration because today most construction workers are rural migrant laborers.

These governmental agencies operate not only at the central level but also at the provincial, prefectural, county and even township levels, and have similar responsibilities for migrant laborers/rural labor migration in local contexts.

2) International organizations and local NGOs

International organizations have intervened in Chinese rural-urban labor migration since the mid-1990s. Most have launched development projects or research programs in cooperation with local partners, including local NGOs/NPOs, the government and private sectors, and have provided them with financial support. International organizations like UNESCO as well as international private funds like the Ford Foundation have significantly assisted local development and exerted influence on governmental policies.

In China, there are two types of local NGOs concerned with internal migration. The first are grassroots and community-based organizations, which operate on a volunteer basis. Most of them seek financial and public support from international donors, media, etc., and so that they can directly work with migrant workers. The other NGOs are more closely related to the government, yet have relatively wide latitude in routine work and project activities. Examples are the Women's Federation, trade unions, voluntary organizations, associations, etc. To some extent, they occupy the role of intermediary between China's government and civil society.

3) Academics

China's academic contingent took an interest in rural labor migration beginning in the late 1980s, including universities, and local research institutes, and "think tanks" like the Chinese Academy of Social Sciences (CASS), the State Council Development Research Centre, etc. Through their efforts, including research, academic seminars, publications and public debates, they brought the issue of rural labor migration to the attention of public policy makers.

4) Migrant laborers and their families

Migration has dubious benefits for migrant laborers and their families. It can be rewarding, but it also carries the risk of descent into poverty. Therefore, the families of migrant laborers must also be a target group of governmental policies and intervention projects. It is also important to note that migrant laborers can help empower themselves/each other when policies or projects create an empowering environment for them.

5) Employers

Governmental authorities must ensure that employers of rural migrant laborers respect the migrants' legal rights, and also encourage them to provide decent living and working conditions for migrant laborers.

6) Volunteers

Since the issue of migrant labor concerns civil society, more and more people have begun to work with migrant laborers as volunteers, such as college students, lawyers, doctors, researchers, etc.

7.2.4 Resources

The role of China's central government in ameliorating the conditions of rural labor migration is undoubtedly the most powerful. They can issue policies, provide financial support, and mobilize the administrative systems from top to bottom. It is the NGOs, however, that have the creativity and flexibility to explore alternative strategies and measures in various local contexts. Academic researchers can provide knowledge, techniques, and skills for policy making and project intervention; moreover, they can incite public awareness of important issues like rural labor migration and as a result have an impact on policy making. Last but not least, the migrants themselves are an invaluable resource in the effort to improve their quality of life. Policies as well as projects must mobilize human resources among the migrant groups so that fellow migrants can assist each other.

7.3 Policy Framework

7.3.1 Current Policies

Since the early 1980s, governmental policies have gradually come to allow rural laborers the freedom to migrate to urban areas. Since 2000, many policies have been made to protect the rights of rural migrants and even promote rural labor migration. These positive changes include:

1) Relaxing the Hukou System

Since 1984, the Hukou system has grown steadily more lenient. Noticeably, on October 1, 2001, China's central government began an experimental reform of the residence registration system in more than 20000 small towns (*Beijing Qingnian Bao* [Beijing Youth Daily], September 28, 2001).

Also, local governments began to reform their individual *Hukou* systems and made urban residency more easily obtainable for rural migrant laborers.

Changes in the Hukou system include:

- Small towns and townships have granted residency to locally employed rural laborers who have obtained jobs and places to live in these communities
- Medium-size cities and some provincial capitals no longer limit the number of rural laborers allowed to apply for permanent residence status
- Mega cities such as Shanghai and Beijing have adopted a soft policy of "widening the gate and raising the price", which still limits the number of rural laborers for permanent residence status.

2) Ensuring fair treatment of rural migrants

In early 2002 the State Council issued the "No. 2 Document of 2002", which designated migrant workers as "members of the working class" rather than peasants, and formally acknowledged their contributions to urban development since the early 1980s, deciding therefore that no unreasonable

limits or biased policies should be inflicted upon rural migrant laborers. The document also set out four principles for new policies: fair treatment, reasonable guidance, improved management, and better services. In January 2003, the State Council Office's "No. 1 Document" drew from these four principles the following commitments:

- Abolish any excessive unfair restrictions on rural laborers seeking either temporary or permanent employment in urban areas
- Ensure that employers of migrant laborers act in accordance with the law concerning contracts and punctual payment of wages
- Improve the working and living conditions for rural migrant laborers, especially women, including health care and personal safety

- Provide legal and skill training for rural migrants: training is strictly voluntary, and no unreasonable fees should be charged;
- Provide access to education for children of migrant workers equal in quality to that afforded the children of urban residents;
- Improve administration of migrant populations, including family planning, education for children, labor employment, health care and legal aid.

3) New concrete measures

To honor the commitments stemming from the "No. 1 Document", the central ministries have issued a series of concrete policies and launched projects to ensure fair treatment and improved social services for rural migrant laborers:

- **Training programs**. In September 2003, the State Council devised *The National Plan of Training Rural Migrants from 2003~2010*, to provide hundreds of millions of migrant workers with introductory training in the areas of law, health, job-seeking, and vocational skills. In March 2004, the MOA launched the "Sunshine Project" to train new rural migrants in their rural home areas, with a concentration on the poorest of these areas.
- **Education services for migrants' children**. In September 2003, the State Council published a document on a plan to improve basic education services in cities for migrant children, who numbered over 6 million in 2003 (*People's Daily*, September 6, 2004). The document assigned urban governments and their public schools the responsibility of educating the migrants' children.
- **No more delayed wages**. In September 2003, MOLSS and MOC jointly issued a document to "Solve the Problem of Delayed Wages of Migrant Workers in the Construction Industry." In September 2004, the two ministries established explicit regulations for the payment of migrant construction workers.
- **Health services and work injury insurance**. In January 2004, the MOH issued a document on the improvement of health services, the prevention of work related illness, and the providing of treatment of work related illness among migrant workers. In June 2004, MOLSS issued a document underscoring the necessity for employers and enterprises to provide work injury insurance for migrant laborers, especially those in high-risk industries, such as construction, mining, etc.

Within the framework of current policies, migrant laborers can, (1) move into and obtain permanent residency in small cities and townships; (2) seek non-agricultural jobs in urban areas; (3) appeal to urban authorities like labor agencies for help and protection; and (4) enjoy improved social services, such as training programs, children's education, health care, etc.

7.3.2 Policy experiences

The current policies have produced positive results. First, rural migrants in cities no longer need to worry about being sent back to their home villages by urban governmental agencies. Second, by the end of 2004, 331 billion RMB (about 4 billion USD), 98.4 per cent of all previously delayed wages were paid back to migrant laborers in the construction industry (*Beijing Daily*, January 10, 2005). Third, the "Sunshine Project" trained 2.4 million rural migrant laborers in 2004, and 87 percent of them succeeded in finding non-agricultural jobs (*Peasants Daily*, February 25, 2005). Fourth, under the guidance of central government policies, more and more urban local governments now provide legal protection and social services for migrant laborers. Last but not least, migrant laborers' social standing has greatly improved and they are increasingly recognized as contributing to development rather than being regarded as "trouble-makers" in urban areas.

Moreover, the Chinese Government has shifted towards a comprehensive approach to development rather than focusing solely on GDP growth. This so-called "New Paradigm for Development", launched by the Chinese Government in October 2003, aims for a more balanced, comprehensive and sustainable development. In this new approach to development, the

five relationships must be balanced, especially the gaps between rural and urban areas and between eastern and western regions. In early 2005, the central government considered the elements of a harmonious society, and found social justice and social inclusion for different social groups to be among the most important. In Premier Wen Jiabao's Government Work Report, released on 5 March 2005, he stressed that migrant laborers' salaries must not be delayed and that the payment for them can be increased without decreasing efficiency. Under the new paradigm, policies concerning rural labor migration can be expected to undergo more positive changes in the coming years.

Despite the positive results seen thus far and the expected continuation of these results, serious issues remain to be addressed. They exist mostly as a result of structural constraints, not current policies. These problems include:

- The average salary of migrant laborers is quite low compared to urban laborers. A large portion of a migrant's earnings are sent back to their home villages, leaving very little for housing, food, etc. Thus they become more vulnerable to health problems and social exclusion. Moreover, migrants' wages are unlikely to increase over time owing to the abundance of labor in China.

- Migrant laborers are largely uneducated and most have not participated in training programs for non-agricultural employment (NBS and MOLSS, 2001). The central government has given some attention to this issue, such as the launch of the "Sunshine Project" in 2004. However, migrants' demand for training programs cannot easily be met when another 150 million "surplus" rural laborers are projected for the coming five to ten years, and as yet no training programs exist in the area of entrepreneurship, which, if provided for migrant laborers who return home, could benefit local development in rural areas.
- Poverty among migrant laborers remains a serious issue. In order to effectively alleviate poverty, it must be understood as multidimensional, encompassing a lack of basic needs, a lack of competence, social exclusion, etc..
- Gender issues in the migrant population are in urgent need of redress, as it is found that they are more acute in this population than among urban residents (Du Jie and Nazneen Kanji, 2003).
- Migrant laborers seek social support through their social network, consisting of families, relatives, village or township associates, friends, etc. However, current policies have paid scant attention to the importance of social capital in the migrant's quality of life.
- The current policy making process functions from the top down, and the policies have not adequately taken regional diversity into account. Some policies that have shown positive results in some regions have been entirely ineffective in others. For instance, in the city of Chengdu in Sichuan Province, one of the pilot sites of the UNESCO project (see below), training programs cannot satisfy the migrants' needs because they have no free time for training or are disinterested because Sichuan is one of the provinces where most rural migrant laborers have years of migration experience. Thus, to a large extent the training programs just target new migrant laborers or those who may become migrant laborers in the future.

These challenges can be summarized as that of a large number of rural migrant laborers who are living and working in poverty, especially female migrants, who have not received attention within the existing policy framework. Thus far, government policy has yet to recognize the role of social capital among migrant laborers or the regional inconsistency in migrants' needs.

7.3.3 Policy options

In light of the current policy framework and its problems, the following policy suggestions are given:

First, policies concerning rural labor migration should focus on poverty reduction among rural migrants in urban regions, to close the gap between policies aimed at urban and rural poverty reduction and bring relief to a population thus far overlooked.

Second, policy must accommodate female migrants' needs and address gender-specific issues faced by the migrant population.

Third, policy must acknowledge the importance of social capital within the migrant population in order to generate a leverage effect, i.e., policy can enlarge its effects and influence through the utilization of social capital.

Fourth, policy must allow for regional flexibility, increased focus on the development of China's largely underdeveloped inland provinces, and encourage local autonomy and creativity in policy making and implementation.

7.3.4 Concrete recommendations

Based on the above policy suggestions, the following concrete recommendations can be posited:

First, the Chinese Government should mobilize more resources, including private funds, to provide rural migrant laborers with non-agricultural training programs; and it should implement a diverse methodology capable of meeting the needs of migrant groups in various regions.

Second, the Government should launch projects to assist female migrants in particular. These projects should address their specific needs, improve their social status, and encourage recognition of their contributions.

Third, the governmental agencies should allow and help migrants to build their own social networks, organizations and communities in urban areas so that migrants can to a large extent organize and support themselves.

Fourth, local governments should make policies and launch projects, financed to some degree by the central government, to solve problems relating to rural migrant laborers in local contexts. For instance, in western regions, especially ethnic autonomous areas, projects can be adjusted to fit local needs and cultural norms.

7.4 Project Practices

7.4.1 Project Initiatives

In 2002, UNESCO, jointly with the Chinese Academy of Social Sciences, launched a six-year project (2002~2007) titled "Urban Poverty Reduction among Young Migrants" (subtitled Together with Migrants in 2003). The project is identified as an action research, which takes action to search for and examine practical ways to solve the problems relating to rural labor migration while simultaneously, social science researchers design, follow, monitor and assess the process of action.

Eight locations in varied regions have been designated as pilot sites for the project. Four are located in western China (Kunming, Yunnan; Diqing, Yunnan; Chengdu, Sichuan; Chifeng, Inner Mongolia) and four in the east (Beijing; Shanghai; Dalian, Liaoning; Zhuolu, Hebei), in all directly involving about 80,000 migrant laborers thus far. Those pilot sites can be categorized into sending and receiving areas, and into small, medium-sized and large cities/prefectures. The project has taken the following basic initiatives:

1) Poverty reduction

The project is designed to reduce poverty through capacity building, empowerment and social network/community building (see Zhan Shaohua, 2005). Capacity building has been identified as a powerful tool in poverty reduction and is employed at all pilot sites. Methods of capacity building include skill training, health education (i.e., sanitation and HIV/AIDS), understanding legal issues, preparation for urban life, etc.

In most pilot sites, institutions responsible for rural or urban poverty reduction such as the offices for rural poverty reduction and labor agencies have been included in project activities. Thus the policy gap between rural and urban poverty reduction has been bridged to some extent at the local level.

These poverty reduction measures serve not only to increase migrants' income but also to promote the development of social capital. At present and even in one or two decades, these methods will be more effective in China than those calling for wage increases or a comprehensive social security system for rural migrant laborers (Huang Ping, 2004b).

2) Gender perspective

At most pilot sites, female migrants are a major focal point of the UNESCO project.

For example, in Chifeng Prefecture, Inner Mongolia, local partner Chifeng Women's Federation has successfully implemented a three level support system for female migrants moving from rural to urban areas. With this support system, female migrants can apply to receive social/administrative support in the form of skill training, consultation, legal aid, rights protection, and provisional food/housing. Also, female migrants are seen as actors and encouraged to organize and empower themselves. Other pilot sites such as Beijing, Shanghai, Kunming, Chengdu, and Diqing have also mainly targeted female migrants in order to promote gender equity and to therefore have an impact on policies in this regard.

Female migrants are more vulnerable than male migrants and female urban laborers. However, it would be a mistake to regard them as disadvantaged/victims in the process of rural labor migration. Actually, they are found to have a strong will to improve their quality of life, and their contributions to both rural poverty reduction and local development are worthy of noting (Tanshen, 2004). Therefore, a poverty reduction project could expect only limited success if it failed to address migrant women or regarded them as helpless subjects rather than recognizing their potential.

3) Network building

There are three types of network in use by the project. The first is a social network among migrant laborers and stakeholders (families and friends of migrants, who are necessary in order to develop social capital among migrant laborers). The second is the network of sending and receiving places, linking local government agencies and forging a cooperative relationship between sending and receiving places (Ma Chunhua, 2005). The third is a nationwide working network/partnership between the eight pilot sites, developed by the joint efforts of UNESCO and CASS. Thus far, the "sending-receiving" networks between Chifeng and Beijing, between Lincang and Kunming, and between Anhui Province and Shanghai have been successfully established.

Migrant laborers typically maintain a social network and identity in both their area of origin and urban destination. They send a substantial portion of their income back to their home villages, and often seek support from their social network back home. Therefore, authorities in sending and receiving places must work together to provide services for migrant laborers, and the policies should take this feature of migrant life into consideration. In terms of regional diversity, a project must adapt to a variety of circumstances in forming a nationwide action research network if it aims to acquire a comprehensive understanding of the issue of rural labor migration in China as a whole.

4) Local development

The UNESCO project concerns local development as well as labor migration, and makes efforts to integrate the two. When designing the project activities at each pilot site, UNESCO and contributing researchers, in cooperation with local partners, investigated the main challenges of development with respect to rural labor migration. For example, Shanghai is a city with an ageing population. More migrant laborers, the skilled in particular, are needed to take care of the elderly. To address this problem, the Shanghai chapter of the UNESCO project seeks to establish a mechanism for recruiting, training, management, employment and services for rural migrants, to care for the elderly in Shanghai (Luo Keren, et al., 2004). Diqing (Yunnan Province) is another good example. As an underdeveloped area, Diqing is experiencing an influx of migrant laborers from outside and as a result it is difficult for locals to find non-agricultural jobs in the local labor market, i. e., they cannot benefit from local development largely due to the absence of non-agricultural skills (Huang Ping and Zhan Shaohua, 2004). To solve this problem, the project at the Diqing pilot site provides skill training for local rural laborers and makes efforts to integrate and work with other resources, such as the funds from the Sunshine Project.

Labor migration can have positive and negative effects on local development. For instance, rural laborers' out flow can become a "brain drain" for sending places, but it can also bring a "brain gain" after the migrant laborers return. Therefore, a project should cultivate a holistic viewpoint while supporting migrants, and integrate labor migration and UNESCO project activities into the process of local development, and as a result assist local development while meeting the needs of migrants and other social groups.

5) Training of trainers

In cooperation with CASS, UNESCO developed a method of training of trainers (TOT). They train the people who will train, directly or indirectly, other trainers and rural migrants. The targeted trainers include local partners, officials, NGOs, and other social actors involved in the project. The TOT program is designed to (a) train local counterparts to understand the project's principles, strategies and methods; (b) involve more governmental agencies and other social actors, build a closer working network and publicize the project among them in pilot sites; (c) strengthen the network among UNESCO, CASS and the eight pilot sites to share information and best practices. Between 2002 and 2004, more than 500 people have been trained by the TOT programs (Please see: Final

Report of TOT Program of the Project "Together with Migrants" in 2004, December 2004, UNESCO Beijing).

As its financial resources are limited, the UNESCO project can only directly benefit a very small portion of rural migrant laborers. It is a more effective use of resources to "train the trainers" to create a leverage effect. In addition, this approach cultivates partnership with local actors and gradually integrates the project's core ideas and methodologies. While the governmental policies show improvement, the UNESCO project promotes more positive and practical policy changes to reduce poverty among rural labor migrants in terms of lack of training and social exclusion, especially from a gender perspective, to promote local development through rural labor migration, and to establish a "win-win" partnership between different regions (sending and receiving areas; western, central and eastern regions; underdeveloped and developed regions).

7.4.2 Intended effects

The project's intended effects are as follows:

- Reducing poverty among migrant laborers
- Influencing local policy makers with the principles and methodology of the project and encouraging them to issue policies to reduce poverty among migrant laborers, especially in regard to gender
- Exploring alternative development strategies in local contexts in terms of rural labor migration, and replicating them in similar contexts
- Influencing central governmental agencies and other policy makers such as the Chinese Communist Party, the People's Congress and the Chinese People's Political Consultative Conference, drawing on project experiences in local contexts, and persuading them to issue practical labor policies
- Assisting institutions and organizations to work together with rural migrant laborers in China and integrating available resources into the UNESCO project.

7.4.3 Aspects of implementation

The project has adopted the following measures/strategies during project implementation:

- **Finding local counterparts**. Different types of organizations have been selected as chief local partner in the project, with one for each pilot site. Three are governmental agencies (Dalian Bureau of Public Security, Diqing Bureau of Agriculture and Livestocks and Zhuolu County Government), another three are academic institutions (Yunnan Academy of Social Sciences in Kunming, Sichuan Academy of Social Sciences in Chengdu, East Normal University in Shanghai), and the remaining two are NGOs/NPOs (Female Migrants' Home in Beijing and Chifeng Women's Federation). However, each selected local counterpart is required to include other agencies (governmental, academic and non-governmental) in project implementation.

- **Triangular partnership network**. At both the national and local level, the project attempts to establish a "triangular partnership network" between governmental agencies (officials), academic institutions (researchers) and NGOs/NPOs. At national level, UNESCO has established a triangular partnership between CASS (academic), All-China Women's Federation (NPO) and ministries such as MOLSS (governmental agency).
- **Participation**. The project encourages migrant laborers (direct beneficiaries) to participate in the project and promotes self-organization and solidarity among them.
- **Publicizing and promoting**. UNESCO, at both national and local level, publicizes and promotes the project through publications, media reporting, academic seminars, art events, etc.
- Policy papers. Almost every year, researchers are asked to draft policy papers/reports on the pilot sites' actions, which are published and discussed with policy makers at both national and local levels.

7.5 Proposed policy implications

7.5.1 Lessons learned

Drawing lessons from past policies concerning rural labor migration, it was found that a good policy cannot be effectively implemented in certain contexts because no specific governmental agency has been designated to address the issues or the designated agency cannot or will not work

with other related agencies; or that a well-intentioned policy cannot be effectively implemented in certain contexts because it has not considered rural migrant laborers' participation during policy implementation and as a result the targeted group rejects the policy or is indifferent to it.

Drawing on the experience of over 25 years of rapid economic growth, the Chinese Government has learned that a policy can be successful if local conditions and input of people of that locale are taken into account. For instance, in 1978, China started its rural reform and replaced the People's Commune System with the Household Responsibility System, which began in a village in Anhui Province in central China. The agricultural production increased tremendously and alleviated the food shortage suffered by locals for many years. Another good example is Township and Village Enterprises (TVEs), which are created by townships and villages themselves. The TVEs, which are the so-called Chinese peasants' "Great Creation", have enjoyed great success in the market economy and employed more than 100 millions rural laborers (Pan Wei, 2003).

7.5.2 Potential problems or barriers

The new policies recommended by the UNESCO project may encounter two problems or barriers in implementation:

One is that some local governments, especially those in regions receiving an influx of migrant labor, may regard the new policies as unfavorable or unrelated to local development, because the policies emphasize protection and services for migrants, who are regarded by some local governments as troublesome "outsiders."

The other is that local governments and even central governmental agencies may not understand the new policies correctly and thus be unable to implement them effectively, partly because concepts like social stigma and gender issues are relatively new to them.

7.5.3 Potentially harmful consequences

The proposed policies are flexible to some extent. If the central government assesses policy implementation of local governments according to rigid standards, however, it could have an adverse effect on local development. If government agencies do not fully understand the challenges faced by rural laborers during policy implementation, migrant laborers may have to shoulder more burdens, in either social or economic form. For instance, training programs may consume migrants' time or money and as a result they could lose their hard-earned jobs or be unable to earn as much as before.

7.5.4 Plans for implementation

In order to overcome these potential problems or barriers and avoid these harmful consequences, plans for implementation are as follows:

First, while issuing the proposed new policies, the policy makers may integrate them into the new development paradigm, and identify them as indispensable components in building a harmonious society.

Second, before and during policy implementation, train the officials or other actors in order to facilitate understanding of the UNESCO project's ideas and principles of poverty reduction and gender equity.

Third, one specific governmental agency should be designated to be responsible for the new policies, and in the meantime, it can be required that the policies be implemented jointly with other related agencies, including the governmental as well as non-governmental actors.

Fourth, academic institutions or research teams can be selected to monitor and assess the implementation of new policies, and on the basis of their work, flexible standards can be made and applied to different local contexts.

Finally, during policy implementation, monitoring and assessment, Beneficiaries' (rural migrant laborers) opinions and feedback should be considered with gravity.

7.5.5 Duplicability/transferability

The UNESCO project is designed to be duplicated in a variety of circumstances. That is why it has selected 8 pilot sites that each demonstrate unique local conditions. For instance, successful projects at Diqing can be reproduced in other underdeveloped western areas, such as Qinghai, Xinjiang, etc., which face similar region-specific challenges.

Moreover, this article's proposed new policies can also be useful for other scenes. A poverty reduction project targeting laid-off workers or another disadvantaged group, can adopt methodologies, policies or measures from the UNESCO project.

7.6 Monitoring and Evaluation During Implementation

7.6.1 Preliminary evaluation

1) Three strengths

First, the proposed policies are according to the experience of different areas (8 different pilot sites), and therefore they carry relative strength in their ability to transfer and duplicate.

Second, the policies are integrated into a socioeconomic structure from a local development perspective. Thus the policies can easily be implemented by local governments and other actors.

Third, the policies stress rural migrant laborers' participation and input, which can ensure a successful implementation.

2) Two Weaknesses

One of two identified weaknesses is that the policies have yet to identify the "poorest" of the poor among rural migrant laborers. Class stratification has emerged among rural migrants in cities during these nearly 20 years of rural labor migration. Many rural migrants have indeed integrated into urban societies and enjoy a high standard of living, and some have not. The other weakness is that the policies have not paid much attention to returned migrant laborers, who are found to have an important impact on local rural development.

3) Two opportunities

One of two identified opportunities is that both local and central governments have come to appreciate the contributions of migrant laborers and have become willing to make policies that are more pro-migrant; the other is that the central government is working towards a new development paradigm and building a harmonious society, with which the proposed policies are in accordance.

4) Two threats

One of two identified threats is that owing to the existing income gap and regional disparity, rural migrant laborers have to work and live in poverty in order to turn a profit; the other is that the large number of rural laborers who leave are mainly relatively young and educated, thus leaving their home villages as migrant laborers can create a "brain drain" effect.

7.6.2 Indicators for assessment

1) Qualitative indicators

- To what extent local governments attach importance to the implementation of the policies and make practical measures to ensure their success.
- To what extent other actors, including NGOs/NPOs, researchers, volunteers, etc., are willing to be involved in and make their contribution to the implementation of the policies.
- To what extent the main targeted group, rural migrant laborers, especially the women, accept and participate in the implementation of the policies.
- To what extent local authorities can cooperate with each other to implement the policies, especially between sending and receiving regions.

- To what extent the policies can facilitate a sustainable, rural-urban balanced local development and promote social justice and gender equity.

2) Quantitative Indicators

- How much money has the government allocated for the implementation of the policies?
- How many officials and other actors are working for the implementation of the policies?
- How many rural migrants, especially the poor and female migrants, benefit from the implementation of policies?

7.6.3 Feedback

While evaluating, monitoring and assessing, the policy makers or experts can receive and collect feedback from the following groups:

- **Government officers**. Meetings or interviews can be held with the officers directly involved in the implementation to survey their opinions and suggestions.
- **Other social actors**. Meetings or interviews can be held with NGOs, local researchers, volunteers, etc., who are directly or indirectly involved in implementation to survey their opinions and suggestions.
- **Migrant laborers**. Discussion or interviews can be held with migrant laborers, especially female migrant laborers, who are the supposed beneficiaries of the policies to survey their opinions and suggestions and understand the results of the policies from their perspective.
- **Other stakeholders**. Other stakeholders such as urban residents, potential rural migrant laborers, employers, etc. can be interviewed by way of questionnaires, telephone or face-to- face communication.

7.6.4 Control

After a trial period of approximately six to twelve months, the policy makers and other concerned parties should evaluate the results of the policies in order to adjust or to improve them. Then the adjusted or improved policies can be applied in additional cities or regions. To guarantee the flexibility and adjustability, the policy makers should make it possible for policies to (1) be designed and adjusted by local governments and authorities; (2) be adjusted according to stakeholders' suggestions, especially migrant laborers; and (3) be in accordance with the strategies of local development (like local five-year development planning).

References

[1] Du Jie and Nazneen Kanji. *Gender Equality and Poverty Reduction in China: issues for development policy and practice.* Beijing: China Office, the Department for International Development, 2003.

[2] Huang Ping. "When Young Farmers Leave the Farm: What Will Happen to Rural Development in China When Rural-Urban Migration Takes Place at a High Pace under Impacts of Globalization?" In *Globalization and its Impact*, ed. Cecilia Lindqvist, pp 56-67. FRN: Stockholm, 2000.

[3] Huang Ping. "Urban Poverty among Young Migrants in China". In *Together with Migrants*. Beijing: UNESCO Office Beijing, 2004a.

[4] Huang Ping, 2004b. "Some Strategic Thinking on Rural-urban Migration in China". In *Together with Migrants*. Beijing: UNESCO Office Beijing.

[5] Huang Ping and Frank N. Pieke. *China Migration Country Report*, DFID Research Report. May 2003.

[6] Huang Ping and Zhan Shaohua. *Capacity Analysis of Skills Training Systems for Migrant Labours in China*. CIDA Working Paper. Beijing, 2004.

[7] Li Yinhe, et al. Nongmin Liudong Yu Xingbie [Rural-urban Migration and Gender]. Zhengzhou: Zhongyuan Nongmin Chubanshe, 2000.

[8] Luo Keren, et al. "Young Migrants' Employment Situation in Shanghai and Policy Suggestions". In *Together with Migrants*. Beijing: UNESCO Office Beijing, 2004.

[9] Ma Chunhua. *Establishing the Network between Origin and Destination of Rural Migrants*. Working paper. Beijing: UNESCO Office Beijing, 2005.

[10] NBS. *China Statistical Yearbook 2004*. Beijing: China Statistics Press, 2004.

[11] NBS and MOLSS. Zhongguo Laodong Tongji Nianjian [China Labour Statistical Yearbook 2001]. Beijing: Zhongguo Tongji Chubanshe, 2001.

[12] Pan Wei. Nongmin Yu Shichang: Zhongguo Jiceng Zhengquan Yu Xiangzhen Qiye [Peasant and Market: China Grassroot Administrations and Townships Village Enterprises]. Beijing: Shangwu Yinshuguan, 2003.

[13] Tanshen. "Leaving Home and Coming Back: Experiences of Rural Migrant Women". In *Together with Migrants*. Beijing: UNESCO Office Beijing, 2004.

[14] Tang Jun et al. Zhongguo Chengshi Pinkun Yu Fanpinkun Baogao [A Report of Urban Poverty and Anti-poverty in China]. Beijing: Huaxia Chubanshe, 2003.

[15] Tang Can. Xingsaorao: Chengshi Wailai Nv Mingong De Shuangchong Shenfen Yu Qishi [Sexual Harassment: Female Migrants' Double Identities and Discrimination in Cities]. *Sociological Studies* 6, no. 4 (1996).

[16] UNESCO. *Together with Migrants*. Beijing: UNESCO Office Beijing, 2004.

[17] Wang Fenyu and Li Lulu. Zongguo Chengshi Laodongli Liudong: Congye Moshi, Zhiye Shengya, Xinyimin [Labour Migration in Urban China: Employment, Career, New Migrants].

Beijing: Beijing Press, 2001.

[18] Zhan Shaohua, 2004. "Prevent Social Exclusions of Rural Migrants: a New Perspective on Rural Development in China". In *Problems of Village and Agriculture during Market Reorientation of the Economy.* Warsaw: IRWIR_PAN.

[19] Zhan Shaohua. *Poverty Reduction among Migrants: Concepts, Practice and Policy Implications.* Working paper. Beijing: UNESCO Office Beijing, 2005.

[20] Zhao Shukai, 2003. Interview records. Interviewed by the author.

8

Policy Considerations on Rural-Urban Migrants: Balancing Legal Rights and Social Order

Huang Ping*

8.1 Defining the Status of Rural Migrants

Hundreds of millions of rural migrants, called *Nongmin Gong*[55] in Chinese, who come to urban areas[56] seeking non-farming jobs since the Reform are becoming the new rank of laborers in China. On the one hand, they are the results of Chinese reform and opening up, social development and urbanization, and on the other hand, they are important contributors to this great social change.

8.2 Significance

Ensuring that the legal rights and interests of rural migrants are protected; improving their working, living and health conditions; and introducing their shift from the agriculture sector to the industrial sector and urban areas are very important in order to facilitate balanced development between rural and urban areas, to build a moderately prosperous society in all respects and a harmonious society, and guarantee social justice and social stability practically and theoretically.

8.3 Consistency in central government policy

The basic principles of the Chinese Government, "treating equally without discrimination,

---

* Translated by Dr. Ma Chunhua, CASS.

55 Speaking strictly, they are not the migrants in English parlance, but mobile laborers or floating laborers for non-agricultural employments or non-agricultural activities.

56 Includes township and county.

providing better service and improving management, planning as a whole and guiding rationally, taking actions that suit local circumstances, standing from the present and looking forward to the future", are playing important guiding roles in current and future work.

8.4 Basic Judgments

(1) In the pasting thirty years, China has pursued a developmental approach which has been unprecedented in the history of China: in a society with 1.3 billion people, the economy keeps on increasing rapidly while more than 300 million of people have risen out of absolute poverty.

(2) During the process, more than 200 million rural laborers transferred from agriculture to industrial sectors[57] without an increase in slums in urban areas and a mass of international migrants.

(3) The rural migrants who come to urban areas for industrial work not only build their capacity and widen their vision, but also contribute to the development and flourishing of urban areas, and provide a large amount of funds, practical skills and related information for rural development.

(4) These rural migrant workers are parts of the Chinese working class, and are important contributors to building a moderately prosperous society in all respects and a harmonious society.

(5) The major issues concerning these rural migrants include: (a) how to protect their legal rights; (b) how to improve their living, working and health conditions; (c) how to push them migrate to industrial sectors and urban areas; and (d) how to make rural-urban migration become the organic component of balanced development between rural and urban areas.

8.5 Cooperation between different parts

In order to deal with these issues, it is not enough to solely depend on governments, or one of the governmental departments (for example the labor and social security department and agricultural departments). It is necessary to build the institutions and foster a public

---

57 The figure includes not only rural laborers who go to urban areas for industrial work and their relatives and children, but also rural laborers who transfer from agriculture to industrial work in their hometown.

atmosphere in favor of understanding, caring, and protecting the legal rights of rural migrants; and all parts, including governments of sending and receiving places, should be involved in providing service and management for rural migrants. These parts should support and cooperate with each other, and gradually improve their service and management.

8.6 Experiences and suggestions

8.6.1 Some discoveries and experiences of this research include:

1) *Establishing the network between sending and receiving places of rural migrants.*

2) *The findings of the project "Together with migrants" and of other research.*

The findings show that hundreds of millions of rural migrant workers are an organic component of Chinese social change and urbanization. Therefore, the issues related to them should be dealt within the framework of a unified developmental design between rural and urban areas. An important approach is to establish the network between sending and receiving places of rural migrants, which is in favor of making use of limited resources, and decreasing the cost of migration. For example, if information on industrial opportunities in urban areas can be acquired in the sending places, then rural laborers will head to urban areas with specific objectives and with pre-established work. If the trainings on housing, skills, health, and legal information can be provided in the sending places, then rural migrants will be able to seek industrial employment opportunities in neighborhoods instead of the alternative migration to large cities.

3) *Combining research and practice*

Another important finding is that studies on rural migrants should: (a) work with other studies on policies of agriculture, rural areas and farmers; (b) combine implementation of policies at different levels; (c) cooperate with social groups and organizations (Women's Federation as an example) at the grassroots level; and (d) especially integrate with rural migrants themselves. Both sides can benefit from their interactions. For example, studies on rural migrants could move forward in depth if they could be based on other studies on agriculture, rural areas and farmers. If the researchers could work with local officials who are in charge of implementing of policies, they could throw off doctrine and make their studies more practical. If the researchers could cooperate with local social groups and organization, with Women's Federation as an example, they could consider the same phenomena from the perspective of social organizations, and even include gender perspective in their studies. Most importantly, if the researchers could integrate with rural migrants themselves, they could understand rural-urban migration from the perspective of rural migrants.

4) *Exploring complementary and win-win mechanisms*

The studies on rural migrants can benefit from interactions between both sides. The experiences of the Project show that it is possible to achieve a win-win situation among governmental departments, social organizations, enterprises and rural migrants. In the Dalian pilot site, for example, (a) governmental departments provide accommodation for (b) rural migrants through encouraging (c) enterprises to contract some old state-run institutional units and make suitable renovations in the form of apartments, and therefore, other governmental departments, such as the Public Security Bureau, Justice Bureau, Labor and Social Security Bureau and Health Bureau, can provide training sessions and related information. In the end, every part can benefit from this model, and in fact are satisfied with its results, especially rural migrants, because these *Nongmin Gong* Apartments are safe, clear and cheap, and they can receive trainings and acquire information in the buildings.

5) *Providing more training sessions*

According to studies of the Project, many types of training sessions have positive impacts on rural migrants. These should be noted here: (1) Training sessions in neighborhoods. This refers to training sessions that are provided for rural migrants in near their hometown. In most cases, the township or county next to their villages are the best choice. (2) Training sessions which are suited to local circumstances. In other words, rural migrants welcome the training sessions which are cheapest for rural migrants and easiest for organizers to conduct. In most cases, these training sessions should be implemented in the township or county next to their villages. (3) Training sessions on skills plus legal and health knowledge. Theses training sessions not only help the rural migrants obtain industrial employment, but it also raises their consciousness so as to protect their legal rights through awareness of relevant laws and regulations, and reduces their possibility of being injured and sick. (4) Training sessions which can establish social networks between trainees. For rural migrants, the content of trainings activities are not always the most important. More importantly, these trainings open a public space for them to interact with and talk to each other, and help them build self-confidence and social network. These characteristics will have a profound impact on their development in the future.

6) *Promoting transfer from agriculture to non-farming sectors in local areas*

Project studies and almost all statistics show that most of the rural laborers seek non-farming opportunities in local areas (local county or urban areas within local province) from the beginning of Reform to present. Furthermore, most rural laborers cannot find a profession or job, but are involved in non-agricultural activities, most of which are included in local "informal sectors." This means that rural "surplus laborers" have to transfer from agriculture to non-farming sectors in local areas. Any policies on promoting urbanization should consider how to impel the development of township enterprises and county economy, increase the capacity of industries in small cities and townships to absorb laborers, and develop local service sectors.

7) *Respecting different situation at local level and their innovation to deal with the issues under the local situation*

The Project only selected eight pilot sites in the country. But it is showed that the situations in eight pilot sites are very different. A previous question about the non-farming transferring process can be repeated again: how do we seek truth from facts and analyze the problems in the local context? In other words, how do we integrate the "general principle", such as respecting legal rights of rural migrants, improving their living and working conditions, and promoting urbanization in local places within the local situation?

In principle, different areas should be treated distinctively, and activities should be taken according to local circumstances. Furthermore, the local innovation, including the exploration of rural migrants in practice, should especially be respected. For the Project, each pilot site has its own characteristics. They can communicate with each other and share the experiences and lessons on the one hand, while some models, which are developed by a pilot site, cannot be adopted by another pilot site. The different situations refer to geographical diversity and differences in population, and disparity in the urban-rural relationship, policy climate, and culture.

It should be emphasized here that innovation of ethnic places should be given more respect. The Project has pilot sites in Yunnan, Sichuan and Inner Mongolia; and one of pilot sites is located in the Tibetan area. The team members are impressed with the innovation of local officials and the ordinary people in these ethnic places, and understand the importance in dealing with rural-urban relationships, including rural-urban migration, with the Concept of Scientific Development as a guide. For example, in Diqing Tibetan Autonomous District, local officials are exploring how to promote local urbanization and therefore benefit the local people through local development. In Chifeng of Inner Mongolia, local officials recognize Chifeng not only as a sending place but also as a receiving place for rural migrants. Few officials in other Han ethnic places have these ideas.

8) *Gender perspective*

Studies on rural migrants should embrace gender perspective because there are an increasing number of rural female laborers who join the rural-urban migration. Gender perspective does not means feminism, but instead equal treatment for female and male. Female migrants have to face more difficulties when they migrate to urban areas. If the industry absorbs a great number of female workers, the trainings for migrant workers should be arranged in terms of circumstances. Compared with their counterparts, female migrants are more active and generate greater initiative in many occasions. At the same time, gender perspective does not mean "sympathy for a disadvantageous group" or "helping them in charity." If training sessions on health, legal areas and employment are targeting the special needs of female migrants, they will become more efficient.

9) *Dealing with issues related to rural migrants within the framework of the new countryside Construction*

The Chinese government recently delivered the theory on the Concept of Scientific Development and Building a Harmonious Society, and intended to achieve the "Five Balanced Development." Five balanced development means scientific development in the areas of rural-urban, inter-regional, socioeconomic, human-environment, and domestic-foreign relations, with an overall comprehensive and sustainable approach to development. One of the most important aspects of this theory is to construct the new countryside. Rural migrants will play a particular important role in the process. They have made a tremendous contribution to urbanization and rural development in China, and are becoming an active force in building a moderately prosperous society in all aspects. In similar fashion, they will also help construct the new countryside.

The new countryside construction does not mean traditional village governance, but instead it is the construction of a new type of rural area under the principle of socialism. In the new countryside, interpersonal relationship is harmonious, and humanity and nature coexists harmoniously, and development of rural and of urban areas are balanced.

It is also reported by the Project that the income of non-farming jobs are not always most important for rural migrants, but instead, that the living and working conditions are most important. While there are many enterprises and managers that refuse to pay wages to migrant workers, the latter have little complaints or do not conflict with the former if the relationships between local government, enterprises, social organizations and rural migrations are harmonious. Conversely, even in the case of high income, without a harmonious environment, the rural migrants are not satisfied, social stability cannot be guaranteed in urban areas, and their families in rural areas always worry about their situation.

The Project suggests that in addition to the urban community and rural community, a new type of rural migrant community should also be constructed, which should be advantageous to the migrants in terms of their working environment in receiving places as well as their hometown area.

10) *Standing from the present and looking forward to the future*

It will take some to solve the problems mentioned, such as ensuring legal rights of rural migrants, improving their working, living and health conditions, establishing a welfare system for them, and enrolling migrant children in urban educational systems. Addressing these issues and resolving them will be a fundamental part to building a prosperous society.

From this perspective, in focusing on how we grasp the relationship between present and future, it becomes necessary to handle the present troublesome problems with a future strategic plan. At present, it is pressing and practical to keep on ensuring that rural workers in cities are paid on time and in full, protecting employment security and health in light of Labor Law and other relevant laws, providing employment information, organizing trainings on vocational skill and knowledge of laws and health, enrolling rural migrant children in educational systems, improving their working and living conditions, establishing a social security and welfare system for them, and helping them find non-farming jobs in local places.

In looking forward to the future, rural migrants' issues refer to development issues, reform issues, and urbanization issues. At the same time, rural-urban migration bridges the gap between rural urban areas, east-west regions, and big cities' small townships. The project's experiences with pilot sites illuminates the important point that if we want to deal with rural migrants' issues, we have to access a problem-solving approach "beyond rural areas", and must ensure that the rural community also benefits from these measures. As a result, rural migrants will be excluded and discriminated in urban areas, and many will not have to flow to large cities.

9

A Brief Introduction of the CASS-UNESCO Project "Poverty Reduction among Young Migrants in Urban Areas"

The CASS-UNESCO Project "Poverty Reduction among Young Migrants in Urban Areas" commenced in 2002. The project advocates social/legal rights and interest protection and a policy development-oriented approach because, firstly, poverty issues among the migrants are not only related to economic factors such as income, but also to social factors that create impoverished conditions; and secondly, could the projects actions would be futile if were not able to improve the relevant government policies. In order to achieve the above goals, in the processes of implementation the project developed two forms or methodologies which proved to be very effective in 8 pilot sites in China.

9.1 Action Research

The Chinese Academy of Social Sciences is the top social sciences research institute in China. However, the researchers in the CASS-UNESCO project do not merely conduct academic studies in their offices but on the contrary they spend a significant time in field research, advocating problem-solving approaches in confronting the issues and problems of migrant laborers. Their research and its investigations related to the migrant laborers' demands directly contributes to the design of the project's activities, and much of the research among the 8 pilot sites is centered on policy issues and measures for policy improvement. In fact, some of the ideas and suggestions have become basic information and recourses for policy makers in different levels of governments. For instance, based on the official data and case documents, the project team of the Dalian pilot site found out through analyses of the possible connections between the lack of social/legal protection and aid for the migrants and the high criminal rate among them, that the project design paid much attention to enhancing the protection of the rights and interests of migrants in Dalian. Tee particular measures taken in order to enhance their protection consisted of building migrants' apartments as a platform for conducting various programs for vocational training, health and sanitation, legal knowledge, to legal aids and job introduction, etc., and the practices proved to be highly effective in improving their living and working conditions and reducing the illegal actions among the migrants in the apartments. In Chifeng, interviews and questionnaire surveys were conducted among female migrants in their working site and in their hometown. The data not only showed their difficulties and needs but also provided concrete information for the local government, the Women's Federation of Chifeng, and the researchers from CASS that helped to develop interest in building a social network for mutual assistance and the guarantee of rights/interests among female migrants, and in turn, which has led to considerable improvements of government policies and financial aid measures from the government.

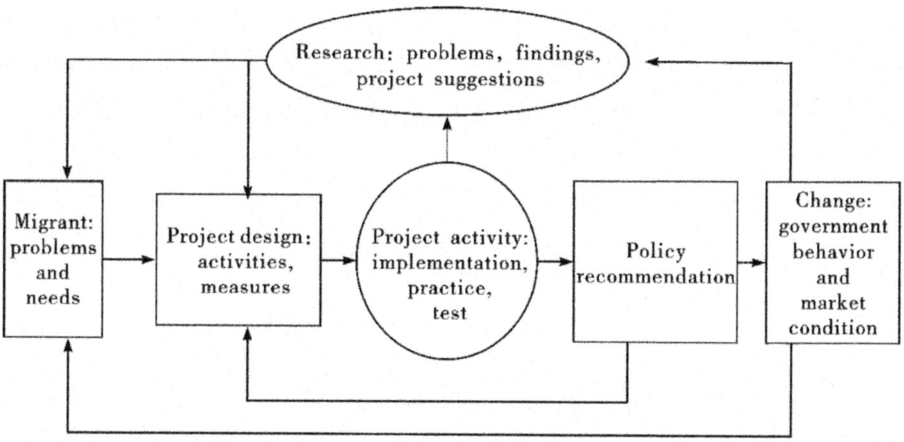

Fig 9-1 Action Research Related to Policy Development

9.2 Triangular Pattern

What we call the triangular pattern here refers to the combination of three resources and advantages from governments, NPOs or international organizations, and research in the implementation of the project activities and policy development of different levels of government. With this combination pattern the projects in 8 pilot sites have achieved rather positive results in pursuit of the improvement of migrants' living and working conditions and policy developments.

The strategy of the project is to generate cooperate between non-governmental institutes (including international organizations), action researchers (such as CASS), and governments (such as the Bureau of Public Security in Dalian) in order to confront these issues.

This strategy attempts to reduce and avoid any possible risk to the government, in terms of both departments and individuals, who are willing to take tentative steps to solve the problems faced but who have no concrete or detailed direction from a formal upper-level governmental document. Firstly, this project of cooperation might give a kind of "validity" to a governmental sector to test something new or innovative. This "validity", introduced through cooperation, makes the governmental system feel that the precise activities would be more acceptable, and the government is then more likely to grant the project activities than if the government alone conducted these activities. Secondly, the cooperation exerts modest pressure upon the local government, which would push it to actively implement the project's measures. Thirdly, the cooperation could generate opinions that would balance different views originally held by each side; it would prove to be an effective way to persuade the governmental officials to accept some new ideas introduced by the project, and for that matter, for the researchers or NPOs, to learn experiences from governmental officials.

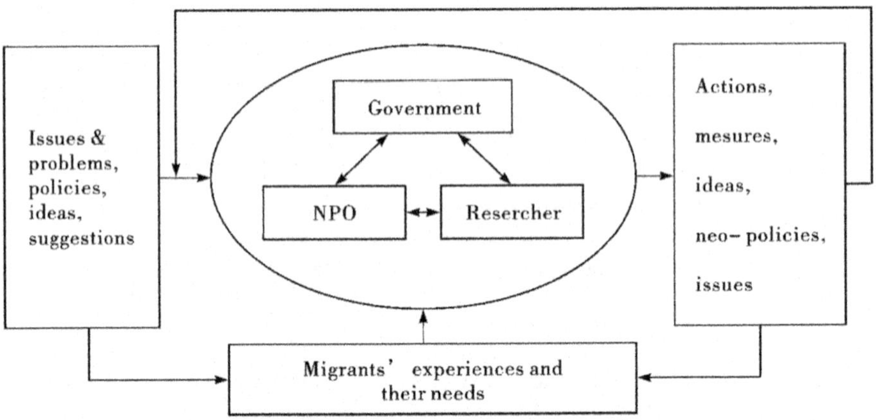

Fig 9-2 Mechanism of project implementation

For instance, in the Dalian case, during the cooperation project the governments gradually realized that the tests or the innovative measures are effective and they could be included into the government's future policy. In Dalian, this transformative attitude of the government was experienced in three stages: (1) Suspicious at the beginning, concerned primarily that the project's activities would not be in accordance with the current policy granted by the upper level; (2) limited support in the mid-term, which meant it thought that the activities would not conflict with central policy and the results would positively impact upon its performance; (3) complete acceptance of the activities at the present stage, which means it believes the activities are really helpful in dealing with the problems, and the measures of the project are capable of introduction into formal policy of the government.

At the same time, the researchers could do more in the way of including and adopting the knowledge and experiences of government officials.

9.2.1 Roles and characteristics of the three respective parties:

(1) Government. The Chinese governmental system has a very strong propensity towards organization, mobilization, and management. However, it still shares the bureaucratic nature of any huge and complicated organization, and sometimes such organizations have difficulties in making innovations and emergent reactions to the reality.

(2) NPOs or international organizations. These organizations usually show their initiatives and can attempt innovation in China. But their independent orientation, and separated and limited activities often fail to have extensive effects in dealing with issues and problems in China. Most of their actions towards poverty reduction among the migrant laborers results in nothing more than an act of charity or a passive critic.

(3) Researchers. Researchers have their independent point of views and can provide new concepts to NPOs or the government. However, as action researchers, they must cooperate with NPOs and the government, otherwise they cannot effectively put their ideas and results into practice.

In order to combine the advantages of the three parties, the CASS-UNESCO project in poverty reduction for urban migrant laborers from rural areas created and developed a pattern of triangular cooperation between these three parties. This practice proved overall to be an effective dynamic in carrying out project activities, as well as a successful combination of powerful resources including government policies and executive ability, NPO initiative, and researchers' intellectual contribution.

9.3 A Brief introduction of project activities and effectiveness of all Sub-Projects

9.3.1 Beijing sub-project

The Beijing sub-project started in 2002. Its local partner is the Migrant Girls' Cultural Development Centre, which has been working on migrant girls for some years and therefore has gained a lot of experiences. It intends to make efforts on improving the social conditions of the female migrants coming to Beijing to work as domestic workers.

9.3.2 The main activities of Beijing sub-project include:

(1) Beijing sub-project provided free trainings, including health and disease prevention, Labor Law, Job-hunting, gender and gynecology, interview skills, and knowledge of social interaction, for young female migrants' groups through face-to-face or VCD

(2) Interviews and research carried out with migrant women doing domestic service.

(3) In order to push the training effectively provided in the sending places, the Beijing sub-project designed training VCD and a practical handbook for the migrants to read and complete as domestic workers in Beijing.

(4) A close relationship was established between sending places (four agencies in Gansu, Shandong, Henan) and receiving places (seven agencies in Beijing) in 2003

(5) In September of 2004, the Beijing team organized the "UNESCO-CASS TOT Partnership Training" "The training focused on how to impact policy makers, how to protect the rights of domestic workers, how to develop of domestic workers' agency, how to provide trainings for these female migrants and push forward the legislation of "Regulations on Domestic Workers in Beijing."

1) Comments

- In 2002, the Beijing team arranged trainings for the trainers and trainings for the migrants, with the cooperation of the governmental agencies, hospitals and Women's Federal Organization, etc. But it seemed they failed to work out a new strategy in persuading the government's in-depth participation or in impacting its policy making.
- In 2003, Beijing sub-project succeeded in building up the relationship between sending and receiving places and organized a series of activities in promoting the communication among the government (Women's Federation, the Labor Bureau), the export agencies and import agencies. However, in 2002 weakness still existed, and the government's participation was limited.
- In 2004, a partner of the Beijing project designed and produced training VCD and a practical handbook for the migrants to do as domestic workers in Beijing, set up a domestic workers self-supporting group and organized the "UNESCO-CASS TOT Partnership Training." At the same time, they began to push forward the legislation of "Regulations on Domestic Workers." Although their activities still lacked the government's in-depth participation, and had little impact on policies related to domestic workers in Beijing, they attracted more attention of the public

and media on migrants, especially on the protection of female domestic workers through several workshops and other activities.

9.3.3 Chengdu Sub-Project, Sichuan

The Chengdu sub-project also started in 2002. Its main local partner is Sichuan Women's Federation, which has gained many experiences from previous projects. It intends to facilitate female migrants in integrating into the urban life.

1) The main activities of the Chengdu sub-project include:

(1) The Research and Service Network for Rural Women Migrant Workers was created in order to facilitate communication among migrants, policy makers and researchers. Participants of the network meet together and discuss the rural migrants' relevant issues regularly.

(2) Publication and distribution of magazines, focused on migrants, which was coined the "Migrant Girls' Mailbox" and "Worry Sharing." Public advertisements about promoting rural migrant workers' integration into urban living in "Worry Sharing" were also designed, published and distributed to migrant workers.

(3) The team continues to compile "Briefing of the Research and Service Network" newsletter and distributes it to researchers and officials of government departments.

(4) Training courses, focusing on the ability to live in urban areas, job seeking, laws and rights protection, physical and psychological health, were provided for rural migrants coming from poor counties. These trainings are controlled by migrants themselves. They discussed how to strengthen their capacity to live and work in urban areas through participatory methods.

(5) The Chengdu sub-project paid more attention to the married migrants and their children, and provided training courses to those groups and their children. The team believed these trainings not only build the capacities of rural migrant workers to live and work in urban areas, but also benefits the new generation of migrants through creating a better educational and family environment for them.

2) Comments

- The sub-project arranged to train officials in three selected communities, and to support the rural migrants through these officials. In the end, this plan had to be aborted because managing the rural labor migrants is not the regular job of the local government in the community, and these grassroots governments have no ability to organize the resources and teachers to train rural labor migrants and residents.

- Consequently, the Chengdu sub-project had to modify the focus in 2003: it had to take advantage of social forces to train the labor migrants and at the same time establish the sub-system of training. The "Research and Service Network for Rural Women Migrant Workers" was one of the resultant fruits of this modified plan. Without working with officials in three communities, the Chengdu team failed to establish some institutional linkage with other agencies, especially with some governmental departments at different levels. Though some participants of the network came from governmental departments, they were independent of their affiliated organ.
- As a result, the relatively few policy impacts on governments were a serious weakness of the Chengdu sub-project, though, the team was rather successful in expanding sub-project influence through the network, media, workshop, trainings and TOT. The situation remained the same in 2004.

9.3.4 The Chifeng Sub-Project, Inner Mongolia

The Chifeng sub-project also started in 2002. Its main local partner is the Chifeng Prefectural Women's Federation (CPWF). It aims to facilitate the integration of female migrants with ethnic backgrounds coming to Chifeng from Inner Mongolia as well as to prepare those migrating to Beijing from Chifeng.

1) The main activities of Chifeng sub-project include:

(1) Through different means, such as the TV program in Chifeng to introduce the project, and participation of local media in large-scale activities, the sub-project attracted the attention and agreement of governmental organizations and other social/civic groups. Then the local government not only provided necessary support, financially and politically, for the team, and even issued a governmental document for the sub-project, but also was active in participating in the activities of the sub-project.

(2) The Chifeng sub-project established a close relationship between receiving and sending places. In order to protect the rural migrants' rights, especially female rural migrants, and meet their needs, the CPWF established the Beijing Migrant's Club and Chifeng Migrant's Center. At the same time, the CPWF took advantage of the current hierarchy within the women's federation system to establish the network between Chifeng (receiving place) and counties/towns/townships/villages (sending place).

(3) There is no doubt that the service organizations for rural migrants (Beijing Migrant's Club and Chifeng Migrant's Center) play an important role in the operating of the network. Through these service organizations, CPWF uses a participatory approach to provide knowledge training, such as law, health, social protection, and how to live in the city. Community-based training for female laborers as well as weekly self-improving activities were organized in order to broaden and strengthen the network among female migrants in Beijing and in Chifeng.

(4) The Chifeng team has successfully created an alternative way to reduce poverty among rural migrants that integrates different forces and resources into the team to help rural migrants. For instance, the Beijing Migrant's Club and the Chifeng Migrant's Center can actually function as platforms for different forces and resources, such as governments, volunteers, and migrants themselves, etc.

2) Comments

- The project is mainly organized by CPWF, though the prefectural government paid attention to this work, and even issued a government document to support it. There are a few other agencies, including governmental and non-governmental organizations, involved in the work initially. In 2004, the situation seemed to improve to some extent.
- The funding which is necessary for supporting the network and activities have to depend on the funding from other resources, such as Hong Kong Oxfam and UNESCO. As soon as they fail to receive this funding, it becomes very difficult to maintain the organization and the network. CPWF is marginalized in the local administration system. It has few resources and little power to support the organization and the network by itself; and it has less capacity to involve other governmental departments.
- The Chifeng sub-project cannot establish a labor service partnership with any department of the Beijing government, or even the Beijing Women's Federation for that matter. This makes it difficult to protect the rights of rural migrants or improve their living and working conditions in Beijing.

9.3.5 The Dalian Sub-Project, Liaoning

The Dalian sub-project also started in 2002. Its main local partner is the Dalian Public Security Bureau. It wants to team up with the Dalian Municipal Government in order to support migrants' integration through housing.

1) The main activities of the Dalian sub-project include:

(1) Three migrant laborer apartments have been constructed in Dalian with more than 2000 migrant laborers, all of which have been provided accommodations and comprehensive services in the apartments in 2002. Learning from these experiences, there were more than 50 migrant laborer apartments with different forms in 2004.

(2) In order to enhance the effectiveness and quality of the comprehensive services in the apartments, the Dalian sub-project launched a comprehensive protection project to carry out an overall social/legal protection for migrant laborers after the establishment of the apartments. Participants include the Bureau of Public Security, the Bureau of Civil Affairs, the Bureau of Labor and Social Security, the Bureau of Legal Service, the Commission of Family Planning, the Bureau of Sanitation and Epidemic Prevention, etc., and the Bureau of Public Security is assuming the role of organizer.

(3) The Dalian sub-project created an extensive employment service, carried out an education program on legal knowledge and legal rights, and provided employment skill training, such as computer operation, house decoration, and housekeeping service; and offered a training program on knowledge of family planning and epidemic prevention for migrant laborers. The Legal Aid Centre, the migrants' mutual assistance organization, has been set up in the community; lawyers from the Legal Office were retained to provide comprehensive legal aid to young migrant laborers.

2) Comments

- The Dalian sub-project has done a great amount of work, which has contributed to the institutional innovation in anti-urban poverty among migrant laborers in cities.
- Compared to other sub-projects, the policy impact of the Dalian sub-project is formidable. The Dalian team included many governmental departments. Furthermore, influenced by the activities of the Dalian sub-project, a formal governmental document has been issued by the Dalian Municipality. The document affirmed the effectiveness of the construction of rural migrants' apartments in Dalian, and has asked relevant governmental departments to try their best to facilitate the project.
- The Dalian sub-project found a new way to provide services for rural migrant workers. It is a "win-win" game: it benefits the government because it reuses state-owned assets; it benefits some bosses because apartments can bring little profit to them; it benefits both the rural and urban segments of society; it benefits

local laid-off workers because it can provide job vacancies for them; and it benefits the whole of society.

- The existing labor training program is controlled by the government, which tend to be one of restricting factors for its development in terms of guaranteeing its quality as well its quantity since there is neither effective competition nor supervision in this domain. Consequently, this has become an obstacle for mobilizing social resources or non-government professional sectors that could benefit the program.

9.3.6 The Diqing Sub-Project, Yunnan

The Diqing sub-project started in 2003, much later than most sub-projects. Its main local partners are the Yunnan Diqing Tibetan Autonomous Prefecture and the Diqing Agriculture and Livestock Bureau. The purpose of the sub-project is to facilitate Tibetan migrant workers' integration by helping them find employment opportunities in tourism activities and help vary their skills in order to avoid job exclusion in the local market.

The sub-project is a significant one in the overall project. It is located in southwestern China and is identified as a Tibetan region where a large number of residents with ethnic backgrounds reside. It presents different challenges when compared to the other projects: on the one hand, the local residents, especially rural residents, have difficulties in benefiting from local development since the migrant laborers from outside occupy a lot of job vacancies, and on the other hand, it is possible for the sub-project to create alternative strategies to cope with the migrant issues through the utilization of local cultural resources.

1) The main activities of the Diqing sub-project include:

(1) The Diqing sub-project has mobilized and integrated many kinds of resources into the project, such as the Sunshine Project. Moreover, the local contracted partner, the Diqing Bureau of Agriculture and Livestock, has established a close relationship with other agencies and actors in terms of project implementation, such as the Bureau of Labor and Social Security, the Office of Poverty Reduction, the Bureau of Education, the training schools, etc. As a result of the above work and effects, the Diqing government has attached much importance to rural-urban labor transferring and labor projection, and has made positive policies towards rural migrants on the basis of the project.

(2) Skill training for migrants, one of main strategies of the project, has been introduced as an important local policy by the local government since the project was initiated. In 2003, the government took skill training as one out of nine most important

policies. In 2004, the government increased its inputs into the skill training programs (including financial contributions) for local rural migrants, partly because of the implementation of the project. Moreover, the new paradigms and measures such as empowerment, capacity building, network building, etc., which are advocated by the project, have been integrated into the skill training programs, to some extent.

2) Comments

- Similar to the Chifeng sub-project, policy impact is also evident in the activities of the Diqing sub-project. The governor and related government agencies attached much importance to this project and set out an official document to ask all governments, at county and township levels, to arrange full-time staff for this project to promote and manage rural-urban labor migration in Diqing.
- As the Diqing government continues to consider its strategic plan for local socioeconomic development in the next 10 to 20 years, it should extend the project partnership to the local Planning and Reform Committee and policy research sector of the municipality of Diqing, such as the Department of Policy Research of the PCP Committee. Through the cooperation with these policy making and research agencies, the training and business creation programs for rural laborers might acquire better integration with the government's policy goals and might also increase chances to coordinate with the higher levels of local authorities in the policy making process.

9.3.7 The Kunming Sub-Project, Yunnan

The Kunming sub-project started in 2003, much later than most of other sub-projects. Its main local partners include the Institute of Philosophy of the Yunnan Academy of Social Sciences and the Lincang Prefectural Women's Federation. Through common action, it attempts to facilitate social and professional integration of migrants coming from Lincang Prefecture.

1) The main activities of Kunming sub-project include:

(1) The Lincang Prefectural Government has established the governmental working offices in Kunming, the capital of Yunnan Province. Through the Lincang Working Office, the network between Lincang (sending place) and Kunming (receiving place) was established.

(2) Through the network, the Lincang prefectural-level and lower governmental

departments recruit rural laborers and send them to Kunming, and then the Lincang Prefecture Working Office in Kunming provides necessary training, including vocational skills training, rights protection, salary management, and job seeking, and helps them find jobs.

(3) In cooperation with Jinniu Neighborhood, the sub-project has been exploring another important way to protect rural migrants in the city: to integrate rural migrants into the existing urban administrative system. Moreover, most residents of the neighborhood have ethnic backgrounds; therefore, residents and migrants can easily share identity thanks to the fact that a large part of migrants in Kunming come from other ethnic prefectures and possess similar ethnic characteristics.

(4) The Kunming sub-project has established close connection and communication channels with some migrant workers; 300 migrant workers' information were collected and preserved. Regular investigation has been carried out among these migrant workers in order to know their difficulties and demands.

2) Comments

- Kunming is the capital city of Yunnan Province. It has a favorable position in having an impact on the process of policy making at the provincial level. In 2003, the sub-project organized an activity of employment promotion in which some provincial officials participated. However, compared with other sub-projects, it had little impact on local policy makers through the project implementation.
- Even though the sub-project has explored two important ways to reduce poverty among migrants, project activities in each way have still remained on a limited scale partly because UNESCO cannot provide large-scale financial support. For instance, only dozens of rural migrants who live in Jinniu Neighborhood are direct beneficiaries of the project.
- Although there is a great deal of demand for rural migrant workers in Kunming, it is impossible for all rural migrant labors to find jobs there. Therefore, the sub-project should consider how to help Lincang Prefectural Government develop a mechanism that can help rural migrants, who come from rural areas directly, or come back from Kunming or other big cities.

9.3.8 The Shanghai Sub-Project

The Shanghai sub-project started in 2002. Its main local partners are East China Normal University, which has conducted long-term research on rural migrants' issues and also has close relationships with local governmental departments and non-governmental agencies, and Shanghai Star International Economy and Technique Corporation. It attempts to explore the connection between training and employment, and to explore training and Employment Qualification Certificates promoted by the government. The principles of the Shanghai sub-project include: *zhengfu zhidao, qiye canyu and shichang yunzuo* (the government gives instruction through issuing related policies, enterprises participate in the establishment of the four-sections employment chain and the network, and the sub-project's implementation in accordance with market principles).

1) The main activities of the Shanghai sub-project include:

(1) A large number of migrants are needed to work in some industries which Shanghai local laborers are reluctant to engage in, such as caring for the elderly, housekeeping, looking after patients, services in hotels, etc. But the fact is that corresponding policies, administration and training systems haven't supported the rural migrants' efforts to work in those industries. The Shanghai sub-project believes employment is most important in supporting a rural migrant's life in Shanghai. How to help trained rural migrants find jobs in the Shanghai labor market is the Shanghai sub-project's focus.

(2) The Shanghai sub-project established a systematic and broad network between university colleagues, local activists from companies, governmental agencies, and the poverty community of the rural migrant laborers. Through the network, the Shanghai sub-project integrated the resources of the government, enterprises and social organizations; established the four-section employment chain, composed of recruitment, training, and recommendation and management; tried to promote and pilot orderly and effective rural-urban laborer migration; and gave rural migrant workers in Shanghai training on legal issues, rights protection, employment, and health care, etc.

(3) Through establishing the four-section employment chain, the Shanghai sub-project has established the network between sending (Shanghai) and receiving places (Jiangxi, Anhui, etc.). This means that when there are some vacant positions, the Shanghai sub-project will recruit rural laborers in their hometown (sending place), send them to Shanghai (receiving place), train them in terms of the requirements for the vacant positions, help them obtain these vacant positions, and provide service and management when they are working in Shanghai. Thus, the four-section employment chain can make sure that trained rural labors can find jobs in Shanghai.

(4) Similar to other sub-projects, the Shanghai sub-project attached more importance to the policy impact of the activities of the sub-project. This was demonstrated through its

cooperation with the government in sending places, the involvement of more governmental departments in activities, the participation of governmental officials at central and local levels in workshops on "Promoting Young Migrants' Jobs in Shanghai", and the combination of the skill training with the requirements of the Employment Qualification Certificate which allows the trained rural migrant workers to obtain the Certificate and find employment in Shanghai.

(5) One of important local partners of the Shanghai sub-project is the Shanghai Star International Economy and Technique Corporation. The corporation is transferring their focus from only high level skill trainings, English training for managers in the foreign corporations as an example, to both high-level and low-level skill training. The Shanghai sub-project thought it was feasible to provide skill training for rural migrants and to protect their economic, social and political rights from the market perspective. It emphasizes it is powerless to help the rural migrants protect their rights without enough money. Through the market, it is possible to achieve a "win-win" outcome for both the corporation and rural migrants; and at the same time, the network established by Shanghai sub-project can maintain its survival.

2) Comments

- The Shanghai sub-project provides a successful and effective model to alleviate poverty among rural migrants in cities. But it is not easy for other sub-projects to copy this model because the Shanghai sub-project has some advantages: (1) as a rapidly developing mega-city, Shanghai provides a large number of non-farming jobs and agricultural opportunities for rural laborers; (2) the Shanghai team has enough resources and is capable of integrating all resources, including the government, enterprises, academic institutions and other social resources.
- In the Shanghai sub-project, the enterprise plays an important role. An enterprise is an economic body at first, and profit maximization is what it pursues. It is why people are worrying about whether or not the enterprise can insist on providing service and management for rural migrants. The sub-project will be implemented in agreement with market principles. This means it is impossible for the enterprise to provide free skill training for rural migrants. Then another potential problem is how the rural laborers pay for the trainings. Or how does the enterprise define the tuition for the training service? How do they know the rural migrants can accept the price? How do the enterprises balance their own interests with the rural migrants' interests? What role does the local government, especially that of the

receiving place, play?

9.3.9 The Zhuolu Sub-Project, Hebei

The Zhuolu sub-project started in 2004. It is the latest sub-project of the entire project. Its main local partners include: the Zhuolu Yanhuang Centre for Peasant Studies, the Zhuolu Labour and Social Security Bureau, the Zhuolu Agriculture Bureau, the Zhuolu Women's Federation, the Zhuolu Youth Federation, and the Zhuolu Education Bureau. It was designed to set up a mechanism to promote the rural migrants' employment, with concrete services and the migrants active participation, and to instil' respect for migrant workers' rights.

1) Main activities of Zhuolu sub-project include:

(1) The Zhuolu sub-project established a villager's Information Centre, located in the township seat and is equipped with books, newspapers, magazines, computers, internet, etc. This is a rural labor training basement which facilitates training of villagers.

(2) The Zhuolu sub-project organizes a villager's forum to provide a platform for returning migrants to discuss their experiences and ideas concerning migration. It is becoming a network between Zhuolu and other cities.

(3) Publication of community newsletters. The newsletter includes information on the latest relevant policies, laws and regulations; information on employment in cities; and practical agricultural knowledge.

(4) A contract model of transferring rural labor to enterprises has been developed.

(5) The working group, local government, local NPO, and volunteers all participate in a mutual training network.

2) Comments

- The project might explore the possibility to undertake some government programs for training rural labors and integrate some government policy financial resources into the project.
- An investigation could be made in terms of who is in most need of training and what type of training is most urgent.

This book is published with financial support from Innovation Project of CASS.

This book is the result of a co-publication agreement between Social Sciences Academic Press (China) and Paths International Ltd (UK).

Title: Urban Migrants And Poverty Reduction in China
Chief Editors: Huang Ping and Genevieve Domenach-Chich
ISBN: 978-1-84464-446-9

CPSIA information can be obtained at www.ICGtesting.com
Printed in the USA
BVOW09s0443220615

404986BV00004B/11/P

9 781844 644469